SAP R/3 ALE & EDI TECHNOLOGIES

SAP R/3 ALE & EDI Technologies

Rajeev Kasturi

RAJCAST, INC.

McGraw-Hill

New York   San Francisco   Washington, D.C.
Auckland   Bogotá   Caracas   Lisbon   London
Madrid   Mexico City   Milan   Montreal   New Delhi
San Juan   Singapore   Sydney   Tokyo   Toronto

McGraw-Hill

A Division of The McGraw·Hill Companies

2 3 4 4 6 7 8 9 0   DOC/DOC   9 0 4 3 2 1 0 9

P/N 0-07-134731-3

PART OF

ISBN 0-07-134730-5

"SAP" is a registered trademark of SAP Aktiengesellschaft, Systems, Applications and Products in Data Processing, Neurottstrasse 16, 69190 Walldorf, Germany. The publisher gratefully aknowledges SAP's kind permission to use its trademark in this publication. SAP AG is not the publisher of this book and is not responsible for it under any aspect of press law. All other products and services mentioned in this book are trademarks/servicemarks or registered trademarks/servicemarks of their respective companies/corporations.

Printed and bound by R. R. Donnelley & Sons Company.

This book is printed on recycled, acid-free paper containing a minimum of 50% recycled, de-inked fiber.

To
Vaishnavi

CONTENTS

vii

Contents

FOREWORD

With the advent of ERP (Enterprise Resource Planning) solutions, there has been an increasing and critical need for powerful interfacing technologies. Application Link Enabling (ALE) and Electronic Data Interchange (EDI) technologies of SAP R/3™ play a key role in the extension of enterprise processes across multiple R/3™ and non-R/3™ systems. Rallying to the cry of "better, faster, cheaper," companies want more tightly integrated business systems. SAP™ has had great success selling R/2™ and R/3™, fully integrated ERP solutions. However, in certain businesses, there are technical, practical, and political limits that prevent an enterprise from running on a single database. With distributed application systems and/or a nexus of disparate systems, ALE provides a solution that enables tightly coupled business integration while maintaining loosely coupled methods to allow local use. EDI provides the exchange of business documents with a company's trading partners that is often mission critical in terms of ensuring fast turnaround of business processes.

ALE and EDI provide the integration layer within SAP's™ Business Framework. This messaging technology ensures business process integration across an enterprise while providing independence to the various business units within the company. ALE can be used to link non-SAP™ applications as well.

ALE and EDI provide the following:

- Data extraction tools
- Guaranteed delivery of the message to the appropriate recipient
- Insulation from the application
- Error-handling tools
- Archival tools
- Audit trail of all the ALE communication
- Customizing tools to address specific customer requirements
- Linkage to third party applications
- Exchange of business documents with trading partners

I have seen many successful SAP™ implementations that have utilized ALE technology. Some were based on organizational splits, where each business unit ran on its own independently operating SAP™ system. Some were based on geographic considerations, with SAP™ systems based on region, area, time zone, or language code page. Others were based on functional divisions within an enterprise, such as sales, manufacturing, human resources, and finance. And finally, some businesses used ALE techniques solely for the purpose of interfacing to non-SAP™ systems. Since your implementation will most likely be some combination of the above, it is important to understand that ALE is extensible enough to be useful in any of these scenarios and that the technology has the flexibility to support many business models.

ALE provides operational independence within the system. Since ALE is implemented with an asynchronous message passing model, every link in your business network does not need to be available at all times. This allows for the possibility of separate release, maintenance, and upgrade schedules.

ALE is not your only option for interfacing separate SAP™ systems. There are many possibilities for meeting your cross-system interfacing requirements. In considering any of these options, you must weigh the costs versus the benefits. Out of the box, ALE provides many tools, all of which would need to be developed for any alternative method to accomplish the same task. With the detailed and logically structured instruction from this book, you will see how quickly you can have a working prototype up and running.

It is important to understand that ALE is not a complete solution in every situation. No matter how many scenarios are provided, they cannot possibly address every business need. The IDOC may not contain the field your team just added to the material master. There may not be an ALE message for the particular business process your customer requires. If this were the case, you will appreciate the extensibility of the ALE technology. It provides the basic building blocks to add fields to an existing message, and it is possible to even create an entirely new scenario to support your business requirements. This book clearly explains the techniques to extend and enhance ALE and EDI scenarios, while also delineating the creation of interfaces from scratch. But remember—if standard SAP™ can't perform the business function required, then neither can ALE. ALE extends a business process across multiple systems. It does not add additional functionality to SAP™.

A word of caution: Due to the tremendous scope of SAP™, its implementation is very complex. ALE is not without limitations. Even though ALE supports integration of technically distinct systems, the extension of business processes across these systems brings with it a need for a level of coordination. Common definition of some, but not all, business objects will be required. How you define and maintain common object definitions can often be the most difficult part of your project. Fortunately, we should expect to see some developments from SAP™ and other vendors in this area.

The other deficiency of ALE is that it is not a real-time interface. This requirement negates more of the benefits of loose coupling, mainly operational independence of the various business systems in the enterprise network. SAP's™ efforts in BAPIs (Business Application Program Interfaces) address many of the synchronous message passing requirements. ALE, EDI, and BAPIs are converging technologies. SAP™ has methods for converting a BAPI into an asynchronous message with a data structure—an ALE IDOC. Both ALE and BAPI are managed in the ALE Customer Distribution Model.

Any treatment of a topic as broad and flexible as ALE and EDI cannot be all-encompassing. This book focuses appropriately and comprehensively on the tools, techniques, and methods to take advantage of ALE and EDI technologies, and the knowledge in this book should equip you with the tools to build and implement a solution. However, it does not explain at length the business reasons for building the interface. The process of developing a vision for a distribution strategy is yet to be a well-defined science. There is not a standardized methodology for resolving the many issues that must be addressed: Why are you distributing? Which is the best approach to take? What additional resources will my project need? There are no simple answers, and these are important questions.

Why are you planning to use ALE? Unless you are only planning to use ALE as an interface method between SAP R/3™ and external systems, a valid approach, you are probably facing one of the following:

- You are finding everything doesn't fit in one system,
- You are trying to get some order out of a landscape of an already implemented SAP™ system, or
- You are dealing with multiple-language code pages, different legal requirements, or organizational issues that prevent physical collocation.

ALE could be the solution to your problems. But I would not recommend undertaking a distributed solution without resolving the following issues: Do you have clear direction and management support? You will need a cornerstone on which you can base your distributed enterprise architecture—a single material master, a consolidated general ledger, or some other compelling business requirement. A management champion is required to gain or force concurrence on common business practices. Unless there is a shared vision, establishing common parties can be a difficult and timely task. I can cite examples where forced commonality was taken too far, losing many of the benefits *loose coupling* provides. Your distribution designs must be driven from your business processes. I can remember long hours mapping business process chains over possible distribution scenarios, ensuring a smooth flow. This required establishing clarity around System of Record (SOR) for various business objects and understanding how users interact with the various SAP™ systems.

I cannot emphasize enough the benefits of prototyping. A prototype project can quickly and easily be set up, even if only two clients on a single system are involved.

This book provides a wealth of information that was unavailable when I was learning this technology. Upon reading the chapters, you will find that, after a brief introduction to ALE and EDI technologies, Rajeev Kasturi delves right into the subject matter. While explaining the steps involved in building the ALE interfaces, he highlights the underlying concepts and associated details. However, the pace is brisk and the book is not padded with fluff! As you progress through the book, the subject matter builds on previous chapters, and the book evolves into an in-depth practical know-how of these two SAP™ technologies, while maintaining its conceptual continuity.

Learn from others. There is an International ALE Users Group, which I currently chair. The only requirement for membership at this time is an active involvement in an ALE implementation. I have found the pooling of experiences to be invaluable. The group meets twice annually and maintains a Web page and a list server. For more information please contact the group through SAP™.

This is a dynamic environment that undergoes rapid change. Expect it. But always be prepared to return to the basic building blocks. From my experiences I can tell you that ALE works. Good Luck, and Cheers!

—Peter Loop
Chairman, International ALE Users Group
ALE Development Manager, Intel Corporation

Introduction to ALE and EDI

Overview

Application Link Enabling (ALE) is SAP™'s proprietary technology that enables data communications between two or more SAP™ R/3™ systems, and/or SAP™ R/3™ and external systems. It is important to realize that when enterprise resource planning (ERP) solutions such as SAP™ R/3™ are implemented, companies have to interface the ERP system with legacy systems, other ERP systems, customers' systems, vendors' systems, or banks' systems. ALE and EDI (Electronic Data Interchange) provide intelligent mechanisms whereby clients can achieve integration as well as distribution of applications and data. ALE technology facilitates rapid application prototyping and development of application interfaces, thus reducing implementation time and effort. The components of ALE and EDI are inherently integrated with SAP™'s applications and are robust in nature, thus leading to a highly reliable system.

SAP™ delivers ALE technology not only with application distribution/integration scenarios, but also with a set of tools, programs, data definition, and methodology that can be configured in a few quick steps to get the interface up and running.

The *message-based architecture* of ALE comprises three layers:

1. *Application Layer:* This layer provides ALE with an interface to R/3™ applications in order to originate or receive messages containing data to or from external (or other R/3™) systems.

2. *Distribution Layer:* The distribution layer is responsible for filtering and converting messages containing data based on predefined or custom-defined rule sets. These conversions may be to ensure compatibility between different releases of R/3™, R/3™-R/2™.

3. *Communications Layer:* ALE communications are carried out both synchronously and asynchronously. Synchronous transmission of messages is typically used for direct reading of control data, whereas the asynchronous method is used for transmission or reception of application data. It is also possible to achieve a pseudo-real-time exchange of application data using tRFC (transactional remote function calls).

ALE scenarios fall into three categories: (1) master data, (2) transactional data, and (3) control data distribution. Although the underlying principles are the same, there are differences in their functioning and configuration. There are over 200 ALE scenarios that are delivered by SAP™; this implies that there are approximately 200 application areas that can leverage ALE technology for distribution or communication of data. A subset of these scenarios is supported by SAP™ R/3™ for purposes of Electronic Data Interchange (EDI).

There are several *advantages* of using ALE technology:

- SAP™ ensures release independence.

- Robust mechanisms capture changes to master data or transactional data.

- Better performance of inbound interfaces over traditional techniques such as Batch Data Communications (BDC) or Call Transactions. ALE does not use screen-based batch input.

- Black box technology—as with an API (Application Programming Interface), ALE user is at a higher level.

- Reduced design and development efforts. Most ALE interfaces can be prototyped in a couple of days, resulting in smaller implementation timelines.

- Little or no ABAP/4 program development. In most cases, the SAP™-delivered ALE functionality meets the requirements.

- Systematic and organized approach to custom enhancements and extensions.

- Due to the structured approach and minimum number of development objects, an ALE interface is easier to maintain.

- ALE is also SAP's™ strategic architecture for "loose coupling" of R/3™ with legacy and third-party applications and is a key element of the Business Framework. ALE provides a message-based architecture for asynchronous integration of Business Framework components including Business Components, Business Objects, and BAPIs.

Electronic Data Interchange (EDI) documents such as an invoice, remittance advice, and purchase order are industry standards based on UN/EDIFACT and ANSI X12, which provide connectivity with business partners such as customers, banks, and vendors. Implementing EDI can enable an organization to improve its competitiveness through enhanced customer services, market differentiation, reduced time to market, and lower cost of doing business with customers, banks, and vendors. Several application areas in SAP™ R/3™ have EDI capability. It is important to note that within the R/3™ system, EDI and ALE use the same set of tools.

Approach to ALE/EDI Development

In order to achieve maximum return on investment, it is important to follow a structured approach to developing ALE and EDI interfaces, as with all software development projects.

After having identified an interface, one must determine if ALE/EDI functionality is supported for that application area. (As mentioned earlier, there are over 200 application areas supported by ALE. In later chapters, a few techniques to do so are explained.)

The first step is to *prototype* the ALE interface in order to determine the standard functionality delivered by SAP™. In most cases, the successful completion of this step itself accomplishes a large percentage of the interface development effort. Most ALE interfaces can be prototyped in a couple of days. This book illustrates an efficient approach to prototyping both inbound and outbound interfaces.

The second step is *gap analysis*. Compare the requirements of the interface with the results of prototyping.

The subsequent steps are to *design* and *develop* the interface to fit the gaps. Enhancing ALE/EDI functionality is greatly simplified through the use of SAP™-delivered tools. Their usage is explained in relevant chapters of this book. *Data mapping* plays a vital role in the case of interfaces between R/3™ and external systems, and also in EDI. (The role of mapping tools and translators is also discussed in this book.)

Testing the interface brings together all the ALE layers—application, distribution, and communications—to work in concert to produce the desired results. This is explained in the section "Working the Interface" at the end of every relevant chapter.

How to Use This Book

This book has been designed to be both a tutorial and a reference. Beginning with understanding the building blocks of ALE and EDI, the book takes you step by step through all the configuration (and programming, if applicable) of various scenarios in order to have a working ALE/EDI interface. The underlying concepts and the possible variations in configuration are discussed as and when needed. In fact, once you are familiar with ALE and EDI, the Table of Contents could serve as a checklist for building an ALE/EDI interface. It should be noted that all steps in building an ALE interface are also applicable to building an EDI interface, unless mentioned otherwise.

Chapter 1 of this book familiarizes you with the building blocks and concepts of ALE, while describing a few practical ALE and EDI interface scenarios.

Chapter 2 explains the configuration and logic behind constructing ALE interfaces for master data distribution, in both settings—R/3™ to non-R/3™ as well as R/3™-R/3™. This chapter also covers the basic and preliminary configuration that needs to be in place for ALE and EDI interfaces to work.

Chapter 3 takes us through ALE interfaces for transactional data interfaces. When you understand this section, you will be able to appreciate the differences between master data distribution and transactional data interfaces in terms of change triggering mechanisms, message control, output determination, as well as configuration settings.

Chapter 4 deals with enhancing ALE functionality and extending IDOCs (Intermediate Documents). This section is useful when SAP™-delivered functionality does not meet all the requirements, and it has to be modified and/or enhanced. Reading this section will also help you to better understand the structure of IDOC and IDOC processing.

Chapter 5 takes us through the exciting and challenging task of creating brand-new ALE functionality. The example illustrated here is for a master data interface. Important concepts such as Change Document objects and change pointer generation are also explained with examples. Reading this section will greatly improve your knowledge of the inner workings of ALE functions as applied to master data distribution.

Chapter 6 deals with the development of EDI interfaces, including the configuration for output determination for transactional objects. The role of IDOC mapping tools is also discussed. As mentioned earlier, many tools and configuration settings are common to EDI and ALE. The commonality will be highlighted here.

Chapter 7 introduces SAP™-delivered programs for periodic processing of ALE and EDI interfaces. These programs are typically used in setting up production jobs and maintaining ALE/EDI databases.

Chapter 8 discusses the error handling mechanisms provided by SAP™ for ALE and EDI processing, using a technology known as Workflow. Steps to configure workflow are described here.

Chapter 9 considers the aspects of IDOC archiving and its importance in a production environment. We also walk through the various steps involved in configuring the R/3™ system for archiving IDOCs.

Chapter 10 describes advanced ALE topics such as optimization and performance tuning. Several optimization techniques are discussed, and recommendations made for the efficient functioning of ALE interfaces. This is an important chapter to read since the inefficient implementation of an ALE interface can become a bottleneck in business processes. Understanding the inner workings of ALE can vastly improve your ability to construct and implement an efficacious ALE scenario.

There are several appendices which complement the information in the chapters, while providing additional information such as authorization profiles for ALE/EDI, message types, IDOC structures, frequently used transactions, and so forth.

Conventions Used in This Book

Following are the conventions used in this book for enhancing readability and understandability.

Menu paths will be represented in Courier font. For example, `Logistics → Central Functions → Distribution`

Transaction codes will be shown in Courier font bold. For example **BALE**.

When a term is introduced it will be in italic. For example *message type*.

Screen objects such as push buttons will be represented by small caps. For example TEST CONNECTION.

Note that most menu paths, transaction codes, and screens are based on SAP™ R/3™ 3.1H; however, these are applicable to other versions because of R/3's™ consistency across versions.

ALE Building Blocks and Concepts

This section introduces the building blocks and associated concepts of ALE/EDI. This terminology is used throughout the book, and the concepts are further explained in detail as and when relevant. These building blocks are fundamental to ALE/EDI functionality, and its creation, linking, and configuration leads to the construction of an ALE or EDI interface.

Logical System

A *logical system* (LS) is the representation of an R/3™ or external system in SAP™ R/3™ for the distribution of data to and from the R/3™ system. (Initially, SAP™ introduced the concept of a logical system in SAP™ R/3™ in order to distinguish the various systems data is being communicated with.) Every R/3™ client used for ALE or EDI has to have a base logical system associated with the client. This logical system becomes the "sender" for outbound messages, and a "receiver" for inbound messages. In addition to the base logical system, an LS should be created within that R/3™ system for each R/3™ or external system used for ALE interfaces. So, in an inbound ALE interface, this logical system represents the sender (another R/3™ or external system) with respect to the base LS (receiver). In an outbound ALE interface, this logical system is the receiver on behalf of the R/3™ or external system with respect to the base LS (sender). The maintenance of logical systems is explained in the next chapter.

Message Type

A *message type* represents the application message being exchanged between R/3™ systems and R/3™ and an external system. A message type characterizes the data being sent across systems, and relates to the structure of the data, an IDOC type (see below). For example, MATMAS is a message type for Material Master, and INVOIC is a message type for an Invoice (Billing Document). There are over 200 message types supported by ALE in SAP™ R/3™. This implies that there are approximately 200 application areas in SAP™ supported by ALE functionality. For a list of message types, see Appendix B. You learn how to create a new message type in Chapter 5.

IDOC Type and IDOC

An *IDOC (Intermediate DOCument) type* represents the structure of the data associated with a message type (DEBMAS02 for message type DEBMAS—Customer Master, WMMBID01 for message type WMM-BXY—Goods Movements, etc.), while an IDOC is an object with the data of a particular message type in it. IDOCs are data containers with intelligence built in. It is important to understand that each IDOC contains one and only one business object; that is, an IDOC of type SHPMNT01, message type SHPMNT, will contain data only of one Shipment Document. Generally, as you will learn, the architecture of an IDOC is independent of the message type by virtue of ALE's capability to redefine it for any message type.

An IDOC consists of three record types: (1) the control record (EDI_DC), (2) the data record (EDI_DD), and (3) the status record (EDI_DS). See Figure 1-1.

The *control record,* or EDI_DC, is a control structure that contains several fields with information about the IDOC, such as what IDOC type it is, the message type, sender and receiver information, direction (1 for outbound, 2 for inbound), and so forth. This information provides control data on the outbound, and processing options on an inbound

Figure 1-1
Structure of an IDOC

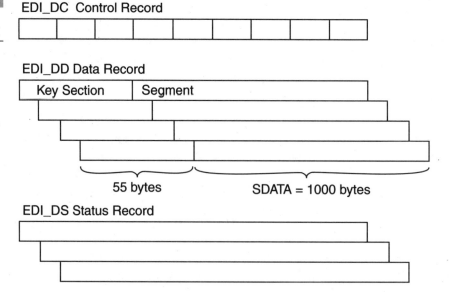

IDOC. It also has as its key the Client (MANDT) and the IDOC number (DOCNUM). The EDI_DC record of an IDOC is stored in table EDIDC. Every IDOC has one control record.

The *data record,* which conforms to the structure EDI_DD, contains the application data. Every EDI_DD record has a key portion 55 bytes in length, which consists of several fields that describe the content of the record. The key of 55 bytes is followed by a field SDATA which is 1000 bytes in length of data type Long Character. The SDATA field holds the application data, and its structure is determined by the key field SEG-NAM (Segment Name). An IDOC consists of one or more data records, and its sequence and structure are dictated by the sequence and structure of segments in a given IDOC type. Hence, the SDATA portion of the data record is being redefined for every occurrence based on the structure of the segment, with the first 55 bytes of the data record identifying the segment name, sequence, hierarchy, and so forth. In an outbound interface, ALE/EDI function modules populate these segments with application data, and in an inbound interface, the application modules process the data contained in the segments. Data records are stored on table EDID2 that belongs to the cluster EDI30C.

NOTE: *In SAP™, from a Data Dictionary perspective, IDOC segments adhere to a naming convention. Each segment has three components—E1 prefix for segment type, E2 for segment definition, and E3 for segment documentation. For example, the first segment of IDOC type DEBMAS02 is E1KNA1M. Its definition is contained in structure E2KNA1M, and documentation in E3KNA1M. When the IDOC is externalized, we see the segment name being addressed by its E2 prefix. For all practical purposes, we will use only the E2 prefix when referring to IDOC segments. Also, note that most segment names represent data dictionary tables.*

The *status record* conforms to the dictionary structure EDI_DS. It contains information on the state of the IDOC as it passed through the various stages of processing. The STATUS field has a length of two bytes (data type CHAR) which has a range of values: 01-41 for outbound and 50-73 for inbound IDOCs. (See Appendix C for a list of status values.) The status record also has date and timestamps of when that particular state was reached; hence, the status records maintain a history of the IDOC states. An IDOC may have one or more status records, which are

Figure 1-2
The IDOC Database

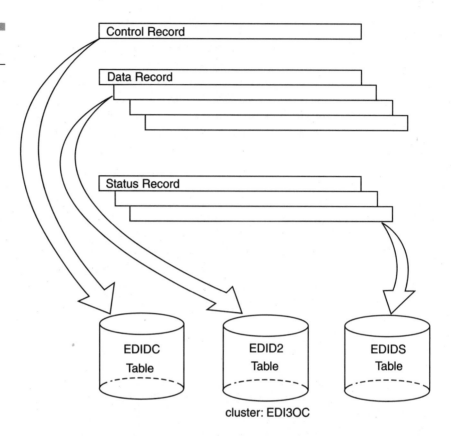

cluster: EDI3OC

stored in table EDIDS (see Figure 1-2). These records can be accessed or created only by SAP™ function modules (APIs), and are not external-ized.

NOTE: *Technically speaking, IDOC objects are known as (1) Basic IDOC type, (2) Extension type, and (3) IDOC type. For now, we address them as IDOC types, until Chapters 4 and 5, where we learn about creating IDOC extensions and new Basic IDOC types.*

In an R/3™ system, IDOCs are identified by a unique IDOC number (field DOCNUM), and all three record types are tied together with this number. The IDOC number is internally assigned by SAP™. It is possi-ble to maintain the number range of IDOCs.

You can display information about IDOC record types by executing transaction **WE61** or following the menu path from the main R/3™ menu: Tools → Administration → Administration → Process Technology → IDOC → IDOC Basis (*) → Documentation → IDOC Record Types. You can reach IDOC Basis (*) by executing transaction **WEDI**, which is frequently used in your adventures with ALE and EDI. (See Appendix E for a detailed description.)

You can display information about IDOC types, such as DEBMAS02, INVOIC01, and so forth by executing transaction **WE60** or following the menu path from **WEDI:** Documentation → IDOC types. (See Appendix F for a description of many commonly used IDOC types.)

Customer Distribution Model

In an R/3™ system, the *Customer Distribution Model* is a tool that stores information about the flow of messages across various systems. The Customer Distribution Model uses an SAP™-delivered *Distribution Reference Model* as its basis. (Note that the Customer Distribution Model can have distribution scenarios other than ones stored in the Distribution Reference Model.) Simplistically, the Customer Distribution Model stores data which dictate as to which messages (message types) flow to which logical systems. Note that many messages can flow to one logical system, and one message can flow to several systems. With the use of filter objects and listings (see below), it is also possible to specify in a model the criteria for filtering information for a specific system. A Customer Distribution Model can be created in an R/3™ system with that client's base logical system as the "sender" logical system.

Use transaction **BD64** to maintain the model. Menu path: From the IMG (Implementation Guide), Cross-Application Components → Distribution (ALE) (*) → Distribution Customer Model → Maintain Distribution Customer Model Directly → Maintain Distribution Customer Model Directly.

The IMG for ALE, Distribution (ALE) (*), can also be directly invoked by using transaction **SALE**. This transaction is used very frequently in this book and in your adventures with ALE.

The process of creating, maintaining, and distributing Customer Distribution Models is discussed in forthcoming chapters.

Filter Object Type and Filter Objects

A *filter object type* is used in the Customer Distribution Model to impose a selection criterion on the message (type) flowing to a logical system. A filter object type with a value associated with it is called a *filter object*. For example, BUKRS (Company Code) is a filter object type available for message type DEBMAS (Customer Master). In order to distribute Customer Master data of only company code "1001" to a particular logical system, you would use filter object type BUKRS to *create* a filter object with value BUKRS = 1001. Note that you can have multiple filter objects with different values for the same message type associated with that logical system. While determining the receiver(s) of a particular message based on the Distribution Model, ALE performs object filtering. As with Customer Distribution Model, filter objects are relevant only to ALE.

We learn the steps to create a filter object in later chapters. Taking it a step further, we also learn how to create a new filter object type.

Listings

Listings are a special occurrence of a filter object type, and are also used to specify a selection criterion for distributing master data. Listings are based on the Classification system (Classes and Characteristics), and are applicable only to Material, Customer, and Vendor master data. Once a list has been created based on certain classification information using the ALE customizing menu, it is associated with a logical system. After this, that listing is used to create a filter object with type LISTING, for a message type associated with that logical system.

Lists can be maintained and allocated to a logical system from the ALE customizing guide, transaction **SALE**, Distribution Scenarios → Master Data Distribution → Distribution via Listings.

Change Pointers

Change pointers are objects in R/3™ that mark changes to SAP™ master data. Change pointers are managed by mechanisms in a tool known as Shared Master Data (SMD), and are based on Change Document (CD) objects. In SAP™ applications, Change Document objects record the changes occurring to master data at a field level. These changes are stored on tables CDHDR (header table) and CDPOS (detail table). ALE configuration provides a link between Change Document objects and change pointers. Internal mechanisms update tables BDCP and BDCPS, which host the change pointers. It is important to note that whereas change document objects are application-data-specific, the processing status of change pointers is message-type-specific. Also, the generation of change pointers by ALE is activated first at a general level, and then at the message-type level.

Using change pointers, ALE provides powerful capabilities of capturing changes occurring to master data and distributing them via the IDOC interface. This feature can be used to keep two or more systems synchronized with respect to master data.

In forthcoming chapters, we learn how to activate change pointers, and also learn to create new function modules for change document objects; we also deal with the steps involved in creating new ALE functionality for master data distribution using change pointers and change document objects.

Ports

A *port* is a logical representation of a communication channel in SAP™, with the data communicated being IDOCs. There are four types of ports that can be defined in R/3™: (1) Transactional RFC (Remote Function Call), (2) File, (3) R/2™, and (4) Internet. ALE can use all types of ports to distribute IDOCs, while EDI typically uses a file-based port. Transactional RFC and File ports can be linked to RFC destinations that are linked to communication connections such as R/3™-to-R/3™ and TCP/IP. By linking ports to RFC destinations, the port can also trigger scripts to invoke EDI subsystems, IDOC mapping software, FTP, and so forth.

We learn more about ports and port definition in subsequent chapters. You can maintain ports by executing transaction **WE21** or **WEDI**, IDOC → Port Definition. RFC destinations can be maintained using transaction **SM59**.

Process Code

Process codes are used in ALE and EDI to identify the function module or API to be invoked for subsequent processing. An inbound interface uses a process code to determine the application module that will process the inbound IDOC to an SAP™ application object such as a sales (customer) order (process code—ORDE), material master record (MATM), or a shipment (SHIP). An outbound interface uses process codes only in the case of applications that use message control (see below). In this case, the process code identifies the application module that populates the IDOC with application data. Each process code is associated with a message type. Outbound process codes are stored in table TEDE1, while inbound process codes are stored in TEDE2.

Use transactions **WE41** to display outbound process codes, and **WE42** to display inbound codes, or **WEDI** → Control → Outbound process codes/Inbound process codes, or from ALE customizing **SALE** → Extensions → Outbound → Maintain process code, or **SALE** → Extensions → Inbound → Maintain process code.

Message Control and Output Type

In an R/3™ system, *message control* is a mechanism by which documents are output based on certain selection criteria, requirements, and sequence. Message control determines the type of document, its timing, number, and medium (print, fax, ALE, EDI, etc.). Outbound messages in SD (Sales and Distribution) and MM (Materials Management, Purchasing) are created and processed by message control records. The output records are stored in the NAST table.

Message control uses the condition technique. The conditions for creation of an output message are stored in condition tables that have selection fields picked from a catalog of application fields/tables. In order to determine if an application document qualifies for output, search strategies are used through access sequences, output procedures, and requirements. Once a message qualifies for output, message control modules use the parameters set in the *condition type* or *output type* to determine the timing of transmission and the medium of the message. The output type also specifies the program or module to be invoked to create the output.

As you might have gleaned, message/output determination are concepts applicable not only to EDI and ALE, but also other output mediums. In this book, we learn how to configure message control and output types for transactional data distribution in ALE and EDI.

Partner Profile

A *partner profile* is an identifier for a system used for communicating messages. There are four types of partner profiles: (1) KU for Customer, (2) LI for Vendor, (3) B for Bank, and (4) LS for Logical System. As you may have realized, KU, LI, and B are used for EDI partners, while LS is used for ALE communications. Every partner profile used for ALE must be based on an existing logical system.

As you will learn, a partner profile brings together several elements of ALE and EDI to define the parameters of communication between two or more systems. Other than general information, you have to maintain inbound parameters, outbound parameters, and message control. The main parameters are message types, IDOC types, process codes, partner functions, application identifiers, message function, output type, and port. There are parameters that also determine the mode of processing and error handling.

Partner profile plays a major role and can be viewed as a gateway for ALE and EDI communications. It routes the specified messages through defined IDOC types to a given port, after invoking the appropriate function modules for outbound processing, while it receives IDOCs of a specific type and identifies modules to post data to the application databases in the case of inbound interfaces.

We deal with partner profiles throughout this book and learn their various aspects. Use transaction **WE20** to maintain partner profiles, or **WEDI** → IDOC → Partner Profile, **or SALE** (ALE Customizing guide) → Communication → Manual maintenance of partner profiles → Maintain partner profiles.

Sample ALE Scenarios

Let us explore a couple of sample ALE scenarios in this section. The first one illustrates a few interfaces with an external warehouse management system using ALE technology, and the second scenario depicts the distribution of master data between two or more R/3™ systems. These scenarios are a small sample of the multitude of ALE interfaces possible. As mentioned earlier, there are over 200 message types supported by ALE in SAP™ R/3™.

Consider a business scenario where SAP™ R/3™ needs to be interfaced with an external warehouse management system (WMS). See Figure 1-3. This scenario assumes that the Inventory management module is being implemented. In an outbound interface, the SAP™ application communicates to the WMS picking requests—materials in the warehouse that need to be picked for packing, shipping, and so forth. Message type PICKSD is used whose corresponding IDOC type is

Figure 1-3
Sample ALE Sce-
nario—Interface with
Warehouse Manage-
ment System

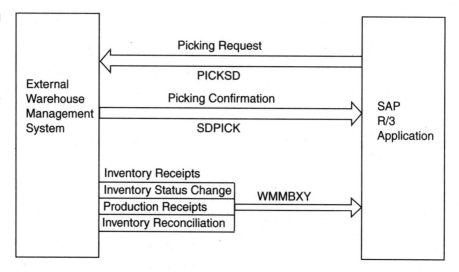

SDPIOD01. This IDOC consists of a header with fields for delivery number, shipping point, total weight of the delivery, units of measurement,
name and address of the ship-to party, and the like. The header is followed by one or more detail segments that contain the delivery items
with fields for item number, material number, quantity, units of measure, and so forth.

After the receipt of the picking request and completion of the operation, the warehouse management system sends back to SAP™ a pick
confirmation. This is an inbound interface to SAP™ from the external
system where message type SDPICK is used. Its corresponding IDOC
type is SDPIID01. This IDOC type also has a header segment followed
by one or more detail segments. The IDOC communicates the material
quantities picked by the warehouse based on deliveries sent earlier. It
can handle batch splits, movement type splits, and also invoke "post
goods issue" process.

As seen in Figure 1-3, there are several inbound inventory interfaces
that can be handled by one single message type WMMBXY. These
inbound interfaces are typically goods movement transactions including
inventory receipts (with or without a purchase order), inventory status
change, goods receipts against production orders, and inventory reconciliation. Most goods movement types are supported by this message
type. The corresponding IDOC type is WMMBID01, which can handle
multiple line items for a single header. In the case of inventory reconciliation, ALE function modules need to be enhanced in order to modify the

data contained in the inbound IDOC for inventory adjustments based on comparing the stock in WMS versus SAP™. This can be easily achieved with a few lines of code in a customer function (user exit) provided by SAP™ in the ALE function module.

Let us consider another simple ALE scenario wherein we distribute master data across multiple R/3™ systems. See Figure 1-4. In large companies, there are advantages of distributing applications and data-bases, especially if the differentiating parameters can be used to seg-ment the data discretely, such as plants, lines of business, geographic locations, departments, and so on. In this example, the headquarters of the company is responsible for maintaining master data such as Cus-tomer Master and Material Master. This is loosely coupled with two dif-ferent plants/companies, 1001/US01 and 2001/EU01, to which master data is distributed. ALE provides the capability of filtering data and dis-tributing them only to relevant systems. Hence, we can distribute the master data pertaining to that particular plant/company code. The filter object type for message type MATMAS (Material Master) used is WERKS (plant), and for DEBMAS (Customer Master) it is BUKRS (company code). Initially, after the customer master and material mas-ter are loaded during conversion at the headquarters, we can transmit ("send") the relevant data to each of the plants/company, and then, on an ongoing basis we can capture the changes occurring to the master data

Figure 1-4

Sample ALE Scenario for Distributing Mas-ter Data

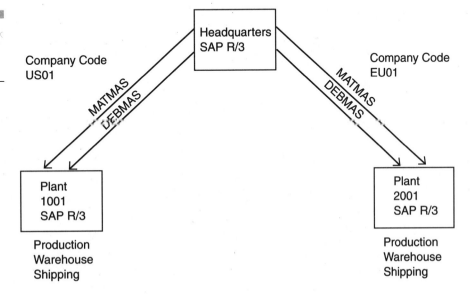

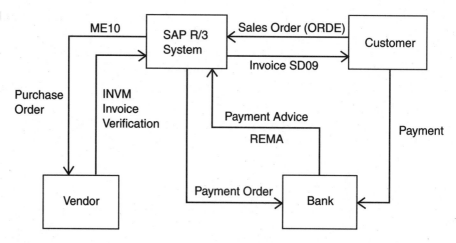

at the headquarters and communicate them to the corresponding plant/company.

Sample EDI Scenario

As discussed earlier, EDI (Electronic Data Interchange) provides companies the capability of communicating business transactions/documents electronically with their partners such as banks, vendors, and customers. This enhanced connectivity greatly improves the turnaround time of business processes and transactions. SAP™ R/3™ supports UN/EDIFACT and ANSI X12 industry standards for EDI.

Figure 1-5 depicts one of the many scenarios possible with SAP™ R/3's™ EDI. In this example, the R/3™ system (company) receives a sales order from its customer (message type ORDERS, process code ORDE). After processing the request, the company could place a purchase order (message type ORDERS, process code ME10) with its vendor to procure raw materials. The vendor delivers the materials and sends an invoice to the company (message type INVOIC, process code INVM—MM Invoice Verification). The company processes the invoice from its vendor and sends a payment order to its bank (message type PAYEXT, document type "PAO") to credit the vendor's account. After manufacturing the product, the company ships the goods to the customer. Then, the company sends an invoice (message type INVOIC, process code SD09) to the customer. Upon receipt of the invoice, the customer instructs the bank to make a payment. The bank in turn sends a remittance advice (message type REMADV, process code REMA) to the company.

As mentioned earlier, these ALE and EDI scenarios represent but a few of the many possible scenarios. A careful study of the various ALE and EDI applications supported by SAP™ R/3™ will enable you to implement most, if not all, interfaces using these two very powerful technologies. With this approach, the advantages are significant and beneficial in both the short and long term.

CHAPTER 2

Master Data
Distribution and
Interfaces

Overview

In this chapter, we learn about the distribution of master data using ALE and the steps involved in building a master data interface. Many SAP™ implementations require the distribution of master data to other R/3™ systems or external systems. For example, certain applications running on legacy systems may require the Customer Master database to process transactions outside of R/3™, or in a distributed environment, the sales department's R/3™ system may need to keep its customer database in sync with headquarters. Master data in SAP™ encompasses a wide range of data such as materials, customers, vendors, classes, classification, characteristics, bills of materials, pricing conditions, general ledger master, cost elements, and so forth. In R/3™, there are over 50 message types available for master data distribution using ALE services.

There are three methods of communicating master data from SAP™ R/3™. The first method is to "send" data directly, that is, an ALE program selects the master data present on R/3™ databases based on user-specified criteria, and creates IDOCs of that type. These IDOCs are communicated to the other system through the ALE communication layer. The second method is to capture all changes occurring to the master data, execute an ALE program to convert the changes to an IDOC, and then communicate it. The third method is to "fetch" the master data from another R/3™ system—this option is available for only a few message types.

Let us further explore the second method. R/3™ provides robust mechanisms to capture changes occurring to the master data through its Shared Master Data tool. As shown in Figure 2-1, when changes (changes are create, change, delete—mark for deletion) are posted to the master data by the application, change document services record these changes in tables CDHDR and CDPOS. These changes are recognized by the Shared Master Data tool which checks if they are relevant for distribution by ALE services. If so, it creates change pointers. These change pointers are maintained in tables BDCP and BDCPS. (Table BDCPS maintains a status flag for a given pointer and message type. This flag indicates if the change pointer has been processed.) An ALE program is run to select all change pointers not yet processed for a given message type, access the master databases through function modules, and populate the IDOC segments pertaining to that IDOC type. The ALE program checks the Customer Distribution Model to determine the receiving logical system(s) for that particular message type, filters the data

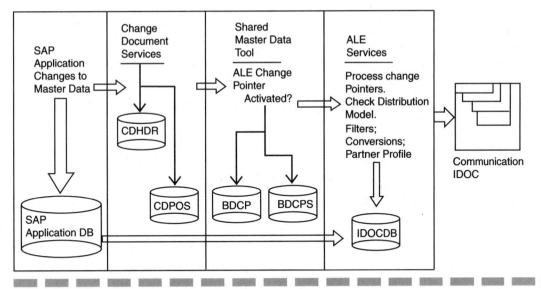

Figure 2-1 Change Pointer Mechanism

based on filter objects, checks the partner profile for the IDOC type, and then creates communication IDOCs.

In this section, we develop an ALE interface for distributing material master data to a non-R/3™ system, using message type MATMAS. We also build an R/3™-R/3™ interface to distribute Class (message type CLSMAS) and Characteristics (message type CHRMAS) data. We will step through the process of "sending" data directly, as well as capturing changes via change pointers, and then communicating them to other systems. This section also teaches you the basic configuration that needs to be in place for ALE and EDI interfaces to function.

Basic Configuration

In order to use ALE functionality in the R/3™ system, you have to configure certain basic elements of the system. This can be performed through the ALE customizing menu (see Figure 2-2). To invoke it, use transaction **SALE** or IMG → Cross-Applications Components → Distribution (ALE) → Basic Configuration.

First, let us set up the base logical system. As mentioned earlier, every client in an R/3™ instance needs to have a base logical system.

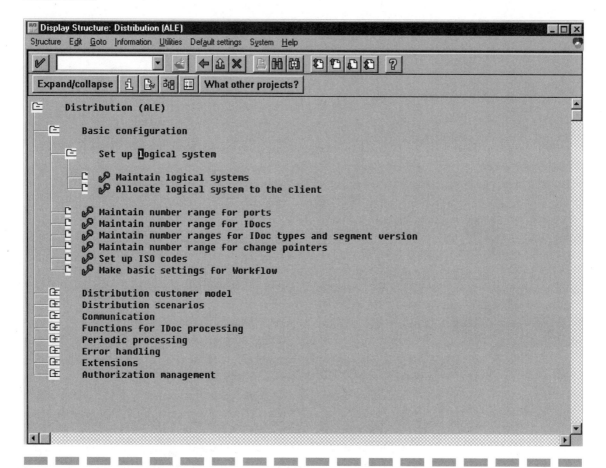

Figure 2-2 SALE—ALE Customizing Menu

This LS will be the "sender" in outbound interfaces and "receiver" in inbound interfaces. To create a logical system:

- Expand the tree Set up Logical System

- Execute Maintain Logical System

- Click on push-button NEW ENTRIES

- Enter the name of the logical system, for example, BK1CLNT010. (You can adopt a naming standard for base LS: aaaCLNTbbb, where aaa is the instance and bbb is the client. This helps in correlating the base LS with its instance and client.)

- Enter a description

- Save

Next, let us allocate the base logical system to its client. This panel can also be accessed by executing transaction **SCC4**.

- **Execute** `Allocate Logical System to the Client`
- You should find an entry for your client, say 010. Select that row, by double-clicking on it, using the push button for details.
- Enter BK1CLNT010 in the field for logical system
- Save

▬ ▬

NOTE: The aforementioned activities are client-independent customizing. These two activities are essential both for ALE and EDI. Data for logical systems is stored in tables TBDLS and TBDLST.

The other activities in this basic setup include number ranges for ports, IDOCs, change pointers, ISO codes, and workflow settings. Other than workflow settings, of which we learn in a later chapter, it is not mandatory to configure the number ranges as these will default to SAP™-supplied intervals.

As part of the elementary configuration, we also have to set up global company codes and business areas. This concept is relevant to ALE distribution for R/3™-to-R/3™ in general. When we distribute data pertaining to a particular company code and business area, they have to refer to the corresponding company code and business area in the target system. Hence, we specify the company code and business area cross-reference in this configuration. ALE requires that we perform this activity for R/3™ to non-R/3™ system interfaces as well. To do this, from **SALE**:

- **Expand tree** `Distribution Scenarios`
- **Expand tree** `Global Organization Units`
- **Execute** `Set up global company codes`
- **Choose** `cross-system company codes`. **Create new entries for the target system's company codes.**
- Save
- **Perform activity** `Assign cross-system company code to chart of accounts`
- **Perform activity** `Assign Company code to cross-system company code.` (**This is where you build a cross-reference of sending and receiving system's company codes.**)
- **Execute** `Set up global business areas`

■ Perform similar activities for business areas as with company codes

Interface to Non-R/3™ System

Let us build a master data interface to a non-R/3™ (external) system. We communicate material master data using message type MATMAS and IDOC type MATMAS02. We then configure the system to "send" material data as well as capture changes via change pointers, and create master IDOCs.

Create a logical system, as explained earlier, to represent the external non-R/3™ system. Let us call it EX1MATMAS2. This logical system will be the receiving LS for MATMAS02 IDOCs.

Configuring the Distribution Customer Model

The *Distribution Customer Model* represents the flow of messages from one system to another. Other than specifying the message type that a logical system will receive from the "sender" base logical system, it also applies filtering criteria to the data being communicated using filter objects. As mentioned earlier, the model is applicable only to ALE.

To configure the model:

■ Execute transaction `SALE`

■ **Expand tree** `Distribution customer model`

■ **Expand tree** `Maintain distribution customer model dircctly`

■ **Choose** `Maintain distribution customer model directly`

■ Enter BK1CLNT010 in the field for logical system. This is the base logical system.

■ Enter a name for the model, say ALEMODEL01

■ Click the CREATE button

■ You will see a tree structure with the base logical system as the parent, and all other logical systems as its children, as seen in Figure 2-3. Place the cursor on the logical system EX1MATMAS2.

■ Click on the CREATE MESSAGE TYPE button. You will get a pop-up screen.

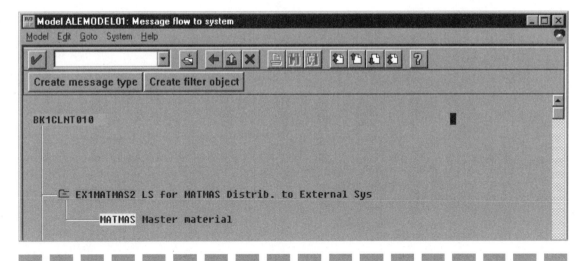

Figure 2-3 Configuring Customer Distribution Model

- Enter MATMAS as the logical message type, and click on the TRANSFER button
- Save

NOTE: *You have the option of maintaining the customer distribution model using the PC tool as well. This provides a graphical interface to the model. In this book, we maintain the model directly using SAP™ screens.*

By configuring the customer distribution model, we have indicated that we want to distribute message type MATMAS to the logical system EX1MATMAS2, with the base system being BK1CLNT010.

Customer distribution model data are stored in tables TBD00 and TBD03. You can access the maintenance of the model by using transaction BD64 as well.

Activating Change Pointers

Change pointers are objects that reflect the changes to master data. They are enabled through change document services and the Shared Master Data tool. ALE programs and APIs use change pointers to select changed master data for populating IDOCs of the relevant message type. Change pointers are stored in database tables BDCP and BDCPS. Table BDCPS maintains the processing status of the change pointer, with its key being a unique change pointer identifier and the message type. Once the change pointer is processed, field PROCESS on table BDCPS is marked with a value of 'X.'

Change pointer generation has to be activated at both the general level and message type. To do this, from **SALE**:

- **Expand tree** Distribution scenarios
- **Expand tree** Master data distribution
- **Expand tree** Activate change pointer
- **Execute** Activate change pointer (generally), **check mark the field Active**
- Save
- **Execute** Activate change pointer for message types
- Choose **the row for message type** MATMAS, **and check mark the corresponding field (see Figure 2-4).**
- Save

Now we have activated change pointer generation at the general level, as well as message type MATMAS. You can use transaction BD61 to activate change pointer at the general level. The flag is stored on table TBDA1. To activate change pointer for message types, you can also use transaction BD50. The data for this are stored in table TBDA2.

After having performed the aforementioned activities, change pointers will be created every time a material master record is created, changed, or marked for deletion. (You can mark for deletion a material at the general level, for a specific plant, storage location, sales organization/distribution channel, warehouse, or storage type.) Note that change pointers for material master are going to be created even if the changes occur through BDCs, Call Transactions, or activation of planned changes.

Communications: Port Definition

A *port* is a channel for communication of IDOCs. There are four types of ports available in SAP™ R/3™: (1) Transactional RFC (Remote Function Call), (2) File, (3) R/2™, and (4) Internet. In this example, we define a

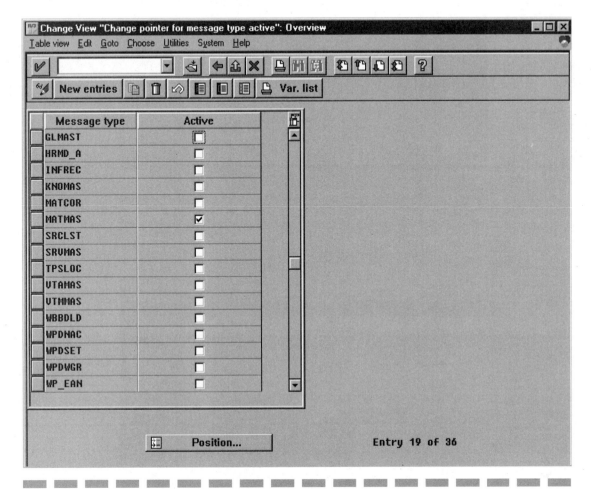

Figure 2-4 Change Pointer Activation for Message Type

file-based port for the communication of material master IDOC to the external system. This will enable us to create a file of IDOCs.

In order to define a port, from **WEDI** → IDOC → Port definition or use transaction **WE21**.

- Choose File-based port
- Click on the CREATE button
- Click on the NEW ENTRIES button
- Enter a name, PT1MATMAS2, and description for the file port (see Figure 2-5)

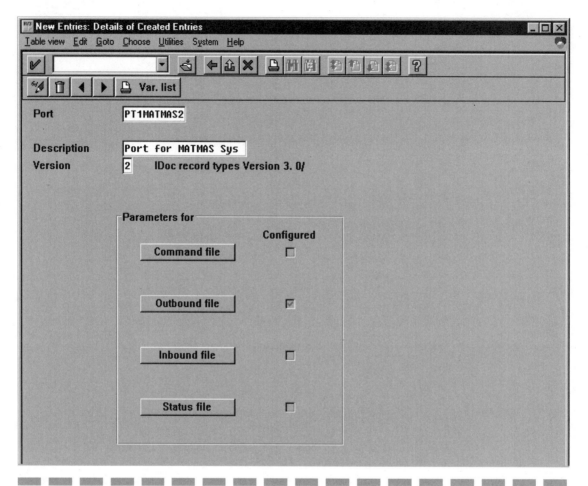

Figure 2-5 Port Definition

- Click on the OUTBOUND FILE button

- You will see a pop-up screen where you can enter a directory, file
  name, and function module. The entry for function module is for
  invoking a routine that generates a file name. There are several
  SAP™-delivered function modules that will create a file in the
  specified directory with the name being a pattern such as user
  name concatenated with the date and timestamp. You can also create your own function module to name the file according to your
  requirements. Use an existing function module as a model to create
  this routine.

- Click on the CHECK button to ensure you can connect to the file server
- If you would like to invoke certain processing on a server once the file is created, such as executing an FTP, you can link this port to a logical RFC destination. Use transaction SM59 to create an RFC destination of type TCP/IP connection. Specify a shell script to be triggered, and the directory it resides in.
- Check
- Save

The data behind the port definition are stored in table EDIPO. This configuration is client-independent and is transportable. We learn more about RFC destinations and transactional RFC ports in subsequent chapters. This configuration is applicable both to ALE and EDI.

Communications: Partner Profile

A *partner profile* is an identifier for the system being communicated with. In ALE, it is based on an existing logical system. The partner profile brings together several elements of ALE and serves as a gateway between systems. Let us create a partner profile for the material master outbound interface (see Figure 2-6).

From WEDI → IDOC → Partner Profile, or from SALE → Communication → Manual maintenance of partner profiles → Maintain partner profile:

- Enter EX1MATMAS2 in the field Partner number. (Remember, we created this logical system in an earlier step.)
- Enter LS for logical system in the Partner type field. All ALE partner profiles will use LS as the partner type.
- Click on the CREATE button
- Enter ALE in the field Partner class
- Enter A in the Partner status field
- Save
- The partner has been created (see Figure 2-7)
- To maintain the outbound parameters, click on the button OUTBOUND PARAMETERS
- Click on NEW ENTRIES

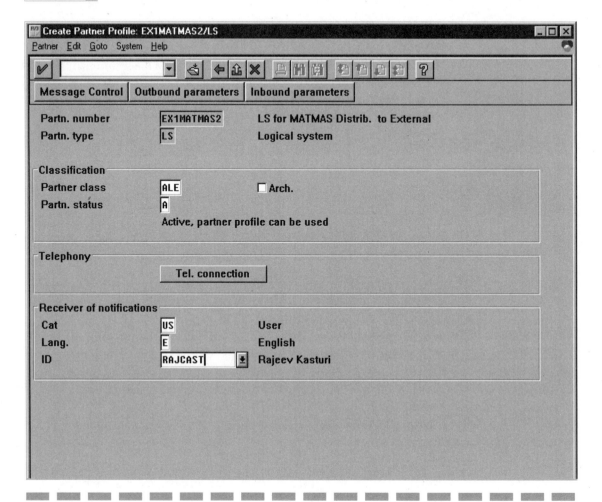

Figure 2-6 Partner Profile—General Parameters

- Enter MATMAS in the Message type field

- Enter PT1MATMAS2 in the Receiver port field

- For Output modes, select Collect IDOCs, and Do not start subsystem. The first parameter instructs ALE communication layer to collect all IDOCs until further processing is requested. The second parameter is typically used for invoking third-party translation software or EDI subsystems. (We discuss these settings and their effects in depth in Chapter 10.)

- Enter MATMAS02 as the IDOC type

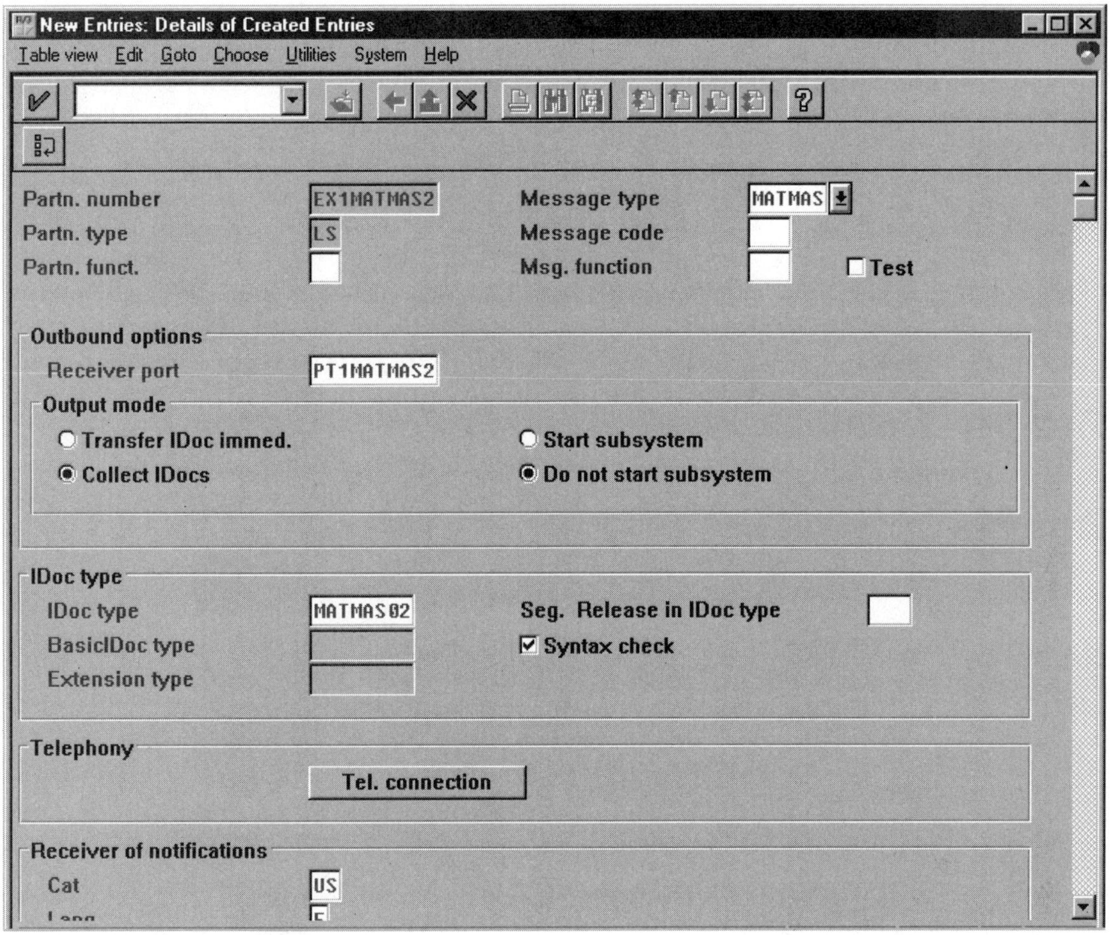

Figure 2-7 Partner Profile—Outbound Parameters

■ Save

We have now created the partner profile for outbound material master interface. Note that the same partner profile can be used for multiple outbound, as well as inbound, messages, given that the communications are for the same logical system. Most of the data regarding outbound partner profile parameters are stored in table EDP13. You can directly access this activity by executing transaction **WE20**.

Note that outbound master data do not use message control parameters or process codes. Also, the fields for notification of messages will default to your user ID. We learn more about its significance in the section dealing with Workflow—ALE and EDI error handling.

Partner profile configuration is client-dependent and transportable. To include the profile in a CTS request, from the initial screen for Partner Profile → Partner → Transport. Enter the relevant CTS values.

IDOC Type MATMAS02   As configured earlier, in this example we are using IDOC type MATMAS02 for the outbound material master interface. MATMAS02 consists of several segments (record structures) in a particular hierarchy. Typically, each segment represents a database table or a material view. For example, segment E1MARAM contains fields for basic data and represents table MARA, segment E1MARCM represents the plant view, E1MARMM has fields for material units of measure, and so forth. When you peruse the documentation for MATMAS02 using transaction WE60, you will notice that some of the segments are required (mandatory), while others are optional. This means that the mandatory segments will always be populated and present in an IDOC, while the optional segments will be present only if there are data available for it, or if it has changed in case of generating IDOCs using change pointers. These segments have several fields that will be populated with data from the database tables by ALE-selection modules. The field names on the segments are usually the same as those on the database tables. As discussed earlier, these segments will redefine the SDATA field on the EDI_DD record of the IDOC. Also, the segment can have a maximum length of 1000 bytes. (See Appendix F for details of some master data IDOC types.)

Based on your application requirements, if you need to eliminate the usage of certain segments, you can perform an activity known as *IDOC reduction*. On the other hand, if you need additional data not present on the Basic IDOC type, it is possible to add segments using a procedure known as *IDOC extension*. We discuss and learn these concepts in Chapter 4.

Working the Interface

Having completed the configuration for the material master outbound ALE interface, we now proceed with the exciting task of testing the interface. There are two ways to work this interface. We can "send" material master IDOCs or capture changes occurring to it, and then convert the changes to IDOCs. Note that there is a third method of "fetching" the data wherein we can request material master data from a reference R/3™ system. This approach uses message type MATFET.

"Sending" Master Data The first approach to communicating master data is to "send" IDOCs using standard ALE programs. In this case, all segments of the IDOC type having data on the master database will be populated, and an IDOC will be created for every master record selected to be sent. To do this:

- Execute transaction **BALE** (Distribution Administration - ALE) → Master Data → Material → Send
- Select a material or range of materials you want to send
- Specify MATMAS as the message type
- Specify EX1MATMAS2 as the logical system
- Execute
- You will receive informational messages indicating the number of IDOCs created. Communication IDOCs are actually the IDOCs that we dispatch to the external system or another R/3™ system. These communication IDOCs are stored on SAP™'s IDOC databases. For example, if in the distribution model(s), we specified that two logical systems will receive message type MATMAS, then for every material selected, there will be two communication IDOCs generated.

You can access this panel by executing transaction **BD10** or executing program RBDSEMAT. If you are sending large volumes of material master data, you can use the parameters Server Group and Number of Materials per process. (This concept is explained in Chapter 10, "ALE Optimization.")

Converting Change Pointers to IDOCs The second method captures all changes occurring to the master data, and an ALE program generates IDOCs based on these change pointers. As explained earlier, ALE has to be configured to activate change-pointer generation at the general level, as well as for that message type.

- Create, change, or mark for deletion materials using transactions **MM01, MM02,** or **MM06**
- Execute transaction **BALE** → Periodic Work → Analyze change pointers

- Enter message type MATMAS
- Execute
- You will receive informational messages indicating the number of IDOCs generated

Once the change pointers have been processed to create IDOCs, they are flagged so that the same changes do not create duplicate IDOCs. Obviously, if changes are made again to the same material, IDOCs will be created again based on the new change pointers. Bear in mind that the IDOC will contain only mandatory segments and segments of fields that were changed on the material master.

You can access this panel by executing transaction **BD21** or executing program RBDMIDOC. When processing large volumes of changes to master data periodically, the change pointer databases could grow to sizes that could degrade performance. In order to maintain these tables, and improve performance of ALE programs and function modules related to creating master data IDOCs from change pointers, you can use program RBDCPCLR. Read Chapter 7 for details.

Displaying IDOCs, IDOC Status   Having created the IDOCs, let us now display the IDOCs and check the results of our tests (see Figure 2-8). The proof of the pudding...

- From **WEDI** →IDOC →IDOC List
- Enter the selection options such as message type, partner number of receiver, date of creation, and so forth
- Execute
- You will see a display with information about the IDOCs matching the selection criteria in the previous panel. The columns are: Direction (1 = Outbound, 2 = Inbound), Status, Message Type, Message Code, Message Function, Number of IDOCs, and Status Description. You will also see lines for subtotals and totals based on status and direction.
- Double-click on the line for message type MATMAS or place cursor on the row and click on button IDOC LIST
- This display will list all IDOCs selected from the previous panel. The columns are: IDOC number—this is a unique number that identifies the IDOC, and is internally assigned; message type; direction; status; sender information; receiver information; and IDOC type.

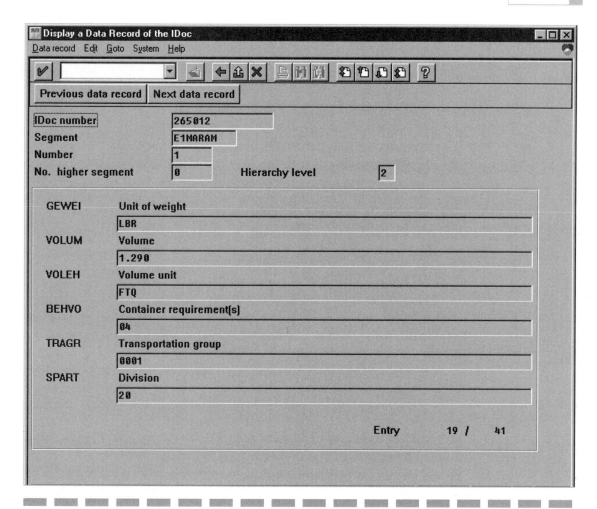

Figure 2-8 Display of IDOC Data

- Double-click on a row or place cursor on the desired row and click button IDOC DISPLAY.
- You will see a hierarchical display of the IDOC number with current status, control record, data records, and status records. Double-clicking or expanding the trees will result in the display of detailed information. For the control record tab, you will see the EDIDC information such as message type, sender and receiver details—partner number, partner type, port. For the data records, you will see a hierarchical display of the IDOC segments that were populated. For the status records, you will see the various statuses

the IDOC has been through, with the current status being the first entry. Each status record may also have associated messages.

- Displaying a segment of the IDOC data record will show you the data contained within the segment. The two columns are the segment field name and its value. You will also see a description of the field.

The IDOC status records, which are stored on table EDIDS, indicate the history of the processing statuses of the IDOC. These values are not externalized and are maintained only within the R/3™ system. SAP™ APIs are used to display the status records. For a list of status codes, see Appendix C.

IDOCs can also be displayed using transaction **WE02** → WEDI → IDOC → Display IDOC or **BALE** → Monitoring → IDOC Overview.

MESSAGE FUNCTION Every segment of master data IDOC types has as its first field MSGFN. This 3-byte field, the Message Function, determines the action to be taken by the IDOC's receiving system. For example, "009" indicates that the data contained in the segment represent an original message, implying that it was newly created. See Table 2-1 for possible values of MSGFN. Note that different segments of the same IDOC could have different values for the message function. For example, segment E1MARAM could have MSGFN = "004," indicating that one or more basic data fields for that material changed, and segment E1MAKTM, being a mandatory segment, could have MSGFN = "018" indicating that the data are being "resent." Also, when master data are "sent" through the ALE "send" process (program RBDSEMAT for material master), the message function fields for the segments of the IDOCs will have a value of "005"—Replace.

TABLE 2-1

Message Function (MSGFN) Values

Message Function	Description
003	Delete: Message contains objects to be deleted
004	Change: Message contains changes
005	Replace: This message replaces previous messages
009	Original: First message for process
018	Wait/Adjust: Data should not be imported
023	Resend

Dispatching IDOCs to Non-R/3™ Systems   One of the settings that we made while configuring the outbound parameters of the partner profile was to "collect" IDOCs. Now that we have created the material master MATMAS02 IDOCs, we need to dispatch it to the external system through the port that we created earlier. (This port was associated with the partner profile in the outbound parameters.) To do this:

- Execute program RSEOUT00
- In the selection parameters, specify the message type, sender and receiver partner details, and so forth
- Execute
- You will receive an informational message indicating the number of IDOCs selected for processing
- Browse the file created on the server. It will be in ASCII (text) format. The file name will be as per the port definition. Each EDIDC record and each IDOC data segment will be a record in the file.
- This file can be translated to the format required by the external system and processed by programs in the non-R/3™ application. The translation can also be accomplished by mapping tools. This is discussed in Chapter 6.

Check the status of these IDOCs through IDOC display. You will see that they are in status "03"—Data passed to port OK.

R/3™-to-R/3™ Interfaces

In this section, we learn how to build interfaces between two or more R/3™ systems. While the underlying concepts are almost the same for either R/3™-to-R/3™ or R/3™-to-external system interfaces, there are important differences in configuration, as well as conceptual differences in the mode of communications. We will work with an example of distributing *Characteristics* and *Classes* from one R/3™ instance to another. While using objects such as materials, customers, vendors, and so forth, it is often required to classify these objects in order to further describe their nature, and to distinguish them from other objects. This concept is called *Classification*. In SAP™, we use Characteristics and Classes to classify objects. Characteristics are attributes that describe the object further. For example, temperature sensitivity of a chemical, and square footage of the shelf at a customer's store are characteristics of objects that can be maintained in the R/3™ classification system. Classes are groups of characteristics that conform to a class type—material, vendor, and so forth. While the term *Classification data* refers to the actual values of the characteristics, Classes and Characteristics can be considered as configuration data. In SAP™, it is not possible to transport Class and Characteristic data using CTS (Correction and Transport System) across systems (development, QA, production). ALE provides message types, IDOC types, and function modules to distribute Class, Characteristics, and Classification data to other systems. The objective of this chapter is to build an interface to distribute Characteristics and Classes from one R/3™ instance to another.

The message types available for this purpose are:

CHRMAS—Characteristics Master

CLSMAS—Class Master

CLFMAS—Classification Data

Note that if you are using the classification system for master data such as Materials, Customers, and Vendors, in addition to distributing the master data, you will need to distribute the classification data as well using message type CLFMAS. In this chapter, we focus on distributing the characteristics and class master using message types CHRMAS and CLSMAS, respectively. We will communicate these messages to another R/3™ system using *Transactional* (tRFC), and learn to configure RFC destinations and R/3™ connections. We also discuss monitoring aspects of tRFC, and get to know programs that will confirm the status of communications. While configuring the distribution model, we will realize the need to create new filter objects in order to distribute only the configuration data that were created in the classification system—SAP™ delivers certain characteristics with the system that we do not need to transport to other systems. Here, we learn the process of creating new filter objects and their usage.

Maintaining the Logical System

Create a new logical system that represents the receiving system, that is, the other R/3™ system. Let us call it CHRCLSR301. Remember that the base logical system for the instance/client that we are sending the master data from is BK1CLNT010, which we defined earlier.

Configuring the Distribution Model

As explained in the last chapter, let us configure the customer distribution model for the message flow of the desired message types.

- Execute transaction **BD64**
- Enter BK1CLNT010 for the logical system
- Enter CHRCLSMODL (as an example) for the name of the distribution model
- Click on button CREATE
- You will see a hierarchical listing with BK1CLNT010 as the parent, and all other logical systems, including CHRCLSR301, under it
- After placing the cursor on CHRCLSR301, click on button CREATE MESSAGE TYPE
- Enter CHRMAS
- Repeat operation for CLSMAS
- If you want to distribute classes pertaining to, for example, material and customers only, then we have the option of specifying a filter object for message type CLSMAS. One of the object types available is KLART—Class Type. To specify the filter, place cursor on message type CLSMAS under logical system CHRCLSR301. Click on button CREATE FILTER OBJECT. You will see a pop-up screen with open fields Object Type and Object. Pull down the list of Object types (F4), and select KLART. Enter value "001" for class type materials in the field Object. Repeat operation for object value "011" for class type customers.
- As mentioned earlier, SAP™ delivers certain characteristics that are used throughout the system. We do not need to transport (distribute) these to the other R/3™ system; hence, we need to use a filter object to restrict the characteristics to perhaps those pertaining to materials and customers. Follow the instructions described in the next section to create new filter object types.

Creating New Filter Object Type   As you know, filter objects are criteria used for selecting data of a particular message type in order to create the required IDOCs. A *filter object type* is basically a field on one of the IDOC segments of the IDOC type corresponding to that message type. Thus, we first need to identify the field on the IDOC that can be used for purposes of filtering data. For example, if we used the field ATKLA (Characteristics Group) to group similar characteristics that we created (configured), then we can use it as the basis for creating the filter object type. Upon scrutinizing the IDOC type CHRMAS01, we find that ATKLA is a field on the segment E1CABNM (see Figure 2-9). Further:

■ From transaction **SALE** (Distribution ALE) → Extensions → ALE Object Maintenance → Maintain object types (for separate message types). **Execute.**

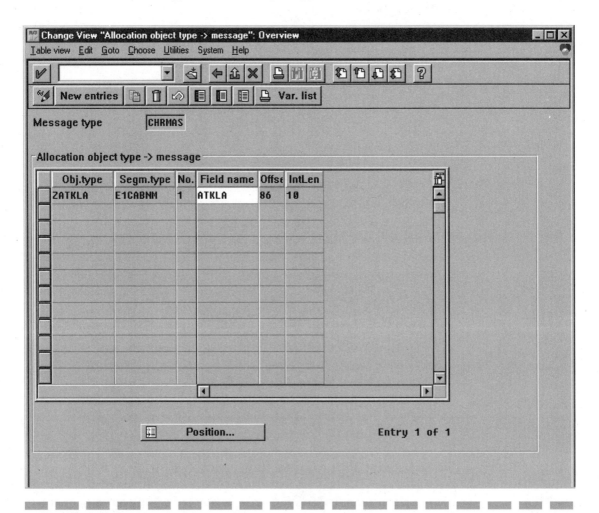

Figure 2-9 Defining a New Filter Object Type

- You will see a pop-up screen for message type. Enter CHRMAS.

- Click on button NEW ENTRIES

- Enter ZATKLA (for example) for Object Type, E1CABNM for Segment Type, 1 for Sequential Number, ATKLA for Field Name, 86 for Byte Offset (from documentation on IDOC type CHRMAS01), 10 for Internal Length

- Save

Now that we have created a filter object type for use with message type CHRMAS, let us complete the configuration of our customer distribution model CHRCLSMODL. Execute transaction **BD64**.

- Expand tree for CHRCLSR301 logical system

- Place cursor on message type CHRMAS

- Click on button CREATE FILTER OBJECT

- Pull down the menu (F4) on field Filter Object Type. You will see the object type that we created—ZATKLA. Choose it.

- Enter value CUSTOMER in the field Object, for example

- Repeat operation and enter MATERIAL in the field Object, for-example (see Figure 2-10)

- Save

Creating CPIC User on Target System

In order to communicate and process messages in the remote system, SAP™ uses a user ID on the target system—this user ID needs to be of type CPIC. Though the user could be a normal dialog user, a user of type CPIC should be used to preclude performance problems such as "maximum number of logons exceeded." Get your Basis Administrator to set up this user ID. Ensure that the ID has all the authorizations required to update that system's databases for characteristics and classes.

Maintaining the RFC Destination

R/3™-to-R/3™ communication uses a method known as *Transactional RFC*. RFCs are Remote Function Calls used to invoke function modules

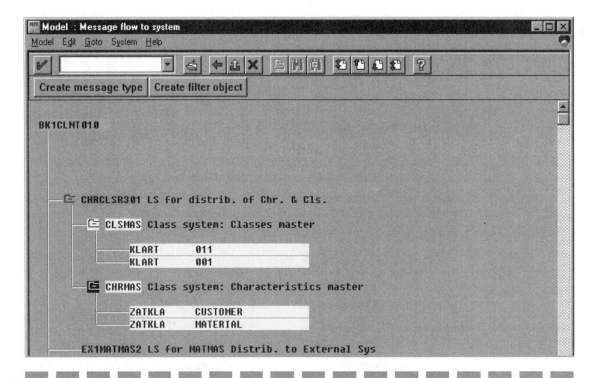

Figure 2-10 Customer Distribution Model for Characteristics and Classes

for transactional or asynchronous activities, typically on remote systems. The word *transactional* prefixed to RFC merely indicates that function is invoked per *logical unit of work,* which for simplicity, could be one material master, one delivery, or one invoice. SAP's™ tRFC and aRFC have advanced mechanisms of tracking the communications of packets of data and maintaining their status. For example, to ensure delivery of data, tRFC calls are "retried" every so often until they are successfully completed. We discuss more about RFCs and their optimization in Chapter 10, "ALE Optimization." To set up an RFC destination for our interface:

- Execute transaction SM59
- Place the cursor on R/3™ Connections. Click on button CREATE.
- Enter the name of the RFC destination, say CHRCLSR301
- Enter "3" for connection type—this is an R/3™ connection
- Enter a description of the RFC destination

- Press ENTER key. You will see a few additional fields appear on the screen.
- Enter the name of the other R/3™ server in the field `Target Machine`. Enter its `System Number`.
- Enter logon information such as Client, Language, User ID (the CPIC user ID defined earlier), and its password
- Save
- Click on button TEST CONNECTION. You will get a list of connection and communication timings for logon and transfer of a certain number of bytes. Note that this does not verify the password entered earlier. If the password is incorrect, you will notice system problems on the target instance.
- Click on button REMOTE LOGON. If you are using a CPIC user ID, then there will be no action taken. If it is a dialog user, you will be logged on to the target system. This is only a test (see Figure 2-11).

It is important to ensure that the name of the logical system and the RFC destination are the same. You can also access this function using **SALE** → Communications → Define RFC destination.

Generating RFC Port and Partner Profile

In the case of R/3™-to-external system interface, we maintained the port and the partner profile manually. Here, we learn how to generate RFC ports and partner profiles for an R/3™–R/3™ interface, using SAP™ functionality. As you will see, the port definition is generated based on the RFC destination that we created in the previous step, while the partner profile is generated based on the customer distribution model we created, as well as the port generated. Follow these steps to generate these objects:

- From **SALE** → (ALE Customizing) → Communications → Generate Partner Profiles
- On the subsequent screen, enter the Customer Model CHRCLSMODL as defined earlier
- Enter details for receiver of notifications. This is to identify the recipient of Workflow messages in case of errors. (This is discussed in detail in a later chapter.)

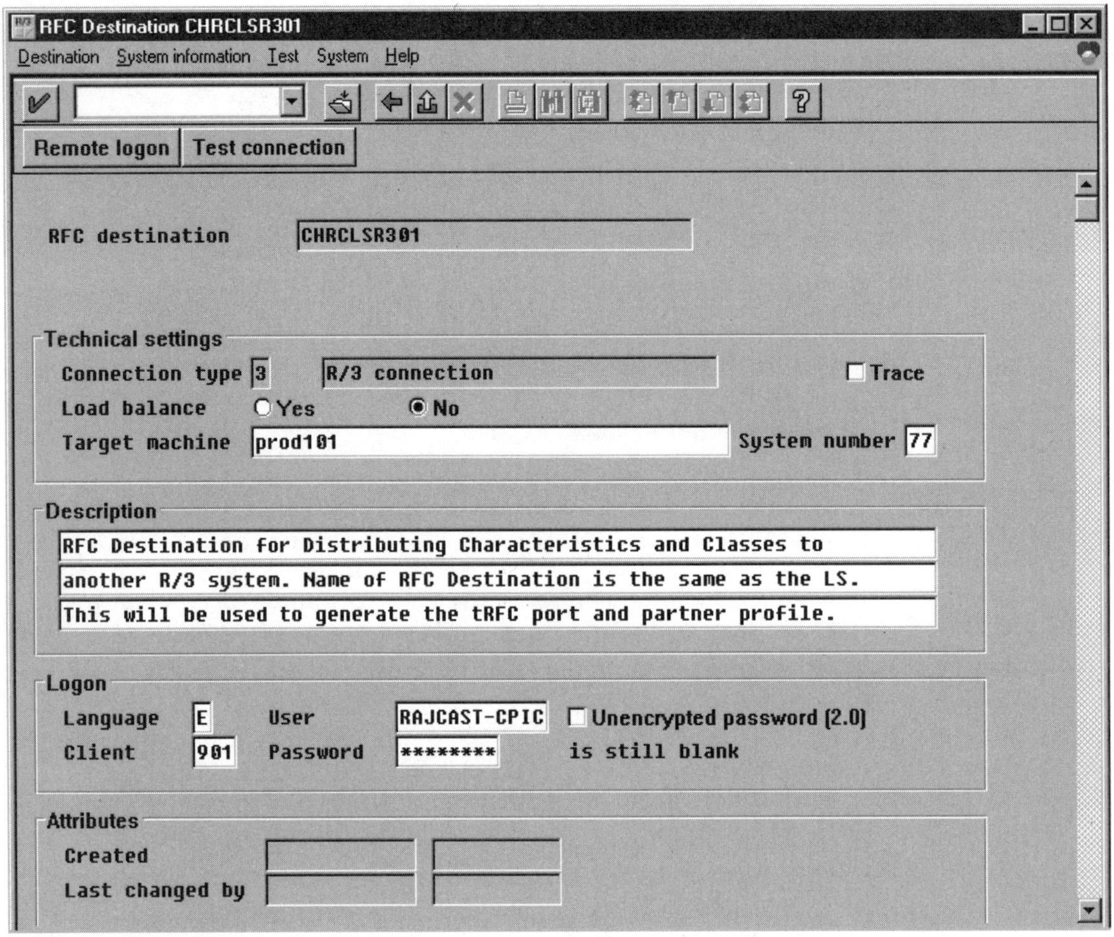

Figure 2-11 Setting up an RFC Destination

- ■ Switch the `Outbound Parameters` to `Collect IDOCs`
- ■ Switch the `Inbound Parameters` to `Background, no over-riding by express flags`
- ■ Execute
- ■ You will see a list of messages confirming the generation of port and partner profile

Note that the transactional RFC port generated has an internally assigned number. If we browse the partner profile CHRCLSR301 generated in this step, we will notice that there are three entries generated for Outbound parameters for message types CHRMAS, CLSMAS, and SYNCH. The message type SYNCH is for synchronous communications between the two R/3™ systems, and is used for validation of ALE functions. Notice that the port associated with the three outbound parameters' entries is the port generated in this step.

The objects created in this process must be generated in the relevant client/instance from which the communications are originating.

Creating Receiving Partner Profile on Target System

We must now create a logical system and partner profile for receiving messages from the sending system. This is a mirror image of the sending logical system on the target system. To do this:

- Create a logical system BK1CLNT010 on the *target system*
- Create a partner profile with partner number BK1CLNT010 on the target system
- Maintain its Inbound Parameters. Create a new entry for message type CHRMAS, with Process code CHRM, and Processing mode Background, with no express override flag. Create a similar entry for message type CLSMAS, with Process code CLSM, and Processing mode Background, with no express override flag.
- Save

We discuss the settings for the processing modes in detail in a later chapter. Suffice it to say that we are choosing a processing mode whereby the IDOCs will be collected by the target system when received from the originating system. These IDOCs will then be processed by a separate program that will post it to the application.

Distributing the Customer Model

The Customer Distribution Model CHRCLSMODL was created on the "sender" system. This determines and dictates the flow of certain message types—CHRMAS and CLSMAS, in this case—to other systems.

This information has to be communicated to the recipient system as well, so that it can accept and process the inbound IDOCs. ALE provides tools to "distribute" customer models. To use this:

- From **SALE** (Distribution ALE) → Distribution Customer Model → Distribute Customer Model → Distribute Customer Model

- Specify the Customer Model to be distributed—CHRCLSMODL

- Specify the Receiving logical system—CHRCLSR301

- Execute

- You should receive a message confirming the success of the action

Browse the Customer Distribution Model on the target (receiving) system, to see it has been created correctly.

Working the Interface

Now that we have configured the system for an R/3™-to-R/3™ interface, let us learn the methods of executing this interface and understand its results. We also learn techniques for monitoring the communications and later discuss performance issues related to R/3™-R/3™ ALE communications.

Sending Data   SAP™ provides standard ALE programs for sending and processing IDOCs. The two programs we are going to use to send data to the target system are RBDSECHR for sending Characteristics Master and RBDSECLS for sending Class Master. Note that characteristics data have to be sent before the class master, since characteristics belong to classes—classes are like envelopes for characteristics. As a first step, we are going to create the communication IDOCs on the sending system. To do this:

- From **BALE** → Master Data → Classification System → Characteristics → Send. This is the same as executing program RBDSECHR or transaction **BD91.**

- Enter the name of the logical system—CHRCLSR301 in this case

- Execute

If the number of characteristics is large, then you should schedule RBD-SECHR as a background job after having defined an appropriate variant. Use transaction **WE05** to view the IDOCs created. They should be in status "30"—IDOC ready for dispatch (ALE service). Browse the IDOCs to understand and verify the data.

For the Class Master:

- From **BALE** → Master Data → Classification System → Class → Send. This is the same as program RBDSECLS or transaction **BD92**.

- Enter the class types—001 for Material and 011 for Customer, in this case. Enter the names of Classes you want to distribute. Enter the name of the logical system—CHRCLSR301 in this case.

- Execute

If the number of classes is large, you should schedule program RBDSE-CLS as a background job with an appropriate variant. Display the IDOCs created and browse them to understand and verify the data.

Dispatching IDOCs to Target System   Once you have created the communication IDOCs, the next step is to dispatch them to the target system. This is when the transactional RFC calls are invoked to connect and communicate to the remote system. Using transaction SM59, test the connection for RFC destination CHRCLSR301 to ensure that the communication channels are open and working.

- From **WEDI** → Test → Outbound from IDOCs. This is the same as program RSEOUT00 or transaction **WE14**.

- Enter the parameters such as message types (CHRMAS, CLS-MAS), partner number of receiver, date last created

- Execute

If there are a large number of IDOCs, schedule program RSEOUT00 as a background job with an appropriate variant. After this processing, you should find all IDOCs to be in a status of "03"—Data passed to port OK. Bear in mind that a status of "03" does not necessarily imply that the transactional RFC communication was successful. We discuss a method of updating this status with the results of the final processing later in this chapter.

Monitoring Transactional RFC   While dispatching IDOCs from one R/3™ system to another using tRFC, it is possible to monitor the communications and take appropriate action to ensure its success. The main tool is the tRFC monitor, which can be accessed via **BALE** → Monitoring → Transactional RFC. This is the same as executing transaction **SM58** or program RSARFCRD. Enter the period and user who initiated the RFC. Note that this log displays only RFC calls that had an error. If you find entries in the log, you can analyze them by reading the system logs and dump analysis for that period using transactions **SM21** and **ST22**, respectively. Carefully analyze these errors in order to take the right action. In many cases, the R/3™ connection may not be active, or the user may not have the necessary authorization for creating entries in the target system. If the problems are other than certain mandatory settings, most RFC transactions might get processed over a small period of time. In case of errors in communication, you might find several jobs in the Job Overview (transaction **SM37**) with a prefix ARFC. These are normal, since the system is scheduling jobs to reprocess the RFC transactions. However, an excessive number of such jobs could bog down the system since all batch processors would get flooded, resulting in a repetitive loop causing more jobs to be created. For your information, the status records of RFC calls sent from the system are stored in table ARFCSSTATE, while those of RFC calls on the receiver system are stored in table ARFCRSTATE. We learn about the process of updating the status of IDOC Dispatch in the next section.

Processing IDOCs on Target System   When the IDOCs arrive on the target system from the host machine, they get created with a status of "64"—IDOC ready to be passed to application. This is because we chose the option of "background" on the target system, rather than processing them immediately. Hence, we need to run a program that will process these IDOCs and post the data to the application. To do this:

- **From BALE** → Periodic Work → ALE Inbound IDOCs → Choose radio button for "64"—IDOC ready to be passed to application. **Execute**. This is the same as executing program RBDAPP01.

- In the panel displayed, enter parameters such as message type (CHRMAS and CLSMAS, in this case), creation date, or IDOC numbers. Execute.

- A list will be displayed indicating the status of the processing

- Also check the status of the IDOCs using transaction **WE02** or **WE05**. All IDOCs must have a status of "53"—Application document posted.

If workflow has been set up, you will receive work items in your inbox in case of errors. There, you can edit the IDOCs if the errors are related to data, and then reprocess them. However, in case of application errors, you can check the logs to determine the cause of these errors and take remedial action. To do this:

■ Execute transaction **SLG1**

■ Enter CAPI for Object (Classification system), and CAPI_LOG for Subobject. If need be, enter time restrictions, user information, and so forth. Execute.

■ You will see a display of errors pertaining to characteristics and classes. Note that you will see log messages for all successful Class (CLSMAS) transactions, too.

In case of errors caused due to system availability, deadlocks, or temporal data problems, it is possible to schedule program RBDMANIN in the background to reprocess the IDOCs in a status of "51," Error—Application document not posted.

How does the sending system know that the tRFC calls to the remote system were successful? There is a program you can execute that collects information about the result of the tRFC call on the remote system, and reports it to the host client. To do this:

■ From **BALE** (Distribution Administration - ALE) → Periodic Work → Check IDOC Dispatch. This is the same as executing program RBDMOIND or transaction **BD75**.

■ Enter the IDOC creation date and the number of IDOCs after which the process can be committed, say 100. This implies that after checking the status of 100 IDOCs, the program will update its status.

If the tRFC calls were successful, the aforementioned process should update the status of the IDOCs dispatched to "12"—Dispatch OK.

Transactional Data Distribution/ Interfaces

Overview

In this chapter, we build transactional data interfaces for a few ALE scenarios. Although some of the concepts we learned in earlier chapters will continue to be used for constructing ALE interfaces, we will learn certain new concepts that are specific to transactional data. One of the main differences between master data and transactional data interfaces is the triggering of the output. Whereas master data has mechanisms such as change pointers, and also the capability of "sending" data as and when required, transactional data in application areas such as SD and MM rely on message control and "output determination." In several other applications, the output (creation of IDOCs) is carried out by specialized programs. This chapter presents the steps involved in configuring both outbound and inbound interfaces. Although these interfaces are set up for communications with external (non-R/3™) systems, they can easily be configured for R/3™-R/3™ connections as well, based on the settings that we learned in the previous chapter.

The two scenarios that we consider are: (1) An outbound purchase order and (2) an inbound goods movement transaction. In the case of the outbound purchase order, we use message control and output determination to qualify purchase order documents on the SAP™ system for the creation of an IDOC. The message type used is ORDERS for the IDOC type ORDERS02. The output type is configured with a vendor as its partner function. As you may be aware, a purchase order is a function of purchasing in the Materials Management (MM) module.

The second scenario prototyped is the inbound goods movement. This functionality is typically used when interfacing external warehouse management systems with the Inventory Management module of SAP™ R/3™. In advanced scenarios, this interface could also be used for mobile data entry in warehouses. Message type WMMBXY is used in conjunction with the IDOC type WMMBID01; this is a very powerful application interface where several goods movement types are supported. You can perform transactions such as goods receipt with or without a purchase order, against a production order, status change of inventory (any combination of unrestricted stock, quality inspection, or blocked stock), inventory lost or found transactions, and so forth. The goods movement transactions supported are MB1A, MB1B, MB1C, MB01, and MB31. By enhancing certain ALE function modules through customer functions (user exits), this message type can also be used for inventory reconciliation. As we prototype this application scenario, we are also building an

IDOC shell program to generate IDOCs that will be imported into the R/3™ system. There, we will also explore the segments available in that IDOC type.

Note that in this chapter we only build interfaces in a fashion that is already delivered by SAP™. We will not be enhancing the functionality of these two message types. (ALE enhancements are dealt with in the next chapter.) It is important to analyze the requirements of the intended interface, and then prototype the SAP™-delivered functionality to evaluate the fit. As discussed earlier, in most cases, the SAP™-delivered functionality will meet your requirements.

Outbound Interface

As mentioned earlier, we first prototype an outbound Purchase Order; this purchase order is a function of the application area "Purchasing" in the Materials Management module. We configure message control and output determination to trigger an output for the creation of a purchase order IDOC of type ORDERS02 based on changes (create, change, line item delete) to a purchase order. The message type used is ORDERS and the corresponding process code is ME10.

Maintaining the Logical System

Using the steps described in an earlier chapter, create a new logical system to represent the external system we plan to communicate purchase orders to. Let us call this logical system ZPOCHG0001. This system is the receiving system on behalf of the external system, while BK1CLNT010 is the sending system that we created and allocated in the previous chapter. Note that you could use a logical system previously created to transmit other message types as well. In order to improve understandability, and preclude confusion, let us use a new logical system for each application area we prototype.

Configuring the Customer Model

Use transaction BD64 to create or maintain the customer distribution model. Here, we create a new model, say POMODEL001, where the base logical system BK1CLNT010 sends messages of type ORDERS to system ZPOCHG0001. The two filter object types available to us are EBELN (Purchase Order number) and LIFNR (Vendor number). If need be, it is possible to use LIFNR filter object type to send purchase order IDOCs for a given vendor to a separate logical system and a port associated with it—simply put, we can differentiate the purchase orders based on the vendor number. Note that we can use the same customer distribution model to transmit and receive different messages from the same or different logical systems.

Defining a Port

Using transaction WE21, let us create a file-based port for creating a file of purchase order IDOCs. Let us name the port POPORT0001. Maintain the outbound file parameters by specifying a directory path and file name or file pattern. Ensure that you can access the specified directory and server by "pinging" the server through the "check" button while defining the port. If need be, you can define a command file whereby a shell script can be triggered at an RFC logical destination. This is especially useful when you need to start an FTP process to a remote server. You can maintain RFC destinations using transaction SM59. The port that we created here is referenced in the partner profile that we maintain in a subsequent step.

Output Determination

In the SD and MM application areas, message control determines the criteria, timing, and medium of output documents such as purchase order, invoice, delivery note, shipment notification, and so forth. *Output determination* is a complex linkage of application objects and concepts, namely Condition Tables, Access Sequences, Output Types, Output Determination Procedures, and Condition Records. We now step through the various actions that need to be taken to configure message control for a purchase order. See Figure 3-1.

From the R/3™ customizing guide (IMG) or transaction SPRO → Materials Management → Purchasing → Message Determination → Message Determination → Condition Table for Messages → Define condition table for purchase order → Messages: Display Condition Table: Purchase order. This leads us

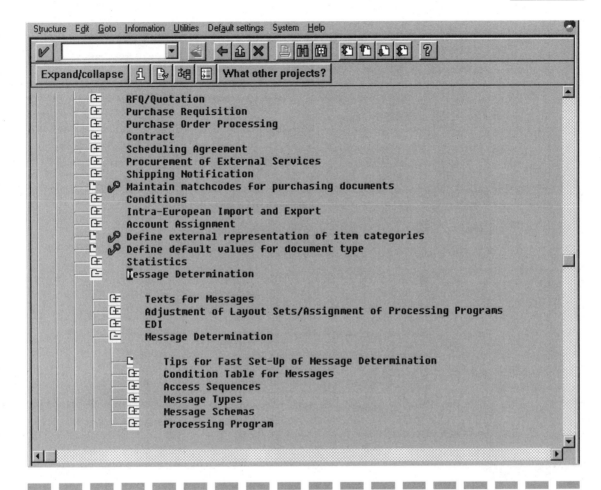

Figure 3-1 IMG for Purchasing Message (Output) Determination

to a screen with a parameter for name of a condition table. A pull down on the field displays the condition tables SAP™ has provided for purchase orders:

025 Purchasing Output Determination: Doc.Type/Purch.Org/Vendor

026 Purchasing Output Determination: Document Type

027 Purchasing Output Determination: Purch. Org./Vendor for EDI

Let us choose condition table 026 (see Figure 3-2). The criterion for selection of the purchasing output is Document Type. The condition table consists of fields selected from a field catalog that has entries of

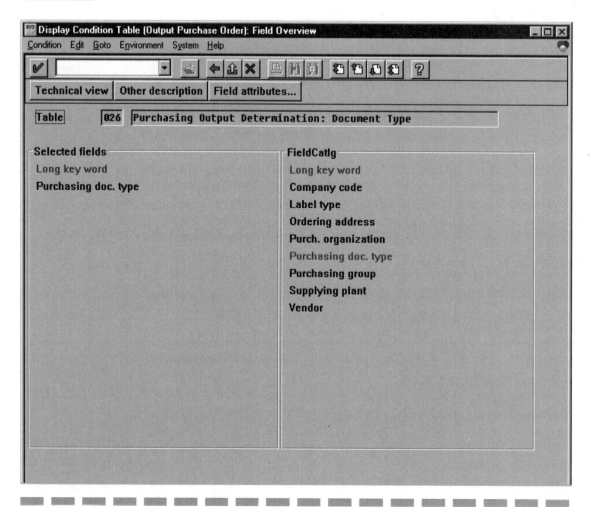

Figure 3-2 Condition Table with Field Catalog and Selected Field(s)

fields that are relevant to the communication of that particular message, namely purchasing output in this case. The selected fields form the criteria for the qualification of the output for further processing. Later, we maintain values for the condition table in "condition records." In this case, the selected field is BSART—Purchasing Document Type. If need be, it is possible to create condition tables with fields selected based on your requirements. In certain cases, it is also possible to add fields to the field catalog, which is based on objects known as "communication structures."

The next step is to define an access sequence for the purchase order. The access sequence dictates the condition tables used to access condition records, the sequence of condition tables, and defining the fields' contents for the criteria for accessing the tables. From the IMG or transaction **SPRO** → Materials Management → Purchasing → Message Determination → Message Determination → Access Sequences → Define Access sequence for purchase order. Let us use an existing access sequence (see Figure 3-3). Sequence 0001 uses condition tables 027, 025, and 026, with 026 being the condition table that we decided to use.

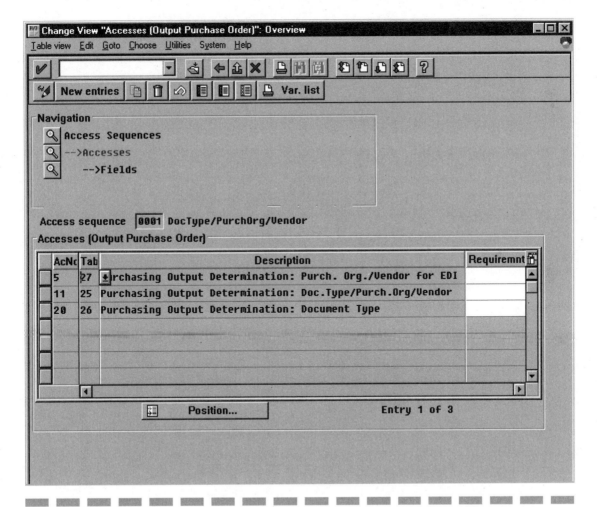

Figure 3-3 Access Sequence for Purchase Order

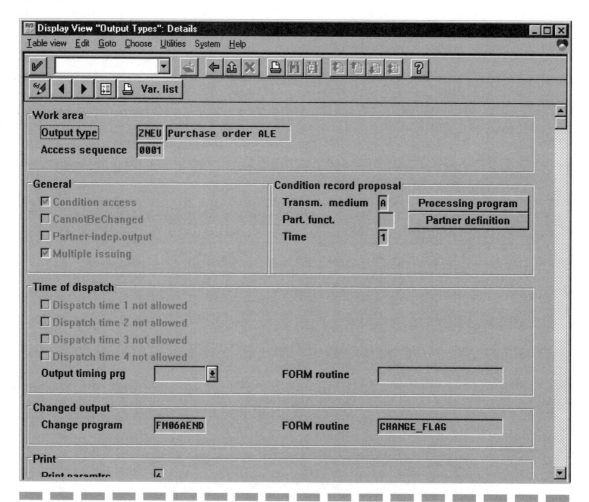

Figure 3-4 Output Type for Purchase Order

The next activity, configuring the *output type* (*message type,* as it is known in Purchasing) is an important step that brings together several elements of message control and specifies the kind of output that will be generated by the system based on requirements specified in the access sequence and condition records (see Figure 3-4). To do this:

- From the IMG or transaction **SPRO** → Materials Management → Purchasing → Message Determination → Message Determination → Message Types → Define message types for purchase order → Maintain output types: Purchase order

- Copy the existing output type NEU to a new output type ZNEU
- Enter a description and access sequence of 0001
- Under the general area, choose condition access and multiple issuing
- Under Condition record proposal, choose transmission medium of A for ALE and time of 1: Send with the next selection run, for example, RSNAST00 Online
- Click on button PROCESSING PROGRAM. Create an entry for ZNEU, with medium A, processing program as RSNASTED, and form routine as ALE_PROCESSING.
- From the previous screen, click on button PARTNER DEFINITION. Create a new entry for output type ZNEU, medium A, partner function VN for vendor.
- You may create another entry for partner function DP—Delivering Plant, for stock transfers
- Save

The next step is to indicate the permitted operations for which the output is activated. This can be done:

- From the IMG or transaction **SPRO** → Materials Management → Purchasing → Message Determination → Message Determination → Message Types → Define message types for purchase order → Fine-Tuned Control: Purchase Order
- Create a new entry for operation "1"—New, for output type ZNEU
- Create a new entry for operation "2"—Change, for output type ZNEU
- Save

Having configured the output type, it is now essential to link it to an output procedure, also known as a *message schema*. We will use the SAP™-supplied output determination procedure RMBEF1. To do this:

- From the IMG or transaction **SPRO** → Materials Management → Purchasing → Message Determination → Message Determination → Message Schemas → Define message schemas for purchase order → Maintain output determination procedure: Purchase order

- Choose the procedure RMBEF1 and click on the button CONTROL
- Add a new entry for output type ZNEU with Step being an incremental number of the previous number. You can leave the field for "Requirement" blank. This field places a selection criterion on the output document. If specified, the document will be a candidate for output processing only if that requirement is met.
- Save
- Go to the option Assign Schema to Purchase Order
- Create an entry with B for output, EF as the application, and RMBEF1 as the procedure
- Save

The last step in this process is to create condition records for the tables that are being accessed in certain sequences that we incorporated in the output type. To do this:

- From SAP's™ main menu, Logistics → Materials Management → Purchasing → Master Data → Messages → Purchase Order → Create
- Enter ZNEU as the output type
- Enter
- Choose the key combination—Purchasing Output Determination: Document Type
- Specify the document type, partner function—VN, medium A for ALE, timing "1" for processing with next run of RSNAST00, and language, for example E for English
- Save

All the preceding steps need to be completed in order for the output to be triggered for processing by ALE. As you may have realized, there are several variations of the configuration that we completed, especially for specifying different criteria, search strategies, requirements, and nature of output. In our configuration, we adopted a simple approach, using SAP™-delivered objects in most cases. This book does not purport to be a treatise on the configuration of output determination; hence, you may use the preceding as a guideline to configure output determination for purposes of prototyping the ALE interface. Contact your functional consultant for more details.

Maintaining the Partner Profile

As we learned earlier, we need to configure the partner profile that is the identifier for the external system. The *partner profile* brings together several elements of the ALE interface and provides a gateway for communications. In the case of transactional data interfaces in the SD and MM modules, we have to define additional parameters based on the output determination that we configured earlier.

First, create a partner profile based on the logical system ZPOCHG0001, with partner type being LS. To do this:

- Transaction **WE20** or **WEDI** → IDOC → Partner Profile, or SALE → Communication → Manual maintenance of partner profile → Maintain partner profile
- Enter ZPOCHG0001 for partner number, and LS for partner type
- Click on button CREATE
- Enter ALE as partner class, and A as partner status
- Save

Outbound Parameters To maintain outbound parameters (see Figure 3-5), follow these steps:

- For partner ZPOCHG0001, click on the button OUTBOUND PARAMETERS
- Click on NEW ENTRIES
- Enter ORDERS for message type, POPORT0001 for receiver port, ORDERS02 for IDOC type
- Select the radio-buttons COLLECT IDOCS and DO NOT START SUBSYSTEM
- Save

Message Control To maintain the message control parameters of the partner profile (see Figure 3-6), follow these steps:

- For partner profile ZPOCHG0001, click on button MESSAGE CONTROL
- Click on button NEW ENTRIES
- Enter EF for Application, and ZNEU for Output type
- Enter ORDERS for message type, and ME10 for Process code

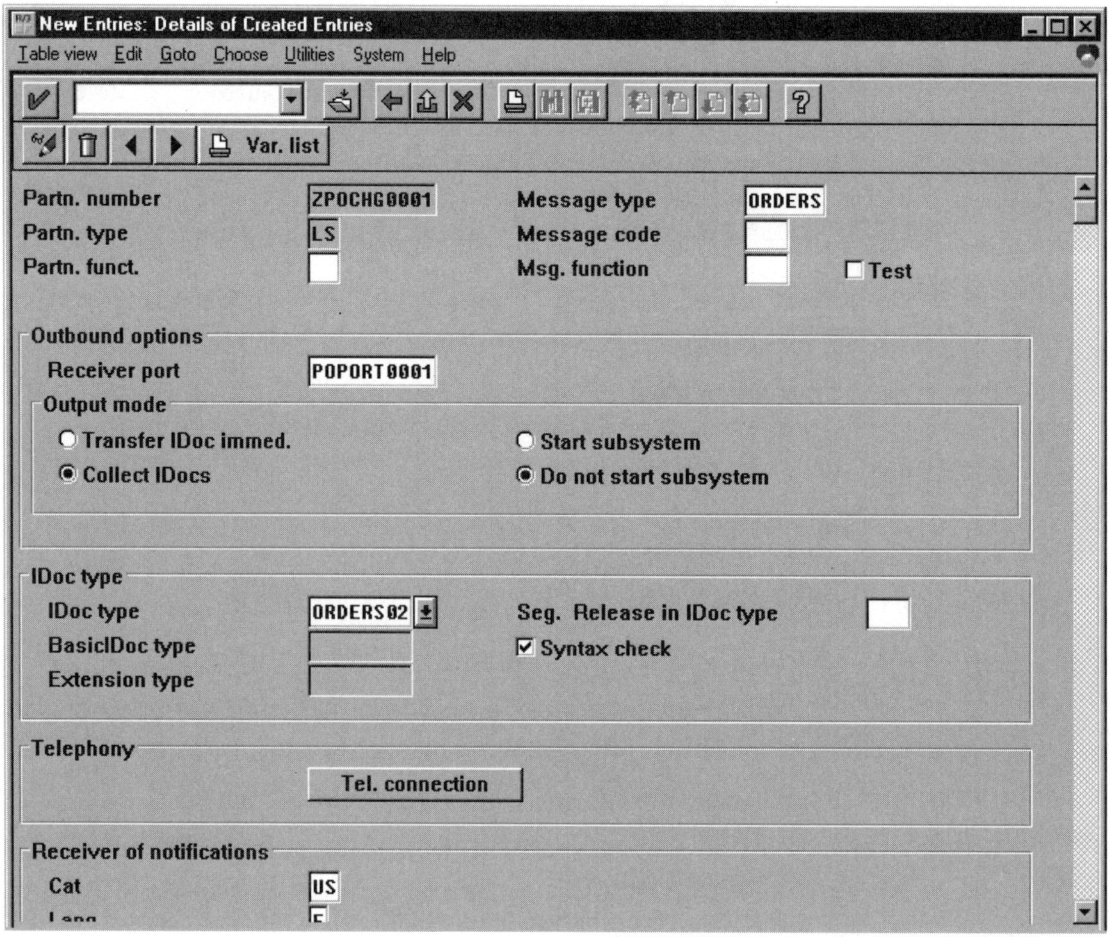

Figure 3-5 Outbound Parameters for Purchase Order

- Save

- Create another Message control entry for Application EF, Output type ZNEU, with the Change message checkbox selected. Use ORDERS for message type and ME10 for Process code. This entry is for accepting changes to purchase orders.

- Save

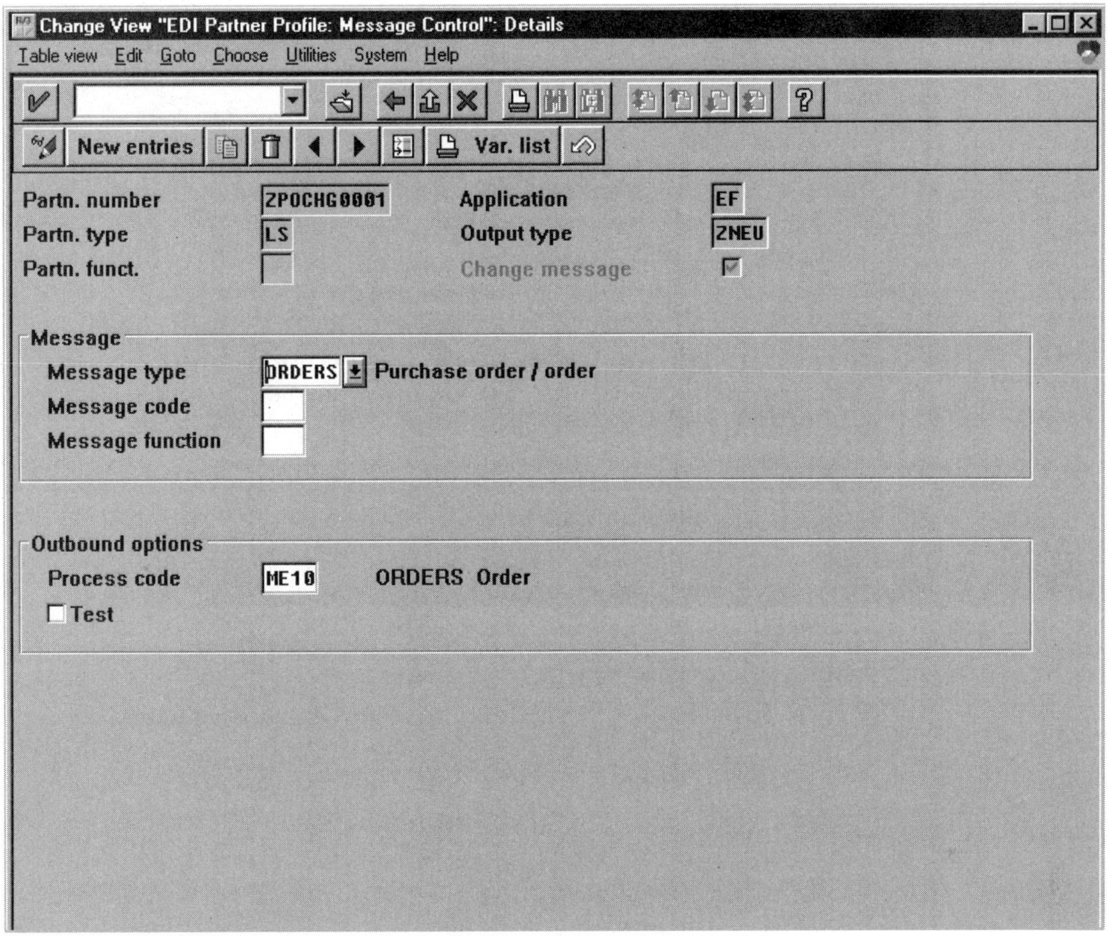

Figure 3-6 Message Control for Purchase Order

Working the Interface

Having completed all the configuration required for generating Purchase Order outbound IDOCs, we now proceed with the exciting task of testing the interface. There are three steps involved in this task:

1. Create or change a purchase order. Ensure that an output (message) has been generated of type ZNEU.

2. Process the preceding output to create an IDOC.

3. Dispatch the IDOC to the external system.

In order to create purchase orders, use transaction `ME21` (Vendor known) or from SAP™ main menu `Logistics` → `Materials Management` → `Purchasing` → `Purchase Order` → `Create` → `Vendor known`. You can also use transaction `ME25`—Vendor unknown. Enter a document type that is valid for message control; that is, enter a purchase order document type that was used for creating condition records during the configuration of output determination. Enter the material number, quantity, plant, storage location, unit price, and the like, for the purchase order. Ensure that the line item has been accepted. To see if the output record has been created:

- From the purchase order overview screen → `Header` → `Messages`
- There should be an entry for output type `ZNEU` with medium `A` for ALE, partner function `VN` for vendor, language `E` for English, and status of 0. The status value 0 indicates that the output record created has not yet been processed
- Save the purchase order
- As you can see in Figure 3-7, if the document has been changed, you will see the flag set for the last column `CHNG`. Only if there exists an entry in the partner profile's message control for change messages will the output be processed into an IDOC in such a situation

Processing Output   When an output record is created based on the output determination that we configured, an entry is created in the NAST table. This table stores output records for all applications using message control. Note that this is not a table specific to ALE, but for the application per se. The NAST table also stores the status of the output record, namely; 0, for not yet processed; 1, for processed successfully; 2, for processed with errors; and 3, for inactive. Programs that process output based on message control, access the NAST table with function modules to gather control information such as the object key (the purchase order number, for example). Subsequently, these programs generate the output in a particular medium, as defined in the output record. After having created the output, the NAST table is updated with the correct status of the output record.

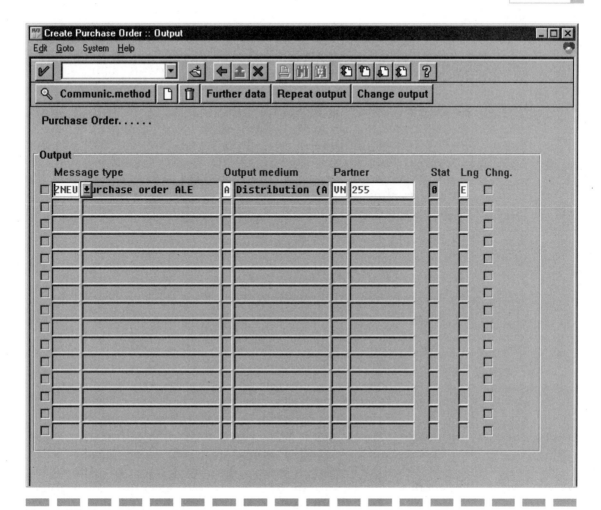

Figure 3-7 Output (message) Record for Purchase Order

In order to process the output record we created earlier, follow these steps:

- Execute program RSNAST00 or from **WEDI** → Test → Outbound from NAST or transaction **WE15**
- Enter EF for Output application, ZNEU for Output type, and A for Output medium
- Execute

- You will receive informational messages regarding the success of the action, along with an IDOC number

Using transaction **WE02** or **WE05**, check the IDOCs created by the preceding process. Inspect the data segments to ensure that the IDOC was populated with the correct information.

Dispatching IDOCs   Now that we have created purchase order IDOCs on the R/3™ system, we need to dispatch it to the external system. Since we defined the port POPORT0001 as a file-based port, we will be creating a file of purchase order IDOCs that can be sent to the external system. To do this:

- Execute program RSEOUT00 or transaction **WEDI** → Test → Outbound from IDOC or transaction **WE14**
- Enter selection criteria such as message type, partner details of receiver, port of receiver, and so forth
- Execute
- You should receive an informational message indicating the number of IDOCs processed

Check the directory on the server designated to receive the file, as configured in the port POPORT0001. SAP™ should have created a file with the name or pattern specified in the port definition. Browse the file's contents and ensure that it is the data that should have been created.

This file can be sent across to the other system by means of an FTP or other such utility. The process can be automated by specifying a command file (shell script) at an RFC logical destination that gets triggered after the creation of the file. It is also possible to define the port as a transactional RFC port, and invoke programs (third-party software) that will communicate the IDOC to the external system. This software may also be capable of translating the IDOC into the format required by the external system. We discuss these options further in a later chapter.

Inbound Interface

In this section, we prototype an inbound interface: a goods movement interface from an external warehouse management system to SAP™ R/3's™ Inventory Management module. The ALE message type used is

WMMBXY with a corresponding IDOC type of WMMBID01. This functionality in SAP™ was originally designed to work with a warehouse system for mobile data entry of stocks. Upon entry of data on the mobile terminal, external software would transmit the data to the SAP™ server where it would get formatted into an IDOC, and imported into the R/3™ system using tRFC for posting to the application. As you can see, ALE is capable of handling real-time or pseudo-real-time interfaces to external systems or other R/3™ systems, using transactional RFC connections. The goods movement interface that is being configured and tested here can be set up in several ways to suit your requirements. WMMBXY is a powerful message type that supports many movement types and goods movement transactions, including and not limited to goods receipt with or without a purchase order, goods receipt against production orders, inventory lost and found transactions, and inventory status change.

There are a few limitations of this message type, too. For example, even though the goods movement IDOC has the capability of creating a material batch when creating a material document, it does not create its corresponding batch characteristic values. To accomplish this functionality, you need to enhance the ALE functionality by extending the IDOC and writing code in the customer functions (user exits) provided by SAP™. (IDOC extensions and ALE enhancements are discussed in the next chapter.) Also, in order to use this interface for inventory reconciliation, you have to enhance the functionality by adding code in the SAP™-provided customer functions. However, as you will discover, this interface provides several powerful functions.

Generally speaking, the steps described below should be sufficient to set up ALE in order to prototype an inbound interface. An important requirement to successfully prototype an ALE interface is to understand the business needs, investigate the capabilities of the message type and ALE function modules by understanding the purpose of the data segments, and testing it with variations of data based on different application scenarios.

An important element in inbound interfaces is the process code. The *process code,* which is maintained in the inbound parameters of the partner profile, determines the application function module that is to be invoked for further processing or for posting the document to the application. This function module also contains code that triggers error processing through components such as Workflow. For example, WMMB is the process code that is used for this interface, and it invokes function module L_IDOC_INPUT_WMMBXY. As discussed earlier, this function module has customer functions (user exits) that can be enhanced to add or modify its functionality.

You can browse or maintain process codes by: **WEDI** → Control → Inbound process codes → Inbound with ALE service, for inbound interfaces; for outbound, **WEDI** → Control → Outbound process codes → Outbound with ALE service. Or, you can use transactions **WE42** and **WE41**, respectively.

Let us proceed with the configuration for our inbound ALE interface.

Maintaining the Logical System

Create a logical system to represent the external system. In this case, the external system's logical system will be the sender system, while the base logical system (BK1CLNT010) will be the receiving system. To do this:

- From **SALE** → Basic Configuration → Set up logical systems → Maintain logical systems. (This is a client-independent activity.)
- Click on button NEW ENTRIES
- Enter the name of the logical system, say GOODSMVT01, and a description
- Save

As mentioned earlier, you can use a logical system for multiple message types for both inbound and outbound interfaces, as long as the correct parameters are maintained in the partner profile that is based on this logical system. However, for better understandability, error handling, and maintenance, it is better to represent each system with its own logical system and partner profile.

NOTE: *It is not necessary to maintain the customer distribution model in this case. It would be needed if communicating with a remote R/3™ system. In such a case, you would distribute the customer model from the remote system to this R/3™ system. Also, for the purposes of this configuration and testing wherein we will be importing a file of IDOCs, it is not required to maintain the port definition.*

Maintaining the Partner Profile

The next step in the process is to create a partner profile for the external system, based on the logical system that we configured. This partner profile will tie together the various ALE objects and settings, and provide a gateway for communications. In this example, we configure only the inbound parameters, since message control and outbound parameters do not apply. Note that you can use a partner profile (and its logical system) for defining multiple inbound and outbound messages. Proceed as follows (see Figure 3-8):

- Execute transaction **WE20** or **WEDI** → IDOC → Partner profile or **SALE** → Communication → Manual maintenance of partner profiles → Maintain partner profiles
- Enter GOODSMVT01 for Partner number, LS for Partner type
- Click on button CREATE
- Enter ALE for Partner class, and A for Partner status
- Save. The partner has been created
- Click on button INBOUND PARAMETERS
- Click on button NEW ENTRIES
- Enter WMMBXY for message type, and WMMB for Process code
- The checkbox for Syntax Check should be checked. This implies that the syntax of the inbound IDOC imported into the system will be checked; that is, it will validate the segments, hierarchy, and other structure-related rules that are defined in the IDOC type. As you will see later, it is our responsibility to maintain the syntax and integrity of the IDOC type. An error message will be issued if the IDOC fails the syntax check; this applies to both the inbound and outbound IDOC types. For your information, syntax data for an IDOC type can be found in table EDISYN.
- Under Processing options, choose the radio-button PROCESS IMMEDIATELY. This implies that the IDOC data will be posted to the application during the process of importing it into the system. In case you choose the option Background processing, no override with express flag or Background processing, override possible with express flag, then you have to schedule program RBDAPP01 to post the IDOC created in status 64—Ready to be passed to application. This mysterious "express"

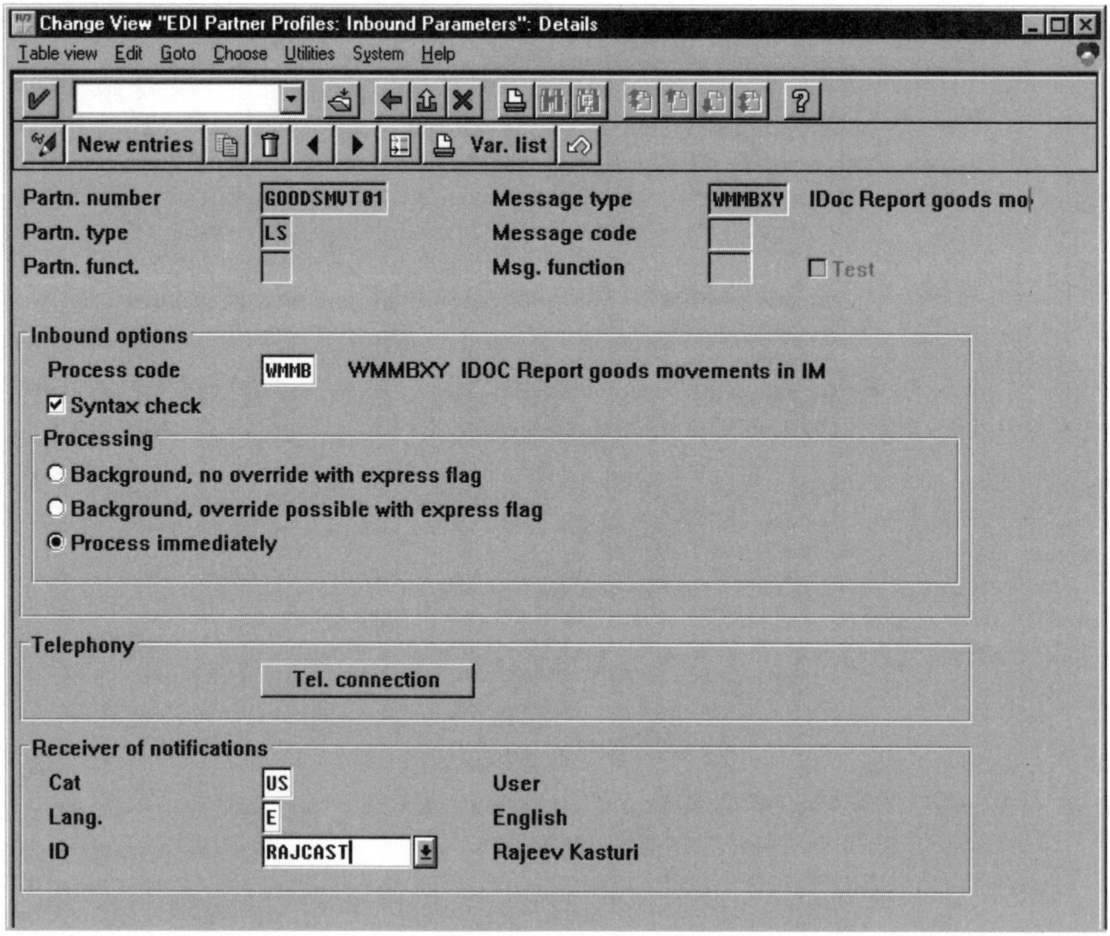

Figure 3-8 Inbound Parameters for Goods Movement Interface

flag is applicable only to inbound IDOCs, and is specified on the EDIDC record of an IDOC in the field EXPRSS. If this field has a value of "X," and if the processing option in the partner profile is set to `Background processing, override possible with express flag`, then that particular IDOC is processed immediately.

■ Save

The partner profile has now been configured for the inbound goods movement interface.

Working the Interface

Having completed the ALE configuration for the interface, we now launch into the exciting task of testing it. In the case of outbound interfaces, it is easy to test the setup since the data either exists in SAP™ or can be created with minimal effort. However, with inbound ALE interfaces, we have to create the IDOC and import it into SAP™ for further processing. For purposes of testing and prototyping, this can be easily achieved by writing a simple ABAP/4 program that creates a file of IDOCs, which can then be imported into SAP™ through normal channels. Also, after having prototyped the interface, it is important to create a mapping document that relates the record layout of the external system to the IDOC type. It is possible to use a mapping tool/translation software that converts the external system records to IDOCs. Some mapping software products have been certified by SAP™ for purposes of ALE/EDI interfaces. They also are equipped with "ALE Adapters" that link with the R/3™ system, thereby providing a seamless interface with the external system. We discuss the role of mapping tools in Chapter 6.

Creating an IDOC Shell Program   In order to test our interface, we need to create an ABAP/4 program that will produce IDOCs. Also, to successfully prototype the interface, it is important to understand the various segments of the IDOC type and its fields. For example, certain values of a particular field could influence the application to process data in a preset manner, or even incorrectly. Read the documentation on that IDOC type (transaction **WE60**) thoroughly before prototyping the interface.

The WMMBID01 IDOC type consists of two segments: (1) E2MBXYH for header data and (2) E2MBXYI for item data. Both are mandatory segments, and every IDOC should be comprised of one E2MBXYH EDIDD record followed by one or more E2MBXYI EDIDD records. Of course, each IDOC will also have as its first record the EDIDC record. The header segment consists of fields such as posting date, document date, document reference number and text, transaction code, and so forth, while the detail segment has several fields that require information such as material number, movement type, plant, storage location, purchase order number, quantity, units of measure, and so on. (See Appendix F for details of the WMMBID01 IDOC type.) There are certain flags on the E2MBXYI segment that indicate or control the processing of the document in the SAP™ application. For example, field E2MBXYI-KZBEW should have a value of "B" for goods receipt against a purchase order, and "F" for a production order. If the interface is handling large volumes of data, or if it is a business requirement, you could package several detail lines for one single header, given that all detail items have the same transaction code; however, from a technical perspective, this is not essential.

Let us inspect the general structure of this IDOC shell program. The first record being written in the file is the EDIDC record, which contains control information about the IDOC such as client, direction, sender partner details, receiver partner details, ports, message type, IDOC type, and so forth. (See Appendix E for details on IDOC record structures.) (Note that the port name by default has to have the value SAP™<SID>, where <SID> is the name of the instance. For example, if the instance is BK1, then the port name would be SAPBK1.) EDIDD records follow the EDIDC record created. We first populate the key information of the EDIDD record structure such as segment name. You can leave fields like segment number and hierarchy level blank, as they will be resolved by SAP™ when the IDOC is added to the system. Then, the SDATA segment is formatted with E2MBXYH header data and moved into field SDATA of the EDIDD record. This record is then written to the file. The same operation is repeated for E2MBXYI detail lines, and the EDIDD records are written to the file. This completes the creation of one IDOC in the file. If need be, you can create several such IDOCs in the same file with different sets of data. See the source listing in Figure 3-9.

NOTE: *In case of message types corresponding to IDOC types that can be used for both outbound and inbound processing, you can use transaction* **WE12** *to modify the IDOC file for inbound processing. For this, you must first create the outbound file.*

Figure 3-9
Sample IDOC Shell
Program

```
REPORT ZWMMBXY1.
*
*********************************************************************
*******
***This is an IDOC shell program to create WMMBID01 IDocs for ***
*** the Goods Movement interface between an external warehouse
***
*** management system and SAP R/3's Inventory Management module.
***
*********************************************************************
*******
TABLES :
    E2MBXYH,                    " WMMBID01 IDoc type's header segment
    E2MBXYI.                    " WMMBID01 IDoc type's detail segment
*       idoc control record
DATA:   BEGIN OF IDOC_CONTROL.
          INCLUDE STRUCTURE EDI_DC.
DATA:   END OF IDOC_CONTROL.

*       idoc data record
DATA:   BEGIN OF INT_EDIDD.
          INCLUDE STRUCTURE EDI_DD.
DATA:   END OF INT_EDIDD.
*
PARAMETERS:
*  SAP IM Inbound Test file of IDocs
    OUTFILE(40)  TYPE C  LOWER CASE      " output filename
                         DEFAULT '/home/rajcast/invadj50.tst'.
*
START-OF-SELECTION.
*
***** Open the output file
*
  OPEN DATASET OUTFILE FOR OUTPUT IN TEXT MODE.
  IF SY-SUBRC NE 0.
    WRITE: / 'Error opening outfile!', SY-SUBRC.
    EXIT.
  ENDIF.
*******
  CLEAR: IDOC_CONTROL, INT_EDIDD.
*********************************************************************
*******
*     SET CONTROL VARIABLES AND WRITE CONTROL RECORD
*********************************************************************
```

Figure 3-9
Sample IDOC Shell
Program (*Continued*)

```
*
   IDOC_CONTROL-TABNAM        = 'EDI_DC'.            "Table name
   IDOC_CONTROL-MANDT         = SY-MANDT.            "Client
   IDOC_CONTROL-DOCREL        = SY-SAPRL.            "SAP release
*  IDOC_CONTROL-DOCNUM        =                      "edi doc number
   IDOC_CONTROL-DOCTYP        = 'WMMBID01'.          "IDOC type
   IDOC_CONTROL-DIRECT        = '2'.                 "Direction
   IDOC_CONTROL-RCVPOR        = 'SAPBK1'.            "Receiver Port
   IDOC_CONTROL-RCVPRT        = 'LS'.                "Receiver Partner
                                                      Type
   IDOC_CONTROL-RCVPRN        = 'BK1CLNT010'.        "Receiver Partner
   IDOC_CONTROL-SNDPOR        = 'SAPBK1'.            "Sender port
   IDOC_CONTROL-SNDPRT        = 'LS'.                "Partner Type for
                                                      sender
   IDOC_CONTROL-SNDPRN        = 'GOODSMVT01'.        "Sender Partner
   IDOC_CONTROL-SNDPFC        = SPACE.               "Sender Partner,
                                                      function
   IDOC_CONTROL-MESTYP        = 'WMMBXY'.            "Message type
   IDOC_CONTROL-IDOCTYP       = 'WMMBID01'.          "IDOC type
*  IDOC_CONTROL-CIMTYP        =                      "Extension type
*  IDOC_CONTROL-SERIAL        =                      "Serial number for
                                                      serlzn
*
   TRANSFER IDOC_CONTROL TO OUTFILE.                 "write control
                                                      record
   IF SY-SUBRC NE 0.
   WRITE: / 'ERROR EDIDC 1'.
   ENDIF.
********************************************************************

********************************************************************
   CLEAR INT_EDIDD.
   INT_EDIDD-TABNAM    = 'EDI_DD'.
   INT_EDIDD-SEGNAM    = 'E2MBXYH'.
*  INT_EDIDD-SEGNUM    =
*  INT_EDIDD-PSGNUM    =
*  INT_EDIDD-HLEVEL    =
*
CLEAR: E2MBXYH.
*
E2MBXYH-BLDAT = '19980825'. "            8    Document date in
                                               document
E2MBXYH-BUDAT = '19980825'. "            8    Posting data in document
E2MBXYH-XBLNR = 'testgood'. "           16    Reference document
                                               number
```

Figure 3-9
Sample IDOC Shell
Program (*Continued*)

```
E2MBXYH-BKTXT = 'testgdsrecp'. "      25    Document header text
*E2MBXYH-FRBNR              CHAR C    16    Number of bill of lading
*E2MBXYH-XABLN              CHAR C    10    Goods receipt/issue slip
E2MBXYH-TCODE = 'MB1C'. "   CHAR C     4    Session: Current trans-
                                            action


*
INT_EDIDD-SDATA = E2MBXYH.
*
TRANSFER INT_EDIDD TO OUTFILE.
IF SY-SUBRC NE 0.
   WRITE: / 'Error writing EDIDD 1'.
ENDIF.
*
  CLEAR INT_EDIDD.
  INT_EDIDD-TABNAM      = 'EDI_DD'.
  INT_EDIDD-SEGNAM      = 'E2MBXYI'.
* INT_EDIDD-SEGNUM      =
* INT_EDIDD-PSGNUM      =
* INT_EDIDD-HLEVEL      =

*
CLEAR E2MBXYI.
*
*2MBXYI-BEAKZ               CHAR C     1    Indicator: line
                                            already e
*2MBXYI-XSTOB               CHAR C     1    Flag: Reverse
                                            posting
E2MBXYI-MATNR = '000000TESTMATERIAL'. "rial number
E2MBXYI-WERKS = 'PLNT'. "   CHAR C     4    Plant
E2MBXYI-LGORT = '0001'. "                   Storage Location
E2MBXYI-CHARG = 'TESTBTCH'. "               Batch number
E2MBXYI-BWART = '561'.      "          3    Movement type
                                            (inventory)
*2MBXYI-INSMK = 'S'         "  CHAR C  1    stock type
*2MBXYI-SOBKZ               CHAR C     1    Special stock
                                            indicator
*2MBXYI-KZVBR               CHAR C     1    Indicator:
                                            consumption po
*2MBXYI-LIFNR               CHAR C    10    Vendor (creditor)
                                            account
*2MBXYI-KUNNR               CHAR C    10    Customer number
*2MBXYI-KDAUF               CHAR C    10    Sales order number
*2MBXYI-KDPOS               CHAR C     6    Item number in
                                            customer or
*2MBXYI-KDEIN               CHAR C     4    Scheduling of
                                            customer or
```

Figure 3-9
Sample IDOC Shell
Program (*Continued*)

```
*2MBXYI-SHKZG                      CHAR C    1     Debit/credit
                                                   indicator
*2MBXYI-WAERS                      CHAR C    5     Currency key
*2MBXYI-DMBTR                      CHAR C    15    Amount in local
                                                   currency
*2MBXYI-BWTAR                      CHAR C    10    Valuation type
E2MBXYI-ERFMG  =  '555.000'. "                     Quantity in unit of
                                                   entry
E2MBXYI-ERFME = 'CS'. "            CHAR C    3     Unit of entry in
                                                   char.for
*2MBXYI-BPMNG                      CHAR C    15    Quantity in order
                                                   price q
*2MBXYI-BPRME                      CHAR C    3     Order price
                                                   quantity unit
*2MBXYI-EBELN =                         "    10    Purchasing docum
*2MBXYI-EBELP =                         "    5     Item number of
                                                   purchasing
*2MBXYI-ELIKZ = 'X'. "             CHAR C    1     "Delivery
                                                   completed" indi
*2MBXYI-SGTXT                      CHAR C    50    Line item text
*2MBXYI-WEMPF                      CHAR C    12    Goods recipient
*2MBXYI-ABLAD                      CHAR C    25    Unloading point
*2MBXYI-KOSTL                      CHAR C    10    Cost center
*2MBXYI-AUFNR =                         "    12    Order Number
*2MBXYI-ANLN1                      CHAR C    12    Asset main number
*2MBXYI-ANLN2                      CHAR C    4     Asset sub-number
*2MBXYI-RSNUM                      CHAR C    10    Number of
                                                   reservation / d
*2MBXYI-RSPOS                      CHAR C    4     Item number of
                                                   reservation
*2MBXYI-KZEAR                      CHAR C    1     Indicator: final
                                                   issue for
*2MBXYI-UMMAT                      CHAR C    18    Receiving/issuing
                                                   material
*2MBXYI-UMWRK =             " CHAR C         4     Receiving
                                                   Plant/Issuing P
*2MBXYI-UMLGO = ' '. "                  C    4     Receiving/Issuing
                                                   Storage
*2MBXYI-UMCHA                      CHAR C    10    Receiving/Issuing
                                                   Batch
*2MBXYI-KZBEW =            "       CHAR C    1     Movement Indicator
*2MBXYI-WEUNB                      CHAR C    1     Indicator: goods
                                                   receipt
*2MBXYI-LGNUM                      CHAR C    3     Warehouse
                                                   number/complex
*2MBXYI-LGTYP                      CHAR C    3     Storage type
```

Figure 3-9
Sample IDOC Shell
Program (*Continued*)

*2MBXYI-LGPLA	CHAR C	10	Storage bin
*2MBXYI-GRUND =	"	4	Indicator:Reason for Good
*2MBXYI-EVERS	CHAR C	2	Shipping instructions
*2MBXYI-EVERE	CHAR C	2	Compliance with shipping
*2MBXYI-IMKEY	CHAR C	8	Internal key for real est
*2MBXYI-KSTRG	CHAR C	12	Cost object
*2MBXYI-PAOBJNR	CHAR C	10	Number for business segment
*2MBXYI-PRCTR	CHAR C	10	Profit center
*2MBXYI-PS_PSP_PNR	CHAR C	8	Project structure plan el
*2MBXYI-NPLNR	CHAR C	12	Network number for account
*2MBXYI-AUFPL	CHAR C	10	Planning number for trans
*2MBXYI-APLZL	CHAR C	8	Counter for distinguishing
*2MBXYI-AUFPS	CHAR C	4	Number of order item in C
*2MBXYI-VPTNR	CHAR C	10	Partner account number
*2MBXYI-FIPOS	CHAR C	14	Commitment item
*2MBXYI-GSBER	CHAR C	4	Business area
*2MBXYI-BSTMG	CHAR C	15	Goods receipt quantity in
*2MBXYI-BSTME	CHAR C	3	Order unit
*2MBXYI-EXBWR	CHAR C	15	Posting amount in local c
*2MBXYI-KONTO	CHAR C	10	G/L account number
*2MBXYI-RSHKZ	CHAR C	1	Debit/credit indicator
*2MBXYI-BDMNG	CHAR C	15	Requirement quantity in C
*2MBXYI-ENMNG	CHAR C	15	Issued quantity in char.f
*2MBXYI-QPLOS	CHAR C	12	Inspection lot number in
*2MBXYI-UMZST	CHAR C	1	Status of receiving batch
*2MBXYI-UMZUS	CHAR C	1	Status key of transfer batch

Figure 3-9
Sample IDOC Shell
Program (*Continued*)

```
*2MBXYI-UMBAR                  CHAR C   10      Valuation type of
                                                transfer
**MBXYI-UMSOK                  CHAR C   1       Special stock
                                                indicator f
*2MBXYI-LFBJA                  CHAR C   4       Fiscal year of a
                                                reference
*2MBXYI-LFBNR                  CHAR C   10      Document number of
                                                a reference
*2MBXYI-LFPOS                  CHAR C   4       Item in a reference
                                                document
*2MBXYI-SJAHR                  CHAR C   4       Material document
                                                year in
*2MBXYI-SMBLN                  CHAR C   10      Number of a
                                                material document
*2MBXYI-SMBLP                  CHAR C   4       Item in material
                                                document
*2MBXYI-EXVKW                  CHAR C   15      Sales value
                                                specified ext
*2MBXYI-QM_ZUSTD               CHAR C   1       Batch status with
                                                status
*2MBXYI-POSNR                  CHAR C   6       Delivery item for
                                                subsystem
*2MBXYI-VBELN                  CHAR C   10      Delivery
*2MBXYI-QM_UMZST               CHAR C   1       Status of receiv.
                                                batch w
*2MBXYI-BWLVS                  CHAR C   3       Movement type for
                                                Whse Mg
*2MBXYI-UMREZ = ' '. "         CHAR C   5       NUMERATOR FOR CON-
                                                VERTING
*2MBXYI-UMREN = ' '. "         CHAR C   5       DENOMINATOR FOR
                                                CONVERSION
*2MBXYI-VFDAT = ' '. "                  8       EXPIRATION DATE OR
                                                BEST-B
*2MBXYI-DABRZ                  .DATS D  8       Reference date for
                                                account
*
***************************** write EDIDD record ************
INT_EDIDD-SDATA = E2MBXYI.
TRANSFER INT_EDIDD TO OUTFILE.
IF SY-SUBRC NE 0.
   WRITE: / 'ERROR EDIDD 2'.
ENDIF.
*****************************************************************
*
```

Importing the IDOC   Having created the file of IDOC/s using the shell program, we are now ready to import the IDOC into the R/3™ system. This is accomplished by using an SAP™ standard program RSEINB00. To do this:

■ Execute program RSEINB00

■ Enter the directory path and name of the IDOC file

■ Execute

■ You should receive an informational message that the file was transferred to the ALE layer

Using transaction **WE02** or **WE05**, display the IDOC that was created. Ensure that its status is 53—application document posted. Remember that we had chosen the processing option to be "immediate." If we had opted for "Background" processing, we would need to execute program RBDAPP01 in order to post the IDOC to the application. Note that the IDOC goes through many statuses, namely 50—IDOC added, 64—IDOC ready to be passed to application, 62—IDOC passed to application, and 53—application document posted.

As you may have realized by reading this section, transactional data ALE interfaces can be configured and prototyped without much difficulty, and within a short period of time. However, it is important to identify the business requirements of the interface and attempt to fit the needs with standard ALE functionality. If gaps exist in SAP™-delivered ALE functionality, we can overcome it by enhancing ALE function modules and/or IDOC extensions. These procedures are discussed in the next chapter.

Upon browsing the message types available in the R/3™ system (see Appendix B or transaction **WE81**), you will find that there are over 200 areas in SAP™ that are supported by ALE functionality. Most of them are for transactional data such as the ones we prototyped in this section. They span almost all the application modules in SAP™. Also, as we will learn in Chapter 5, we can create new ALE functions with a relatively minimal effort if need be. As part of the high-level design process for R/3™ implementations, it is important to consider the powerful and robust ALE scenarios *delivered* by SAP™ in order to reduce implementation costs and efforts, and put in place a reliable system.

ALE Enhancements; IDOC Extensions and Reductions

Overview

Having familiarized ourselves with prototyping master data and transactional data ALE interfaces, we now turn our attention to the techniques involved in enhancing ALE functionality. After prototyping the ALE interface for an application area, you may find that your requirements are not being fully satisfied by SAP™-delivered functionality, and there exist gaps in the desired results. In such cases, it is possible to add functionality to the IDOCs and associated ALE-function modules. For example, if in an outbound interface you find that the IDOC type does not contain all the data you need to pass to the other system, you can "extend" the IDOC to accommodate those additional fields, and enhance the ALE-function modules to populate the fields. Similarly, if in an inbound interface, there are additional data that need to be posted to the R/3™ application, you can extend the IDOC type to have these additional fields populated by the external system or translator, or the other R/3™ system, and then enhance the inbound ALE-function modules to post the additional data to the R/3™ application.

On the other hand, if in the case of certain master data ALE interfaces, you plan to use only a limited number of fields and segments in the IDOC type, it may be a good idea to restrict the transfer of data through these interfaces only to the required segments and fields. This process is called *IDOC reduction*. Reduction of IDOC results in greater throughput of the interface, and could possibly improve performance, reduce disk space required, as well as reduce the processing time. This feature is available only for master data IDOC types. As we will learn, the primary benefit of reducing an IDOC type is achieved with the elimination of nonessential IDOC segments.

In this chapter, we learn methods for IDOC extensions, ALE-function module enhancements, and IDOC reductions. After having read this section, you will realize that the approach to these processes is very well structured, and that SAP™ provides mechanisms for maintaining and tracking these "projects." We will work with message types DEBMAS (Customer Master) for IDOC extension, and the now familiar MATMAS for IDOC reduction. Other than IDOC reduction, these enhancement techniques are applicable to EDI as well.

Understanding the concepts and techniques explained in this chapter could greatly improve your insight into some of the underlying mechanisms of ALE. For example, if you follow the code associated with the IDOC extension in the ALE-function module, you will understand how

SAP™-function modules build the IDOC data. Also, you will realize that the amount of ABAP/4 code required to achieve the desired results is minimal.

Let us now proceed with the IDOC extension and ALE enhancement of IDOC type DEBMAS02 and message type DEBMAS.

IDOC Extensions

The IDOC type DEBMAS02 is used to communicate Customer Master data. Upon perusal of the IDOC type (use transaction **WE60**), you will see that there are a number of hierarchical segments whose fields contain almost all the data needed to describe a customer and its attributes. However, after having maintained a customer using the Customer Master application in SAP™ (transactions **XD01**—create, **XD02**—change, **XD03**—display), specifically the customer contact person screens (see Figure 4-1), you will realize that even though the application has a screen to enter and store the contact person business address (see Figure 4-2), the IDOC type DEBMAS02 does not have a segment or fields that communicate the contact person's business address. If your business requires that this business address be communicated to the other system through the ALE interface for Customer Master, then we have to extend the DEBMAS02 IDOC type, and enhance the corresponding ALE-function module.

Let us first understand the concept of IDOC extension. As mentioned in the introductory chapter, SAP™ delivers Basic IDOC types such as DEBMAS02, MATMAS02, ORDERS02, and WMMBID01. By extending the *Basic IDOC* type, we are actually creating a *new IDOC* type. To do this, we first create a *new segment* with the additional fields. This new segment has to be associated with one of the existing segments of the Basic IDOC type. The result is the creation of a new *extension type,* which is then associated with the Basic IDOC type, thus creating a new IDOC type. In order for ALE-function modules to relate to this new IDOC type, the IDOC type is *linked* to the corresponding message type. Note that you should not add fields to existing segments, but create a new segment and associate it with an existing segment. This, in a nutshell, is the process of creating IDOC extensions.

In our example of Basic IDOC type DEBMAS02, research will show that the customer contact person fields are present in segment

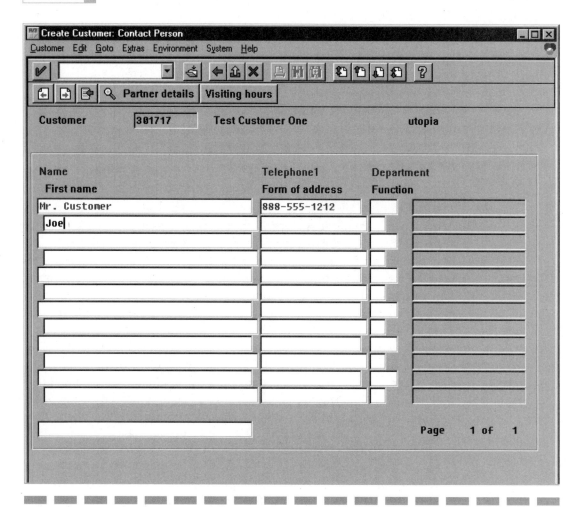

Figure 4-1 Customer Master Contact Person Screen

E1KNVKM. Also, the business address of the contact person is stored on an SAP™ table SADR. Since we have to extend the IDOC to contain the business address of the customer contact person, we will create a new segment Z1SADRX that is associated with E1KNVKM. This will be done in the process of creating an extension type ZDEBMASX. This extension type will then be associated with a new IDOC type ZDEBMASZ. As a penultimate step, IDOC type ZDEBMASZ is going to be linked to message type DEBMAS for Customer Master. The final step in the IDOC extension process is to "check" the new objects we created. This also verifies the structural integrity of the IDOC type.

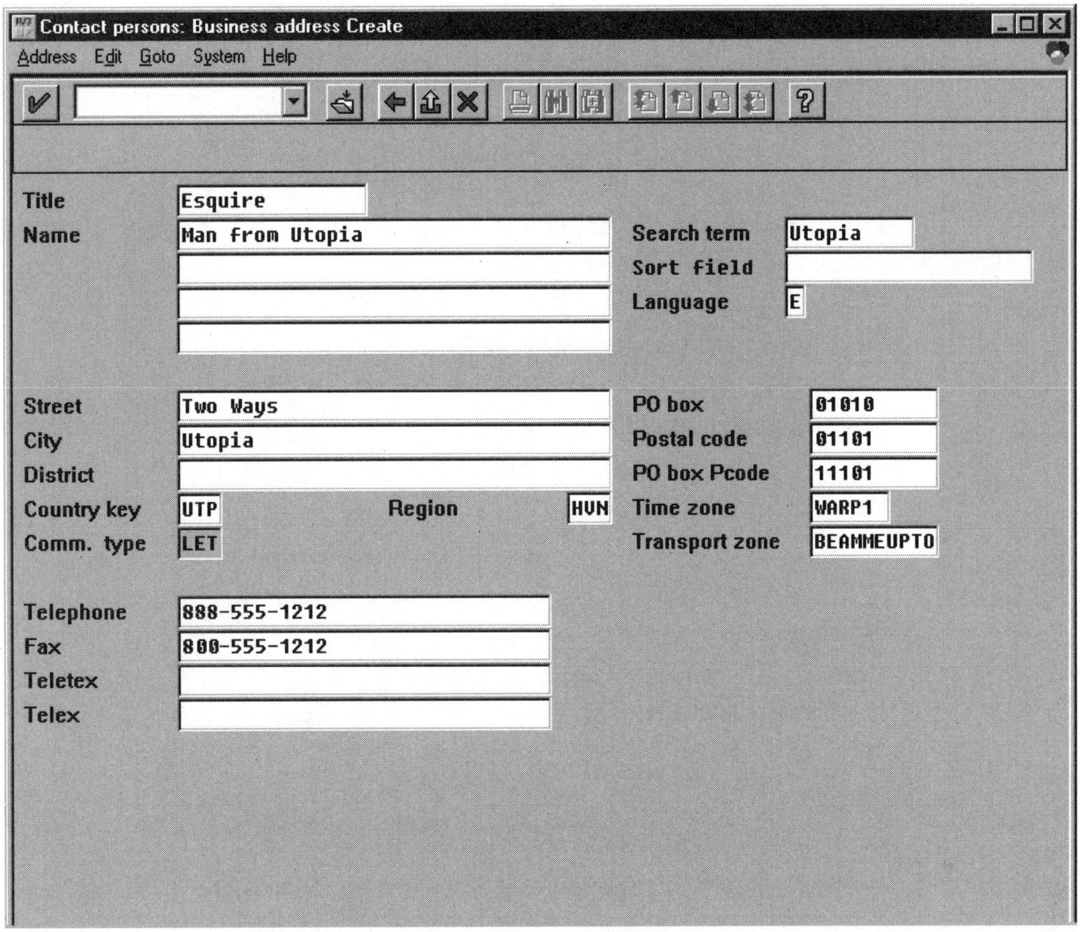

Figure 4-2 Customer Master Contact Person Business Address Screen

Creating an Extension Type and a New Segment

Let us first determine the fields on table SADR that we are going to provide for in our new segment Z1SADRX. We need to have the fields for name, street, city, region, and country. In addition to these basic fields giving the business address of the contact person, we also need to have a couple of fields for the address number. ADRNR is a field in SAP's™ tables such as SADR that uniquely identifies the address of an entity. This field is cross-referenced from other tables to the SADR table to obtain the full description of the address. Since this is an IDOC type for master data, we will have the first field of the new segment as MSGFN. The message function field informs the receiving system regarding the action to be taken for that particular segment. (See Chapter 2 for more details.) As you will notice in the code that we write for populating the new segment, the value of the message function is the same as that of the parent segment E1KNVKM. In all, we will have 12 fields in segment Z1SADRX. See Table 4-1 for details.

To create an extension type and new segment:

- Use transaction **WE30** or from **WEDI** → Development → IDOC types
- Enter ZDEBMASX for Object Name
- Choose radio-button EXTENSION TYPE
- Click on CREATE icon
- You will see a pop-up screen. Choose radio-button CREATE NEW and enter a description.
- Enter
- You will see a screen with ZDEBMASX and its description in the first line. Click on this line, and press icon CREATE.

Table 4-1

List of Fields for
New Segment
Z1SADRX

#	Field Name	Data Element Structure	Field Length	Data Element Documentation	Data Type
1	MSGFN	MSGFN	3	MSGFN	CHAR
2	PARNR	PARNR	10	PARNR	NUMC
3	ADRNR	CADNR	10	CADNR	CHAR
4	NATIO	INTER	1	INTER	CHAR
5	ANRED	ANRED	15	ANRED	CHAR
6	NAME1	NAME1_BAS	35	NAME1_BAS	CHAR
7	NAME2	NAME2_BAS	35	NAME2_BAS	CHAR
8	STRAS	STRAS_GP	35	STRAS_GP	CHAR
9	ORT01	ORT01_GP	35	ORT01_GP	CHAR
10	REGIO	REGIO	3	REGIO	CHAR
11	LAND1	LAND1	3	LAND1	CHAR
12	PSTLZ	PSTLZ_BAS	10	PSTLZ_BAS	CHAR

- You will see a pop-up screen. Enter E1KNVKM as the reference segment. Enter.

- You will see a line appear with E1KNVKM hierarchically below ZDEBMASX, with a description "Customer master contact person (KNVK)" (see Figure 4-3).

- Click on this line and press the icon for CREATE. You will receive a message indicating that the new segment being created will be a child segment of E1KNVKM. Enter. A pop-up box appears for the new segment.

- Enter Z1SADRX as the Segment type, 1 for Minimum, 1 for Maximum. Leave Mandatory segment unchecked. These entries imply

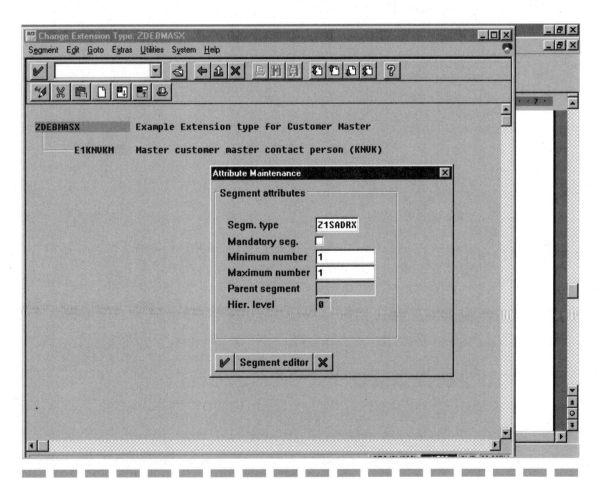

Figure 4-3 Extension Type and Creating a New Segment

that there is only one Z1SADRX segment for every occurrence of the E1KNVKM segment, and also that this segment is not mandatory. Note that if the parent segment is not mandatory, then the child segment should not be mandatory, since this could result in a syntax error during the creation or processing of the IDOC.

- Click on button SEGMENT EDITOR

- On the next screen, click on icon CREATE. Enter a development class for the object. Enter.

- This will take you to the screen for segment definition (see Figure 4-4). Enter a description for the segment. Enter the field name, data element, and the data element documentation name. In most cases, all three fields may have the same values. If you are using a field in the segment that is not present in the ABAP/4 data dictionary, you have to first create the domain, data element, field, and appropriate documentation before using it in the new segment.

- After entering these three columns for all 12 fields (see Table 4-1), save

- Click on the GENERATE/ACTIVATE button. F3 to step back.

- **From screen** `Maintain Segment: Segment type` → `Go To` → `Release`. A checkbox now appears beside the segment definition Z1SADRX (see Figure 4-5). Check this box. Save.

- Save again to save the descriptions of the segment. F3 to step back.

- Save the extension type

- We have now created an extension type (see Figure 4-6)

Note that it is possible to have several new segments with relevant parent segments of the Basic IDOC type in a single extension type. However, you can form only one IDOC type based on a single extension type, as you learn next.

Creating an IDOC Type

The next step is to create an IDOC type by associating the extension type that we created with the Basic IDOC type. This is a simple process:

- From transaction **WE30** or **WEDI** → `Development` → `IDOC Types`

- Enter ZDEBMASZ for Object name

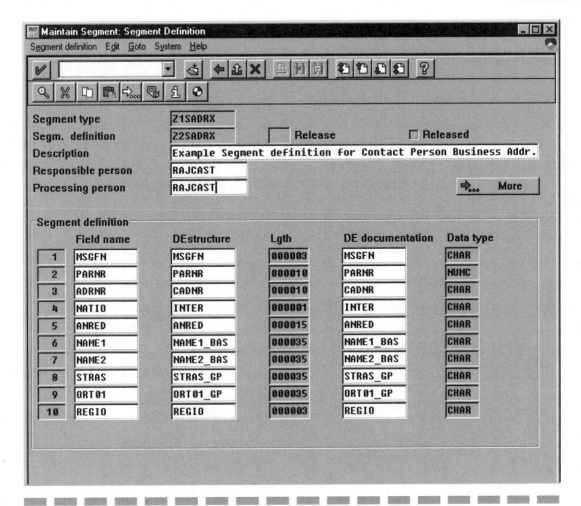

Figure 4-4 The Segment Editor

- Click on radio-button IDOC TYPE
- Click on CREATE
- Enter DEBMAS02 for Basic IDOC type
- Enter ZDEBMASX for extension type
- Enter a description
- Hit ENTER

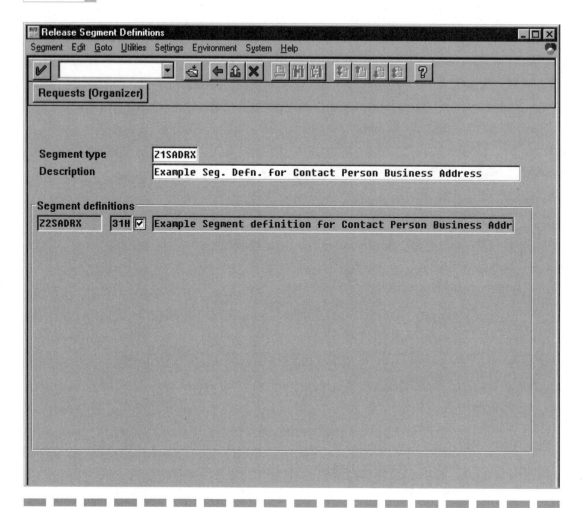

Figure 4-5 Releasing the Segment

■ You will see a display of the composite IDOC type with all segments, including Z1SADRX (see Figure 4-7)

As you might have realized, it is possible to associate only one extension type with a Basic IDOC type, for a given IDOC type. However, you can have multiple new segments in an extension type.

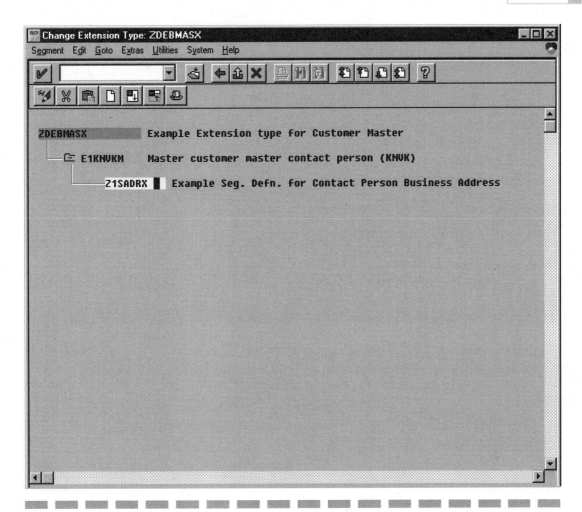

Figure 4-6 The New Extension Type

Linking IDOC Type to Message Type

The next step is to link the new IDOC type that we created to its corresponding message type. This is important since this relationship is referenced in the partner profile parameters where we specify the message type and IDOC type to be used for that particular representative system. To link the message type:

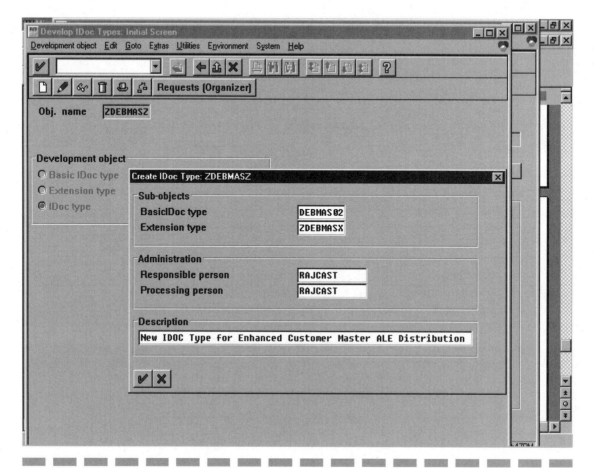

Figure 4-7 Associating Extension Type with Basic IDOC Type to Create New IDOC Type

- Use transaction **WE82**, or from **WE30** → Environment → IDOC Type / Message Type, **or from WEDI** → Development → IDOC Type → Environment → IDOC Type / Message Type

- Click on the DISPLAY <-> CHANGE icon

- Click on NEW ENTRIES

- Enter DEBMAS for message type

- Enter DEBMAS02 for Basic IDOC type

- Enter ZDEBMASX for extension type

- Enter your SAP™ R/3™ release number for Release

- Save

These data are stored on the EDIMSG table and are accessed by several ALE processes to relate the message type to the IDOC type.

Checking the IDOC Type

Before checking the IDOC type for consistency, it is important to perform another step that "releases" the extension type to the IDOC type. This is done by:

- **WEDI** → Development → IDOC Types → Extras → Release Type **or from transaction WE30** → Extras → Release Type
- For the Object name ZDEBMASX and radio-button EXTENSION TYPE, click YES
- The extension type has now been "released"

Note that you cannot edit the extension type once it has been released. To cancel the release for further editing or deactivation: **WE30** → Extras → Cancel release. The final step in the IDOC extension process is to check the validity of the IDOC type we created. This is easily done by:

- Transaction **WE30** or **WEDI** → Development → IDOC types
- Enter ZDEBMASX for Object name
- Click on radio-button EXTENSION TYPE
- From the Development Object menu, select CHECK
- Repeat the operation for IDOC type ZDEBMASZ
- A check log will be generated for each run with details of correctness or errors. See Figure 4-8.

In certain situations, it is possible to receive errors during the check process, especially segment length errors. In this case, the IDOC segment in error can be repaired and corrected. To accomplish this, execute program RSEREPSG. This program checks the formal consistency and repairs incorrect segments. In test mode, this program will generate a log of formal correctness for the specified segment only. For the program to repair segments in normal mode, the underlying IDOC structures (DDIC structures) have to be active. This program rectifies the lengths of the DDIC structures, and not the fields themselves. RSEREPSG can also be used to change the person responsible for the object and the release flag.

Figure 4-8
Sample Logs of
Formal Checks for
IDOC Extensions

```
|Check extension types (report RSECHK03)                              |

|ZDEBMASX                                           RC =      0|
|                                                             |

|IDoc definition is formally correct                RC=       0|
|304 Extension type is released                               |

|Segments used are formally correct                 RC=       0|
|Z1SADRX                                            RC=       0|

|100 IDoc is linked to the following messages:               |
|DEBMAS   Customer master                                    |


|Check IDoc types (report RSECHK03)                          |

|ZDEBMASZ                                           RC=       0|
|New IDOC Type for Enhanced Customer Master ALE Distribution |

|IDoc definition is formally correct                RC=       0|
|302 Basic IDoc type used is released                        |
|306 Extension type used is released:                        |

|Segments used are formally correct                 RC=       0|
|E1KNA1M                                            RC=       0|
|E1KNA1H                                            RC=       0|
|E1KNA1L                                            RC=       0|
|E1KNVVM                                            RC=       0|
|E1KNVPM                                            RC=       0|
|E1KNVDM                                            RC=       0|
|E1KNVIM                                            RC=       0|
|E1KNVLM                                            RC=       0|
|E1KNVVH                                            RC=       0|
|E1KNVVL                                            RC=       0|
|E1KNB1M                                            RC=       0|
|E1KNB5M                                            RC=       0|
```

Figure 4-8
Sample Logs of
Formal Checks for
IDOC Extensions
(*Continued*)

```
|E1KNB1H                                                RC=    0|
|E1KNB1L                                                RC=    0|
|E1KNBKM                                                RC=    0|
|E1KNVAM                                                RC=    0|
|E1KNVKM                                                RC=    0|
|Z1SADRX                                                RC=    0|
|E1KNVKH                                                RC=    0|
|E1KNVKL                                                RC=    0|
|E1KNEXM                                                RC=    0|
|E1KNASM                                                RC=    0|
|E1KNKAM                                                RC=    0|
|E1KNKKM                                                RC=    0|
|E1KNKKH                                                RC=    0|
|E1KNKKL                                                RC=    0|

|100 IDoc is linked to the following messages:         |
|DEBMAS  Customer master                                |
```

ALE-Function Module Enhancements

Having extended the IDOC type to contain additional fields for an inbound or outbound application, we now proceed with the task of enhancing ALE-function modules for populating the additional segment on the outbound, or applying the additional segment data on the inbound. Note that it may be necessary to enhance an ALE-function module even in situations where an IDOC extension has not been performed, for other reasons that require modifications to the IDOC data being passed to and from the application. The approach discussed in this section applies to both the situations.

The core working code for ALE processes for a given application area is always encapsulated in ABAP/4-function modules. These function modules are associated with message types and/or process codes. Hence, the ALE process checks the control information such as message type or process code and derives the name of the function module to invoke for that particular IDOC processing from certain database tables. These function modules contain objects known as *customer functions,* which can be considered as SAP's™ enhanced user exits. It is actually a function module that is called at a particular point in processing of the main program or function module, and can be used to influence the processing of the data at that particular point by adding code to the customer function. The customer function behaves like a normal function module and has import and export parameters, tables (internal tables) statement, and exception processing. As you will see, unlike a conventional user exit, customer functions give you the capability of modifying only data that are made available to you by the function module's parameters and internal tables. While most ALE/EDI-function modules are supported by customer functions, note that there are ALE/EDI processes that still use conventional user exits. How do we find which function module to enhance for a given message type/process code? There are a few ways to figure this out:

- For master data distribution, from **SALE** → Extensions → Master data distribution → Setup additional data for message types. Search for message type, say DEBMAS in this example. You will see an entry for DEBMAS associated with function module MASTERIDOC_CREATE_SMD_DEBMAS. (These data are stored on table TBDME.) By browsing the other entries on this table you will realize that all master data message types have their function module names in this pattern: MASTERIDOC_CRE-ATE_SMD_messagetype. This function module calls another function module of name MASTERIDOC_CREATE_DEBMAS or MAS-TERIDOC_CREATE_messagetype. Search for the words *customer function,* and you will find several hits that can be used to add code to the function module.

- From **WEDI** → Control → Inbound process codes → Inbound with ALE service → Processing by function module (transaction **WE42**) or **WEDI** → Control → Outbound process codes → Outbound with ALE service → With function module (transaction **WE41**). There will be function modules associated with the process codes. For inbound, the function modules usually follow this pattern: IDOC_INPUT_messagetype, for example IDOC_INPUT_CHRMAS for inbound characteristics master.

- Use transaction **WE57** or **WEDI** → Development → Message/Application Object. The entries list the function module, business object, message type, and IDOC type that are used for inbound ALE/EDI interfaces.

Customer functions are not specific only to ALE and EDI, but also to all programs/modules in SAP™ R/3™. Customer function is a type of component of an SAP™ enhancement; the other two types are menu and screen enhancements. All customer function exits are maintained in SAP™ enhancements and can be found by using transaction **SMOD**. After executing transaction **SMOD**, pull down (F4) on the enhancement name field, and execute again. This will provide you with a list of all SAP™ enhancements available. SAP™ enhancements are grouped by development class pertaining to an application area. By browsing the list you will come across the enhancement "Application development R/3 SD master data distribution" for development class VSV. Choosing that will lead to a screen listing VSV00001 as an enhancement (see Figure 4-9).

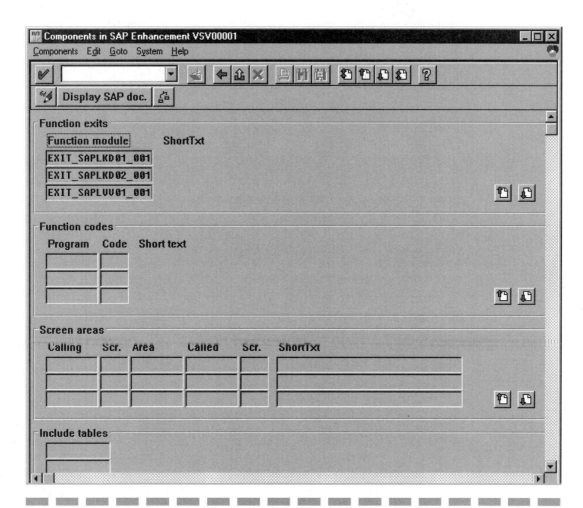

Figure 4-9 SAP™ Enhancements and Components

Press the button COMPONENT +/- to display its function exit components. There are possibly four components listed, all of which are function exits, and are actually function modules themselves, that are called from the ALE function modules in the form "Call Customer Function '001'." This is a special occurrence of the ABAP statement "Call...." Reading the documentation on the components will lead you to item EXIT_SAPLVV01_ 001, which we need to enhance for our Customer Master outbound example of IDOC extension. In the ALE-function module MASTERIDOC_CREATE_DEBMAS, the statement "Call Customer Function '001'" is translated in the background to call component EXIT_ SAPLVV01_001. Although this function exit can be edited using transaction **SE37**, we will follow a more understandable approach.

Creating a Project Using CMOD

When we use SAP™ enhancements and their components, we have to manage them with an SAP™ object known as a *project,* which is like an envelope containing the selected enhancements and their components that can be used to control the execution of components, as well as be transported by CTS to other clients/instances in SAP™. Basically, the process involves creating a project, including enhancements and components that are to be enhanced, editing the components, and then activating the project. Let us proceed by creating a project for our example of IDOC extension, the Customer Master.

- Execute transaction **CMOD**
- Enter name of project, say CSTMAST1
- Click on CREATE
- Enter a description of the project
- Save
- Click on button SAP ENHANCEMENTS
- Enter VSV00001 for Enhancement
- Save

Once the project is created, edit the function exit components as described next, and activate the project. Remember that the code in the function exit enhancement is going to be executed only if the project is activated. In fact, this is a convenient feature of SAP™ enhancements,

whereby the work in progress—developing code in the customer function—will not affect users of that application. When the code is completed, the project can be activated for the enhanced functionality to
take effect. Note that it can also be deactivated for maintenance.

Customer Function Enhancements

As mentioned earlier, customer functions (function exits) are embedded
in ALE-function modules, and can be used to influence the creation/
modification of IDOC data on an outbound, or post additional or modified IDOC data to the R/3™ application on an inbound. Function exits
are similar to regular function modules and they have import/export
parameters, tables (internal tables), and exceptions. The two important
factors to consider while developing the customer function are (1) the
point in the ALE-function module where the function exit occurs and (2)
the data that are made available by the customer function that can be
modified or posted to the R/3™ application, based on the direction. Since
there are function modules with several customer functions, it is critical
to choose the right function exit suited for that particular enhancement.
Do not attempt to perform activities that the function exit is not
designed for.

Outbound   In an outbound ALE interface we can use function exits
(customer functions) to populate additional segments created by an
IDOC extension, or modify the existing IDOC data segments as per our
business requirements. Previously, we identified that enhancement
VSV00001 has a component EXIT_SAPLVV01_001 (function exit), which
can be used for populating the additional data segment Z1SADRX that
we created in the IDOC extension ZDEBMASX (IDOC type ZDEBMASZ,
based on Basic IDOC type DEBMAS02). We also learned that the ALE-
function module that calls this function exit is MASTERIDOC_CRE-
ATE_DEBMAS, which has a statement "Call Customer Function '001'."
Browse the function module MASTERIDOC_CREATE_DEBMAS using
transaction **SE37**. You will find that this customer function is being
invoked for every segment of IDOC type DEBMAS02. In fact, the function exit is called soon after the creation of an existing segment has been
populated with data and appended to the IDOC data table (internal
table). Also, the function exit is exporting the message type, IDOC type,
and the segment name; importing the IDOC extension type; and passing

the IDOC data internal table. This indicates to us that the ALE-function module is providing us the opportunity of populating additional segments for every existing segment if need be, and/or modify the existing segment's data. Having realized this, let us write ABAP/4 code to accomplish our task—populate IDOC segment Z1SADRX with the contact person's business address. To do this:

- From **SE37**, display function module MASTERIDOC_CREATE_DEB-MAS

- Find Customer Function '001'

- Double-click on 001

- The function EXIT_SAPLVV01_001 will be displayed

- Double-click on INCLUDE ZXVSVU01

- You will be asked to create a new include object. Proceed as desired.

- Enter code as in Figure 4-10

- Be sure to perform a main program check (Function Module → Check → main program) and extended program check (Function module → Check → Extended check)

Following is a brief explanation of the code in Figure 4-10.

- The import parameter CIMTYPE is populated with the extension type ZDEBMASX

- Determine if the segment being currently processed is E1KNVKM

- Read the last line of the internal table T_IDOC_DATA for E1KNVKM data

- Move SDATA component of the EDIDD record to structure E2KNVKM

- Select ADRND (address number) from table KNVK based on the contact person's number

- Select address from the SADR table based on ADRND

- Move the SADR fields to corresponding fields in segment structure Z2SADRX

- Move Z2SADRX into the SDATA component of the EDIDD record (IDOC_DATA)

- Specify the segment name as Z1SADRX

- Append the IDOC data internal table

Figure 4-10
Sample ABAP/4 Code
for ALE Function Exit
Customer Master
Enhancement

```
*********************MODIFICATION*********************************
* Programmer      :   Rajcast                                    *
* Task #          :   BK1K901289                                 *
* Changes         :   This include is for the Customer Function  *
*                     001 enhancement of MASTERIDOC_CREATE_DEBMAS, *
*                     customer master ALE distribution of        *
*                     changes to master data. This CF is being   *
*                     used to populate IDOC extensions such as :  *
*                                                                *
*     1. Business/mailing address of customer Z1SADRX.           *
*       *                                                        *
*     This enhancement is a component of project CSTMAST1.       *
*****************************************************************
CONSTANTS: C_CIMTYPE LIKE EDIDC-CIMTYP VALUE 'ZDEBMASX',
           C_E1KNVKM LIKE EDIDD-SEGNAM  VALUE 'E1KNVKM'.


*
DATA: V_LINENO TYPE I.
*
TABLES: SADR, KNVK, Z2SADRX, E2KNVKM.
*
*
IDOC_CIMTYPE = C_CIMTYPE.
*
CASE SEGMENT_NAME.
WHEN C_E1KNVKM.
*** This section creates segment Z1SADRX with Business       ***
*** Address  info.It will be created only if the            ***
*** Business/Mailing address has been maintained            ***
     V_LINENO = 0.
     DESCRIBE TABLE IDOC_DATA LINES V_LINENO.
     READ TABLE IDOC_DATA INDEX V_LINENO.
     CHECK SY-SUBRC EQ 0.
     E2KNVKM = IDOC_DATA-SDATA.

     SELECT SINGLE ADRND FROM KNVK
       INTO KNVK-ADRND
      WHERE PARNR = E2KNVKM-PARNR.
*
     CHECK SY-SUBRC EQ 0.
     SELECT SINGLE * FROM SADR
      WHERE ADRNR = KNVK-ADRND
        AND NATIO = SPACE.
*
     CHECK SY-SUBRC EQ 0.
     CLEAR: Z2SADRX, IDOC_DATA.
```

Figure 4-10
Sample ABAP/4 Code
for ALE Function Exit
Customer Master
Enhancement
(*Continued*)

```
      MOVE-CORRESPONDING SADR TO Z2SADRX.
      MOVE E2KNVKM-PARNR TO Z2SADRX-PARNR.
      Z2SADRX-MSGFN = E2KNVKM-MSGFN.
      IDOC_DATA-SEGNAM = 'Z1SADRX'.
      IDOC_DATA-SDATA  = Z2SADRX.
      APPEND IDOC_DATA.
   ENDCASE.
```

Working the Interface Now that we have extended the IDOC, and enhanced the ALE-function module based on our requirements for the contact person's business address on the Customer Master, let us test the interface. You should create a logical system and define a port for this interface. You should also configure the Customer Distribution Model to indicate that message type DEBMAS is being distributed to this logical system. The only difference in configuration between a regular outbound ALE interface and an enhanced one is the partner profile definition. While maintaining the outbound parameters of the partner profile, ensure that the IDOC type is ZDEBMASZ. The fields for Basic IDOC type and extension type are automatically populated with DEBMAS02 and ZDEBMASX, respectively.

Maintain the contact person's business address of a customer. Using transaction **BD12** or **BALE** → Master Data → Customer → Send, **send** that customer master record by executing the transaction after having filled in the relevant fields like customer number, message type, and logical system. Use transaction **WE02** or **WE05** to verify the IDOC created. You should see the new segment Z1SADRX populated with the right data.

Note that with the standard SAP™ functionality, you cannot capture changes to business address through change pointers because a change document object is not available for it, and also it has not been configured to write change documents for a contact person's business address. If you would like this functionality, you can either create change document objects, generate function modules to create change documents, and perform ALE configuration to tie it in as explained in the next chapter, or make a cosmetic change to the contact person screen data, while changing the contact person's business address, so that it gets captured as a change to the customer master. Subsequently, the ALE enhancement that we performed captures the contact person's business address.

Inbound The process for enhancing inbound ALE interfaces is similar to the outbound, with a few exceptions, especially in the coding of customer functions (function exits) for the ALE/EDI-function modules. Create an IDOC extension for the specific Basic IDOC type by adding new segment(s) at the appropriate hierarchy level, that is, associated to the relevant existing segment. The data field(s) on the new segment(s) will have to be populated with application data by the translator or external system/program before being imported into the R/3™ system. Find the ALE-function module that is invoked by the inbound processing, as explained previously. By browsing through the code or reading the documentation on the function-exit enhancements using the SMOD transaction, identify the right function exit to place your code in. The technique used in the code to post the additional or modified IDOC data to the application can vary, based on the application rules and requirements; the data available at that point in processing; and the application function modules available, if any, to update the application tables. It is important to first search for application modules that process the data, and see if they can be called within the function exit. If the additional data in the extended segments are specific to a custom table or reside in nonkey fields of a single or small set of tables, you may be able to update them directly by SQL statements in the function exit. This approach should be carefully evaluated, and is certainly not highly recommended.

The other option is to use "Call Transaction" from within the function exit to process the additional data. For example, in the case of message type WMMBXY for inbound goods movements from a warehouse management system, the standard interface creates "batches" for materials, but does not update its characteristics. In such a case, you can "Call Transaction" MSC1 to create the batch and assign characteristic values to it from within the function exit provided. A very important consideration while making enhancements to inbound ALE/EDI objects is error handling. In ALE and EDI inbound processing, workflow is used for handling errors at different levels such as technical and application. If workflow has been configured for the interface, the error messages and workflow item flow to the inbox of the named recipient(s). An important consideration while modifying the inbound ALE/EDI process is to enhance the workflow handling as well. In most scenarios, this is not a very difficult task since SAP™ provides the capability of influencing the workflow parameters and messages in function exits (customer functions). These are typically in the form of flags and message codes that trigger certain specific actions by the workflow. If you conform to the status codes and flags stipulated for workflow processing, the enhancement could be error-free and seamless.

Note: In the case of an inbound IDOC with an extension, populate the EDIDC fields IDOCTYP (new IDOC type) and CIMTYP (extension type) accordingly.

IDOC Reductions

When distributing or communicating master data to other systems, R/3™ or external, the volumes of data being transmitted over communication lines could be large. This could result in performance problems and/or excessive usage of resources such as disk space and bandwidth. Careful scrutiny of the master data Basic IDOC type might reveal that many of the segments are redundant or simply not being used. If this is true, then it is a candidate for a technique known as *IDOC reduction*. The R/3™ system provides us with the capability of eliminating unused segments and irrelevant fields of segments from the Basic IDOC type. This procedure is relatively simple and easy to implement. IDOC reduction is available for only a few message types such as DEBMAS, CREMAS, GLMAST, MATMAS, and certain POS messages.

Basically, when performing an IDOC reduction, a new message type is created based on an existing message type. The IDOC segments associated with that message type are proposed for editing. Obviously, mandatory segments of the IDOC type cannot be excluded. Also note that by default, the optional segments are excluded. You have the choice of including an optional segment, and furthermore including only certain fields of the optional segment chosen. Note that if you have extended the Basic IDOC type and created a new IDOC type associated with a corresponding message type, and you are creating a new message type (view) based on it for purposes of IDOC reduction, then the enhanced IDOC type is presented for editing along with the additional segments.

Let us take the example of the Vendor Master IDOC type CREMAS01 for IDOC reduction. As you are aware, message type CREMAS is used for communicating Vendor Master data to other R/3™ or external systems. Browsing the IDOC type CREMAS01 indicates that it has 10 segments with E1LFA1M being a mandatory segment (see Figure 4-11). To reduce this IDOC type, follow these steps:

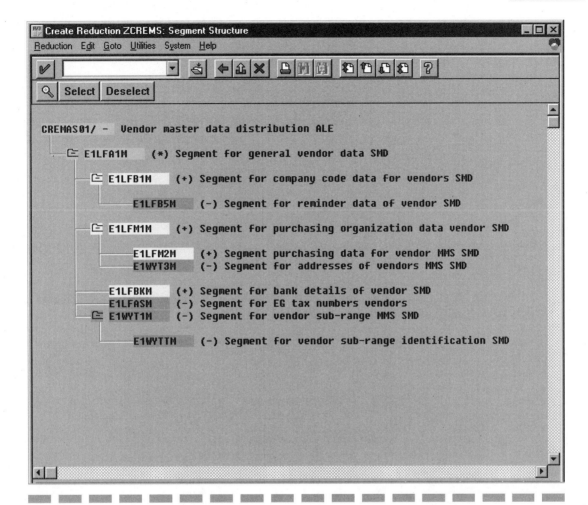

Figure 4-11 IDOC Reduction of Segments

- Transaction **BD53** or from **SALE** → Distribution scenarios → Master data distribution → Reduce IDOC type for master data

- Enter **ZCREMS** for View (message type)

- Click on CREATE icon

- You will see a pop-up box. Enter CREMAS in the Derived From field. Enter.

- Enter a description. Enter.

- You will see a list display with segment E1LFA1M in green and with a (*) symbol. The symbols used in IDOC reduction are: * for mandatory, + for selected, - for deselected, x for core selected, '.' for core not selected. Also, elements are highlighted in green, white, red, violet, and gray, respectively.

- Expand all trees. You will see nine other segments in red.

- Place your cursor on E1LFB1M, segment for company code data, and click on SELECT. It turns white with a + symbol.

- Double-clicking on it will display a list of fields, with the usual conventions as mentioned previously. You can select fields that you require (see Figure 4-12).

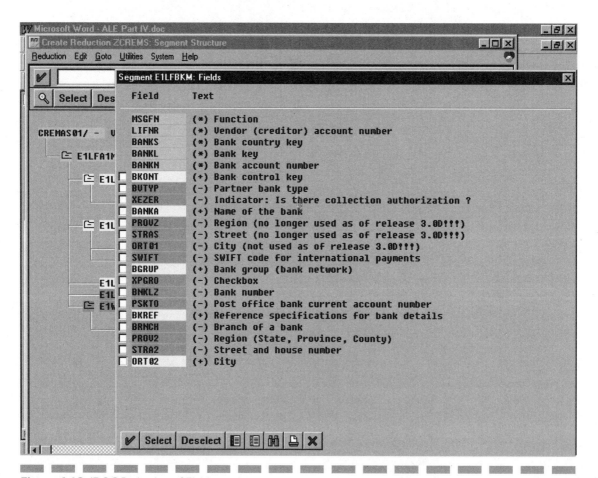

Figure 4-12 IDOC Reduction of Fields

- Note that if a child segment is selected, its parent is also selected automatically in order to maintain the hierarchical integrity
- After having selected the segments required and its fields, save
- From the main screen, click on button ACTIVATE

Activating the new message type ZCREMS will turn on change pointer generation of this message type on that particular client. Note that, while creating a reduced IDOC type message is a client-independent activity, activation is client-dependent. An entry is created in table TBDA2 for that message type in that client and is activated; hence, in order to delete this message type, you need to deactivate it from all clients on that instance. These message types are transportable.

Working the Interface

Having created a new message type for a reduced IDOC type, let us build the rest of the ALE configuration to work the interface.

- Define a logical system to represent the other R/3™ or external system
- Configure the customer distribution model to send message ZCREMS to this logical system
- Define a port, if needed, for this system
- Define a partner profile based on the logical system, and maintain its outbound parameters. Ensure that you use ZCREMS as the message type, and CREMAS01 as the IDOC type
- Use transaction **BD14** or execute program RBDSECRE or from **BALE** → Master Data → Vendors → Send. Specify a vendor or range of vendors, enter message type as ZCREMS, and its target logical system. Execute
- You can also capture changes to Vendor Master data, and create IDOCs by executing transaction **BD21** or program RBDMIDOC

Use transaction **WE02** or **WE05** to view the IDOCs created as a result of the preceding test. Notice the segments populated and the basic segments that are absent due to the reduction. You will find that the fields deselected from the segments have a value of '/'. This is equivalent to a null value. As you might have realized, elimination of segments might result in saving resources, while elimination of fields might not, unless the data are compressed. Also, perusal of the master data ALE-function modules for these few message types will reveal that a function module IDOC_REDUCTION_FIELD_REDUCE is called for every segment being populated. This in itself might be an overhead. Hence, it is important to weigh the pros and cons of IDOC reduction before implementing it. Of course, in certain cases, it may be a necessity for adjustment of data.

As you may have concluded, enhancements to ALE/EDI, IDOC extensions, and IDOC reductions are fairly simple procedures, and can be developed with reasonable efforts. However, before proceeding with tasks, one must carefully research the many options available in ALE and EDI and develop a design that is most appropriate for the business scenario. It should be mentioned that it is also possible to handle very complex situations within ALE and EDI enhancement objects.

Creating a New Basic IDOC Type and ALE Functionality

Overview

As mentioned earlier, there are over 200 message types delivered in the R/3™ system for building ALE and EDI interfaces. These message types are across all application modules of the R/3™ system, and most application areas are supported by ALE/EDI functionality. However, there are certain application areas that lack ALE/EDI support, and it is possible to build brand-new ALE/EDI functionality for it. In this section, we take the example of a master data application that is not supported by SAP's™ ALE: the SD Customer Hierarchy. *Customer hierarchy* is used to represent the organizational data and hierarchy of a company's customers. For example, a company that distributes and sells products to its customers' stores may need to maintain the organizational structure and reporting chain of its customers based on a combination of Customer/ Sales Organization/Distribution Channel/Division. Each occurrence of this combination is considered a *hierarchy node* and is assigned to other hierarchy nodes, thus forming a hierarchical chain. The assignment is also based on partner functions of the nodes, each of which has a validity period. SAP™ allows for building complex chains and relationships, including future assignments and multiple future overlapping assignments. Customer hierarchy can be maintained using transaction **VDH1** and can be displayed with transaction **VDH2**.

Since there is no ALE functionality to capture the changes occurring to the SD Customer Hierarchy, we will build all the components to accomplish this task and communicate changes to the external system via the IDOC interface. The steps involved in constructing this functionality include:

- Creating a new Basic IDOC type
- Creating a new message type
- Linking the Basic IDOC type to the message type
- Creating/using Change Document Object for generating function module for updating the Change Document tables CDHDR and CDPOS
- Activating change pointer generation for the new message type with respect to the change document object
- Creating new ALE function modules for populating the IDOCs
- Enhancing the SAP™ program for SD Customer Hierarchy to log changes

■ Configuring ALE objects such as logical system, distribution model, port, and partner profile

The preceding steps essentially describe the process of accomplishing our task. It is important for the reader to understand all these steps as detailed in this chapter, since there are a few intricacies with the development of new ALE functionality for master data distribution. We also learn the use of change document objects, which is common to several types of application data in the R/3™ system. Many elements of this approach are also applicable to building new transactional data ALE interfaces, with the important difference being the triggering mechanism for the creation of change object or output type. It is possible to create new change document objects and generate function modules that update the change document tables; however, the calls to these change document function modules have to be embedded in SAP™ application programs. Also, as you will learn, most of the steps involve configuration, which is done without difficulty using SAP™ transactions and parametric tables.

Let us proceed with the various steps listed earlier to construct this interface. Each step describes in detail the considerations for building the ALE or application objects.

Creating a New Basic IDOC Type

As we know, an *IDOC type* represents an intelligent data container that is used to transport application objects to and from the R/3™ system. To build a new Basic IDOC type, we need to research the application so that we can define IDOC segments that contain the various data elements of the application object. In the case of SD Customer Hierarchy, we will find that a single table, KNVH, represents the hierarchical relationships of the customers and hierarchy nodes. The data behind the customer nodes are stored in a set of Customer Master tables that can be transported by SAP™-delivered IDOC type DEBMAS02, message type DEBMAS. The KNVH table consists of 16 fields that represent the hierarchy type, customer, sales organization, distribution channel, division, start of validity, end of validity, the higher-level customer, its sales organization, distribution channel and division, flag for rebates and pricing, and hierarchy level number. Understanding the application will reveal to us that the KNVH table structure itself can completely represent the hierarchical relationship of a customer node. To this, we need to add the field "message function" on the segment that will indicate the action taken to generate the change to the hierarchy.

Let us create a new Basic IDOC type with one segment mirroring the KNVH table. To do this:

- Execute transaction **WE30** or from **WEDI** → Development → IDOC types or from SALE → Extensions → IDOC types → Maintain IDOC type

- Enter ZKNVHM01 for object name

- Choose radio-button BASIC IDOC TYPE

- Click on the CREATE icon

- On the pop-up window, choose radio-button CREATE NEW, and enter a description of the Basic IDOC type. Enter.

- Place cursor on ZKNVHM01 and click on the CREATE icon

- A pop-up panel will appear. Enter Z1KNVHM for Segment type; check the Mandatory segment flag, since this segment is mandatory; enter 1 for minimum number and maximum number of segments, since every IDOC will contain only one segment, that is, Z1KNVHM. Leave the field for Parent Segment blank. Click on button SEGMENT EDITOR.

- On the next panel. Maintain Segment, click on the CREATE icon after ensuring the segment name is Z1KNVHM. Enter a development class for this object on the pop-up window

- You will be taken to the segment editor. Enter the components of the segment with details as shown in Table 5-1.

- Save the segment definition and activate it by clicking on the GENERATE/ACTIVATE button. Step back to the previous screen, Maintain Segment.

- Release the segment: from GoTo → Release. Save.

- Enter a description for the segment and save again

- Check the segment definition by clicking on icon CHECK

- Step back to the Basic IDOC type screen. Ensure the Z1KNVHM segment appears hierarchically below Basic IDOC type ZKNVHM01. Save.

- From the main screen (transaction **WE30**), release the Basic IDOC type: Extras → Release type

TABLE 5-1

Segment Fields for
Z1KNVHM

#	Field Name	Data Element Structure	Length	Data Element Documentation	Data Type
1	MSGFN	MSGFN	3	MSGFN	CHAR
2	HITYP	HITYP_KH	1	HITYP_KH	CHAR
3	KUNNR	KUNNR_KH	10	KUNNR_KH	CHAR
4	VKORG	VKORG	4	VKORG	CHAR
5	VTWEG	VTWEG	2	VTWEG	CHAR
6	SPART	SPART	2	SPART	CHAR
7	DATAB	DATAB_KH	8	DATAB_KH	DATS
8	DATBI	DATBI_KH	8	DATBI_KH	DATS
9	HKUNNR	HKUNNR_KH	10	HKUNNR_KH	CHAR
10	HVKORG	HVKORG	4	HVKORG	CHAR
11	HVTWEG	HVTWEG	2	HVTWEG	CHAR
12	HSPART	HSPART	2	HSPART	CHAR
13	GRPNO	GRPNO	3	GRPNO	NUMC
14	BOKRE	BOKRE	1	BOKRE	CHAR
15	PRFRE	PRFRE	1	PRFRE	CHAR
16	HZUOR	HZUOR	2	HZUOR	NUMC

The Basic IDOC Type ZKNVHM01 has now been created. Before checking for consistency in definition, we need to link it to a new message type. (See Appendix F for a detailed description of the IDOC type we created.)

Creating a New Message Type

The next step is to create a new message type. In a message-based architecture of ALE, *message type* represents the type of information being communicated through the IDOC interface. We need to define a new message type that will denote the SD Customer Hierarchy master data, and be associated with the IDOC type that we created. This message type will also be used to invoke the ALE-function modules that we are going to create in a subsequent step; hence, message type plays a pivotal role in an ALE interface. Let us proceed with this task:

- From **SALE** → Extensions → IDOC types → Maintain message types for intermediate structures → Create logical message type
- Click on icon for DISPLAY <-> CHANGE
- Click on NEW ENTRIES
- Enter ZDEBHI for message type and a description
- Save

This information is stored in tables EDMSG and EDIMSGT.

Linking IDOC Type to Message Type

The next step is to link the two objects we created, the Basic IDOC type, and the message type, so that the corresponding ALE-function modules we will create can populate the IDOC segments with the right data. This can be easily accomplished by:

- **SALE** → Extensions → IDOC types → Maintain message types for intermediate documents → Assign message type to IDOC for ALE **or transaction BD69**
- Click on NEW ENTRIES
- Enter ZDEBHI for message type and ZKNVHM01 for Basic IDOC type. Leave the field extension type blank (see Figure 5-1).
- Save

Change Document Object/Generate Update Function Module

Change document objects capture changes occurring to master data, tables, and application objects in the R/3™ system. SAP™ has an extensive change document service, which tracks approximately 140 objects in the system and is enabled through components known as *change document objects* and *change document update function modules/programs*.

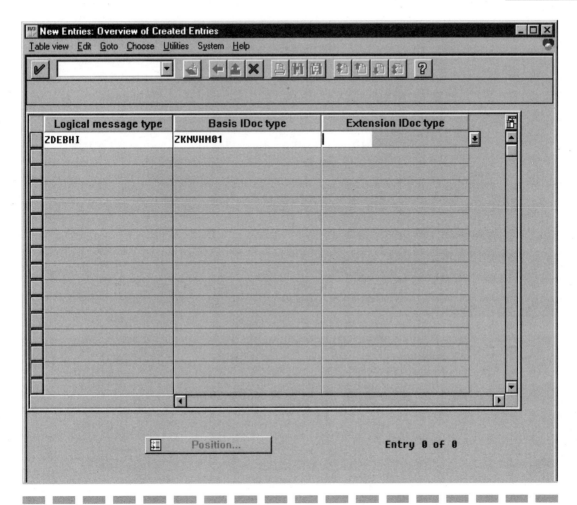

Figure 5-1 Linking Basic IDOC Type with Message Type

The change documents based on CD objects are stored in tables CDHDR (CD header information) and CDPOS (CD detail information). Most change documents report information about the change at the field level. Other than the table name and field name, it stores the key of the table, as well as the nature of the change, namely insert, update, or delete. As we learned earlier, ALE leverages the change document services through its shared master data (SMD) tool to capture changes to master data by objects known as change pointers. The change pointers, which are stored in tables BDCP and BDCPS, actually point to the change documents that were created by the application's change document update programs/function modules. ALE's APIs collect this information, and based on the table key and type of change, populate the IDOC segments. Subsequently, these IDOCs are distributed via the communications layer.

If a change document object—the seed for development—does not exist, it can be created through tools provided by SAP™. Use transaction **SCDO** to review the change document objects existing in the R/3™ system. A search will reveal that change document object KUNHIER exists for Customer Hierarchy. We can use this as the seed for change tracking of Customer Hierarchy objects, namely data on the KNVH table. Inspection of the CD object KUNHIER will show that all the fields on the KNVH table are tracked for changes. The next step is to generate an update program/function module based on this change document object. This is easily accomplished by choosing the option "Generate update pgm" from transaction **SCDO,** or by executing program RSSCD000. Note that this activity is classified as a "repair" to the R/3™ system by CTS (correction and transport system). Accept the default parameters of the program such as development class, function group, and so forth. Set the processing option to "Immediate update." The successful execution of this program will result in the generation of a new SAP™ function module, namely KUNHIER_WRITE_DOCUMENT. (Note that this is the naming convention SAP™ uses for such modules: <cdobject>_WRITE_ DOCUMENT.) Figure 5-2 shows the code in this function module.

Enhancing the SAP™ Program

The function module KUNHIER_WRITE_DOCUMENT that we generated needs to be incorporated in the SAP™ application program for maintaining Customer Hierarchy. This program, RVKNVH00, which is invoked by transactions **VDH1** (maintenance) and **VDH2,** has to call the update function module at an appropriate point in processing of customer hierarchy data. Browsing the RVKNVH00 program will show that this call can be made right after SAP's™ call to module CUSTOMER_HIERARCHY_UPDATE, which updates the KNVH table with changes in that session of **VDH1** transaction. Note that the call is being made "IN UPDATE TASK," and we need to call our update function module in update task, too. The program RVKNVH00 populates two internal tables XVKNVH and YKNVH that store the new and old image of the customer hierarchy record. We can use these two tables to process the

Figure 5-2
Change Document
Update Function
Module for Customer
Hierarchy

```
FUNCTION KUNHIER_WRITE_DOCUMENT    .
CALL FUNCTION 'CHANGEDOCUMENT_OPEN'
              EXPORTING OBJECTCLASS = 'KUNHIER    '
                        OBJECTID    = OBJECTID
              PLANNED_CHANGE_NUMBER = PLANNED_CHANGE_NUMBER
          PLANNED_OR_REAL_CHANGES = PLANNED_OR_REAL_CHANGES
              EXCEPTIONS SEQUENCE_INVALID = 1
                         OTHERS          = 2.


CASE SY-SUBRC.
   WHEN 1. MESSAGE A001 WITH 'SEQUENCE INVALID'.
   WHEN 2. MESSAGE A001 WITH 'OPEN ERROR'.
ENDCASE.

IF UPD_KNVH        NE SPACE.
    CALL FUNCTION 'CHANGEDOCUMENT_MULTIPLE_CASE'
              EXPORTING  TABLENAME         = 'KNVH        '
                         CHANGE_INDICATOR  = UPD_KNVH
                         DOCU_DELETE       = 'X'
              TABLES     TABLE_OLD         = YKNVH
                         TABLE_NEW         = XKNVH
              EXCEPTIONS NAMETAB_ERROR         = 1
                         OPEN_MISSING          = 2
                         POSITION_INSERT_FAILED = 3
                         OTHERS                = 4.

    CASE SY-SUBRC.
       WHEN 1. MESSAGE A001 WITH 'NAMETAB-ERROR'.
       WHEN 2. MESSAGE A001 WITH 'OPEN MISSING'.
       WHEN 3. MESSAGE A001 WITH 'INSERT ERROR'.
       WHEN 4. MESSAGE A001 WITH 'MULTIPLE ERROR'.
    ENDCASE.
ENDIF.

IF UPD_ICDTXT_KUNHIER    NE SPACE.
    CALL FUNCTION 'CHANGEDOCUMENT_TEXT_CASE'
              TABLES    TEXTTABLE = ICDTXT_KUNHIER
              EXCEPTIONS OPEN_MISSING         = 1
                         POSITION_INSERT_FAILED = 2
                         OTHERS               = 3.

    CASE SY-SUBRC.
       WHEN 1. MESSAGE A001 WITH 'OPEN MISSING'.
       WHEN 2. MESSAGE A001 WITH 'INSERT ERROR'.
       WHEN 3. MESSAGE A001 WITH 'TEXT ERROR'.
ENDCASE.
```

Figure 5-2
Change Document
Update Function
Module for
Customer Hierarchy
(*Continued*)

```
ENDIF.

CALL FUNCTION 'CHANGEDOCUMENT_CLOSE'
            EXPORTING  OBJECTCLASS    = 'KUNHIER    '
                       OBJECTID       = OBJECTID
                       DATE_OF_CHANGE = UDATE
                       TIME_OF_CHANGE = UTIME
                       TCODE          = TCODE
                       USERNAME       = USERNAME
    OBJECT_CHANGE_INDICATOR = OBJECT_CHANGE_INDICATOR
            EXCEPTIONS HEADER_INSERT_FAILED = 1
                       OBJECT_INVALID       = 2
                       OPEN_MISSING         = 3
                       NO_POSITION_INSERTED = 4
                       OTHERS               = 5.

CASE SY-SUBRC.
   WHEN 1. MESSAGE A001 WITH 'INSERT HEADER FAILED'.
   WHEN 2. MESSAGE A001 WITH 'OBJECT INVALID'.
   WHEN 3. MESSAGE A001 WITH 'OPEN MISSING'.
   WHEN 5. MESSAGE A001 WITH 'CLOSE ERROR'.
ENDCASE.

ENDFUNCTION.
```

request for updating the CDHDR and CDPOS through the call to the update function module.

As you may have noticed, the program RSSCD000 that we used to generate the update function module also created a form routine CD_CALL_KUNHIER for use in program RVKNVH00. See Figure 5-3. We have to add this form routine to program RVKNVH00, and call it in the main code of RVKNVH00 after the call to CUSTOMER_ HIERARCHY_ UPDATE. The block of code shown in Figure 5-4 processes the XVKNVH and YKNVH tables. For every row of the internal table XVKNVH, which is the new image, it builds a reference internal table I_XVKNVH. Then it checks for an occurrence of the key data in internal table YKNVH, which is the old image of database table KNVH. If a match is found, it builds a reference internal table, I_YVKNVH. These two reference internal tables, I_XVKNVH and I_YVKNVH, are passed as parameters to the form routine CD_CALL_KUNHIER. The form then calls the update function module KUNHIER_WRITE_DOCUMENT. This module updates tables

Figure 5-3
Form Routine for
KUNHIER Update
Function Module

```
*********** Insert Form here ********************************
* Form routine to create change documents. This function module *
* was "generated" based on CD object KUNHIER.                   *
****************************************************************
FORM CD_CALL_KUNHIER
              TABLES FXKNVH STRUCTURE VKNVH
                     FYKNVH STRUCTURE VKNVH
              USING  UPD_KNVH OBJECTID.
***
   IF  ( UPD_KNVH        NE SPACE ).
     CALL FUNCTION 'SWE_REQUESTER_TO_UPDATE'.
     CALL FUNCTION 'KUNHIER_WRITE_DOCUMENT        ' IN UPDATE TASK
         EXPORTING
             OBJECTID                 = OBJECTID
             TCODE                    = 'VDH1'
             UTIME                    = SY-UZEIT
             UDATE                    = SY-DATUM
             USERNAME                 = SY-UNAME
             PLANNED_CHANGE_NUMBER    = SPACE
             OBJECT_CHANGE_INDICATOR  = 'U'
             PLANNED_OR_REAL_CHANGES  = SPACE
             UPD_KNVH                 = UPD_KNVH
             UPD_ICDTXI_KUNHIER       = SPACE
         TABLES
             ICDTXI_KUNHIER           = I_ICDTXI_KUNHIER
             XKNVH                    = FXKNVH
             YKNVH                    = FYKNVH.
   ENDIF.
ENDFORM.
```

CDHDR and CDPOS, creating a change document based on the reference internal tables I_XVKNVH and I_YVKNVH. The nature of the update—insert, update, or delete—reflected in field KZ of the internal tables, is also taken into consideration while creating the change document. Note that you need to define these two internal tables using the ABAP/4 data statement.

It is highly recommended that you make a copy of program RVKNVH00, say ZVKNVH00, and then make the aforementioned changes to it. If you do so, you need to point transactions **VDH1, WDH1, VDH2,** and **WDH2** to program ZVKNVH00, using transaction **SE93**—Maintain SAP™ transactions. Also note that you may need to make additional changes to program ZVKNVH00 to handle special situations for future assignments of customer hierarchy. This can be easily incor-

Figure 5-4
Changes to Program
RVKNVH00

```
IF CHANGE_LINK = 'X'.
CALL FUNCTION 'CUSTOMER_HIERARCHY_UPDATE' IN UPDATE TASK
        TABLES
              T_XKNVH = XVKNVH
              T_YKNVH = YKNVH.
***** Insert code here ******************************************
* This block of code has been added to create Change Documents  *
* on CDHDR/CDPOS tables via the function module -               *
* KUNHIER_WRITE_DOCUMENT (called in the form).                  *
* XVKNVH is the new image of changes, whereas YKNVH is the      *
* old image.                                                    *
* For every line of change in XVKNVH with a corresponding old   *
* image in                                                      *
* YKNVH, a Change Document is written.                          *
****************************************************************
    LOOP AT XVKNVH.
      CLEAR: I_XVKNVH, I_YVKNVH.
      REFRESH: I_XVKNVH, I_YVKNVH.
      I_XVKNVH = XVKNVH.
      APPEND I_XVKNVH.
      READ TABLE YKNVH WITH KEY
                    MANDT = XVKNVH-MANDT
                    HITYP = XVKNVH-HITYP
                    KUNNR = XVKNVH-KUNNR
                    VKORG = XVKNVH-VKORG
                    VTWEG = XVKNVH-VTWEG
                    SPART = XVKNVH-SPART
                    DATAB = XVKNVH-DATAB.
      IF SY-SUBRC EQ 0.
         I_YVKNVH = YKNVH.
         APPEND I_YVKNVH.
      ENDIF.
      PERFORM CD_CALL_KUNHIER
              TABLES I_XVKNVH
                     I_YVKNVH
              USING 'U' I_XVKNVH-KUNNR.
    ENDLOOP.
*****
***** Code changes end here ***********************************
*****
*—— Änderungsmeldungen ausgeben _____
   MESSAGE S028.
 ELSE.
   MESSAGE S033.
 ENDIF.
```

porated in the same block of code that we added, as shown in Figure 5-4.

Creating ALE-Function Modules

Having enhanced the SAP™ application program to create change documents for customer hierarchy, we now need to create ALE-function modules to read the associated change pointers and populate the ZKNVHM01 IDOC type that we created. Most master data ALE-function modules follow a standard approach to gathering data, populating IDOCs, and distributing them. First, there is a function module that collects all unprocessed change pointers of that particular message type and builds an internal table of its keys. This internal table is passed on to another function module that populates the corresponding IDOC type and, with the aid of a standard ALE-function module, distributes this IDOC to the communication layer.

Let us build these two function modules. In keeping with SAP™ naming conventions, we will call them ZMASTERIDOC_CREATE_SMD_ ZDEBHI and ZMASTERIDOC_CREATE_ZDEBHI. Figures 5-5 and 5-6 show the source code of the first and second function modules, while Figure 5-7 gives us the global data. A synopsis of these two function modules follows.

Function module ZMASTERIDOC_CREATE_SMD_ZDEBHI first collects all unprocessed change pointers for message type ZDEBHI using an SAP™ standard API "CHANGE_POINTERS_READ" that accesses the BDCP and BDCPS tables. Then, it creates the keys of these change pointers and stores them in an internal table. The message function of each of the keys is determined based on the change document change ID. The internal table is sorted by its key, and subsequently for every row in this internal table it calls function module ZMASTERIDOC_ CREATE_ZDEBHI, which populates and distributes the IDOCs. After this processing, it appends all processed pointers to another internal table which is passed to function module CHANGE_POINTER_ STATUS_WRITE. This API updates the BDCPS table to indicate that the change pointer has been processed.

When function module ZMASTERIDOC_CREATE_ZDEBHI is called from the first module, it selects data from table KNVH based on the key passed to it. It populates IDOC segment Z1KNVHM with this data. Subsequently, the EDIDD key fields are filled appropriately and segment

```
FUNCTION ZMASTERIDOC_CREATE_SMD_ZDEBHI.
*"_____
*"*"Local interface:
*"      IMPORTING
*"            VALUE(MESSAGE_TYPE) LIKE  TBDME-MESTYP
*"_____
*

************************MODIFICATION****************************
* Programmer   :   Rajeev Kasturi                          *
* Date         :   Feb. 1998                               *
* Description   :   This function module has been created   *
* anew for generating Customer Hierarchy IDOCs used in ALE  *
* distribution of changes (creates/changes/deletes) of SD   *
* Customer Hierarchy. The new message type for this purpose is *
* ZDEBHI, and the custom "Basic IDOC" type is ZKNVHM01.      *
***************************************************************
    DATA: BEGIN OF F_KNVHKEY,
            MANDT    LIKE KNVH-MANDT,
            HITYP    LIKE KNVH-HITYP,
            KUNNR    LIKE KNVH-KUNNR,
            VKORG    LIKE KNVH-VKORG,
            VTWEG    LIKE KNVH-VTWEG,
            SPART    LIKE KNVH-SPART,
            DATAB    LIKE KNVH-DATAB,
          END OF F_KNVHKEY.
*
  DATA: BEGIN OF F_KNVH.
          INCLUDE STRUCTURE ZKNVHKEY.
  DATA: END OF F_KNVH.
*
  DATA: BEGIN OF T_KNVHKEY OCCURS 10.
          INCLUDE STRUCTURE ZKNVHKEY.
  DATA: END OF T_KNVHKEY.
*
  DATA: BEGIN OF T_CHGPTRS OCCURS 10.
          INCLUDE STRUCTURE BDCP.
  DATA: END OF T_CHGPTRS.
  DATA: BEGIN OF T_CPIDENT OCCURS 10,
          CPIDENT LIKE BDCP-CPIDENT,
          END OF T_CPIDENT.
  DATA: BEGIN OF T_CPIDENT_KNVH OCCURS 10,
          MANDT    LIKE KNVH-MANDT,
          HITYP    LIKE KNVH-HITYP,
          KUNNR    LIKE KNVH-KUNNR,
          VKORG    LIKE KNVH-VKORG,
```

Figure 5-5
ALE-Function Module
to Process Change
Pointers (*Continued*)

```
                    VTWEG   LIKE KNVH-VTWEG,
                    SPART   LIKE KNVH-SPART,
                    DATAB   LIKE KNVH-DATAB,
                     CPIDENT LIKE BDCP-CPIDENT,
                  END OF T_CPIDENT_KNVH.


*  created idocs
*  SAP created variables - does not follow naming stds.
   DATA: CREATED_M_IDOCS LIKE SY-TABIX.
   DATA: CREATED_COMM_IDOCS LIKE SY-TABIX.
   DATA: CREATED_C_IDOCS LIKE SY-TABIX.
   DATA: DONE_SINCE_COMMIT LIKE SY-TABIX.


*  read all not processed change pointers for the given
*  messagetype,
*  object class KUNHIER
*  return code is not checked for since no exception is raised by
*  the function module.
   CALL FUNCTION 'CHANGE_POINTERS_READ'
       EXPORTING
            CHANGE_DOCUMENT_OBJECT_CLASS = 'KUNHIER'
            MESSAGE_TYPE                 = MESSAGE_TYPE
            READ_NOT_PROCESSED_POINTERS  = 'X'
       TABLES
            CHANGE_POINTERS              = T_CHGPTRS.


*
   REFRESH T_KNVHKEY.
*
*  create all keys from the change pointers
   LOOP AT T_CHGPTRS.
*      table KNVH
*      table KNVH of the change document equals the table KNVH
       PERFORM MOVE_X_TO_Y USING T_CHGPTRS-TABKEY+0(3)
                                   F_KNVHKEY-MANDT.
       IF F_KNVHKEY-MANDT = SPACE.
         F_KNVHKEY-MANDT = T_CHGPTRS-MANDT.
       ENDIF.
*
       PERFORM MOVE_X_TO_Y USING T_CHGPTRS-TABKEY + 3(1)
                                   F_KNVHKEY-HITYP.
*
       PERFORM MOVE_X_TO_Y USING T_CHGPTRS-TABKEY+4(10)
                                   F_KNVHKEY-KUNNR.
*
```

Figure 5-5
ALE-Function Module
to Process Change
Pointers (*Continued*)

```
      PERFORM MOVE_X_TO_Y USING T_CHGPTRS-TABKEY+14(4)
                                F_KNVHKEY-VKORG.
*
      PERFORM MOVE_X_TO_Y USING T_CHGPTRS-TABKEY+18(2)
                                F_KNVHKEY-VTWEG.
*
      PERFORM MOVE_X_TO_Y USING T_CHGPTRS-TABKEY+20(2)
                                F_KNVHKEY-SPART.
*
      PERFORM MOVE_X_TO_Y USING T_CHGPTRS-TABKEY+22(8)
                                F_KNVHKEY-DATAB.
*
      READ TABLE T_KNVHKEY WITH KEY F_KNVHKEY.
*
      MOVE F_KNVHKEY-MANDT TO T_KNVHKEY-MANDT.
      MOVE F_KNVHKEY-HITYP TO T_KNVHKEY-HITYP.
      MOVE F_KNVHKEY-KUNNR TO T_KNVHKEY-KUNNR.
      MOVE F_KNVHKEY-VKORG TO T_KNVHKEY-VKORG.
      MOVE F_KNVHKEY-VTWEG TO T_KNVHKEY-VTWEG.
      MOVE F_KNVHKEY-SPART TO T_KNVHKEY-SPART.
      MOVE F_KNVHKEY-DATAB TO T_KNVHKEY-DATAB.
*
      PERFORM CONVERT_CDCHGID_TO_MSGFN USING T_CHGPTRS-CDCHGID
                                            T_KNVHKEY-MSGFN.
      IF SY-SUBRC <>0.
        APPEND T_KNVHKEY.
      ELSE.
        MODIFY T_KNVHKEY INDEX SY-TABIX.
      ENDIF.
*
*       add pointer to processed pointers
      MOVE-CORRESPONDING F_KNVHKEY TO T_CPIDENT_KNVH.
      MOVE T_CHGPTRS-CPIDENT TO T_CPIDENT_KNVH-CPIDENT.
      APPEND T_CPIDENT_KNVH.
    ENDLOOP.
*
    SORT T_KNVHKEY BY MANDT HITYP KUNNR VKORG VTWEG SPART DATAB.
    SORT T_CPIDENT_KNVH BY MANDT HITYP KUNNR VKORG VTWEG SPART
    DATAB.
*
* initialize counter variables for created idocs
    CREATED_M_IDOCS = 0.
    CREATED_C_IDOCS = 0.
    DONE_SINCE_COMMIT = 0.
```

Figure 5-5
ALE-Function Module
to Process Change
Pointers (*Continued*)

```
        CLEAR T_CPIDENT. REFRESH T_CPIDENT.

* call of the idoc creator
    LOOP AT T_KNVHKEY WHERE MANDT = SY-MANDT.
      CLEAR   F_KNVH.
      MOVE-CORRESPONDING T_KNVHKEY TO F_KNVH.
* return code is not checked for since no exception is raised by
* the function module.
*

      CALL FUNCTION 'ZMASTERIDOC_CREATE_ZDEBHI'
          EXPORTING
                KNVHKEY               = F_KNVH
                RCVPFC                = ' '
                RCVPRN                = '       '
                RCVPRT                = ' '
                SNDPFC                = ' '
                SNDPRN                = '        '
                SNDPRT                = ' '
                MESSAGE_TYPE          = MESSAGE_TYPE
          IMPORTING
                CREATED_COMM_IDOCS = CREATED_COMM_IDOCS.
*
    CREATED_M_IDOCS = CREATED_M_IDOCS + 1.
    CREATED_C_IDOCS = CREATED_C_IDOCS + CREATED_COMM_IDOCS.
    DONE_SINCE_COMMIT = DONE_SINCE_COMMIT + 1.
*
* append all processed pointers
    LOOP AT T_CPIDENT_KNVH WHERE MANDT = F_KNVH-MANDT
                             AND HITYP = F_KNVH-HITYP
                             AND KUNNR = F_KNVH-KUNNR
                             AND VKORG = F_KNVH-VKORG
                             AND VTWEG = F_KNVH-VTWEG
                             AND SPART = F_KNVH-SPART
                             AND DATAB = F_KNVH-DATAB.
*
      T_CPIDENT-CPIDENT = T_CPIDENT_KNVH-CPIDENT.
      APPEND T_CPIDENT.
*
    ENDLOOP.
    IF DONE_SINCE_COMMIT >= C_IDOCS_BEFORE_COMMIT.
      DONE_SINCE_COMMIT = 0.
*
* write status of all processed pointers
* return code is not checked for since no exception is raised by
* the function module.
```

Figure 5-5
ALE-Function Module
to Process Change
Pointers (*Continued*)

```
        CALL FUNCTION 'CHANGE_POINTERS_STATUS_WRITE'
             EXPORTING
                 MESSAGE_TYPE              = MESSAGE_TYPE
             TABLES
                 CHANGE_POINTERS_IDENTS = T_CPIDENT.
*
     COMMIT WORK.
* return code is not checked for since no exception is raised by
* the function module.
     CALL FUNCTION 'DEQUEUE_ALL'.
*
     CLEAR T_CPIDENT. REFRESH T_CPIDENT.
*
   ENDIF.
*
  ENDLOOP.                                 "at t_knvhkey
*
* commit if necessary
  IF DONE_SINCE_COMMIT > 0.
*
* write status of all processed pointers
* return code is not checked for since no exception is raised by
* the function module.
     CALL FUNCTION 'CHANGE_POINTERS_STATUS_WRITE'
          EXPORTING
              MESSAGE_TYPE              = MESSAGE_TYPE
          TABLES
              CHANGE_POINTERS_IDENTS = T_CPIDENT.
*
     COMMIT WORK.
* return code is not checked for since no exception is raised by
* the function module.
     CALL FUNCTION 'DEQUEUE_ALL'.
*
  ENDIF.
*
  MESSAGE ID 'B1' TYPE 'I' NUMBER '038'
          WITH CREATED_M_IDOCS MESSAGE_TYPE.
  MESSAGE ID 'B1' TYPE 'I' NUMBER '039'
          WITH CREATED_C_IDOCS MESSAGE_TYPE.
ENDFUNCTION.
*&_____*
*&      Form  MOVE_X_TO_Y
*&_____*
*       text
```

Figure 5-5
ALE-Function Module
to Process Change
Pointers (*Continued*)

```
*_____*
*        →P_T_CHGPTRS-TABKEY+20(2)  text                *
*        →P_F_KNVHKEY-SPART  text                        *
*_____*
FORM MOVE_X_TO_Y USING X Y.
*
  Y = X.
*
ENDFORM.                                    " MOVE_X_TO_Y
*&_____*
*&       Form   CONVERT_CDCHGID_TO_MSGFN
*&_____*
*        text                                            *
*_____*
*        →P_T_CHGPTRS-CDCHGID  text                      *
*                                                         *
*        →P_T_KNVHKEY-MSGFN  text                         *
*_____*

FORM CONVERT_CDCHGID_TO_MSGFN USING CDCHGID LIKE BDCP-CDCHGID
                                    MSGFN LIKE Z1KNVHM-MSGFN.
*
  MSGFN = SPACE.
*
  CASE CDCHGID.
    WHEN 'I'.
      MSGFN = C_MSGFN_I.
    WHEN 'U'.
      MSGFN = C_MSGFN_U.
    WHEN ' '.
      MSGFN = C_MSGFN_R.
    WHEN 'D'.
      MSGFN = C_MSGFN_D.
    WHEN 'E'.
      MSGFN = C_MSGFN_D.
    WHEN 'S'.
      MSGFN = C_MSGFN_S.
  ENDCASE.
*
ENDFORM.                         " CONVERT_CDCHGID_TO_MSGFN
*&_____*
*&       Form   FILL_SEGMENT_Z1KNVHM
*&_____*
*        text                                            *
*_____*
```

Figure 5-5
ALE-Function Module
to Process Change
Pointers (*Continued*)

```
*         →P_KNVHKEY-MSGFN  text                                        *
*_____*
FORM FILL_SEGMENT_Z1KNVHM USING MSGFN.
*
  CLEAR Z1KNVHM.
*
  Z1KNVHM-MSGFN  =  MSGFN.
  Z1KNVHM-HITYP  =  KNVH-HITYP.
  Z1KNVHM-KUNNR  =  KNVH-KUNNR.
  Z1KNVHM-VKORG  =  KNVH-VKORG.
  Z1KNVHM-VTWEG  =  KNVH-VTWEG.
  Z1KNVHM-SPART  =  KNVH-SPART.
  Z1KNVHM-DATAB  =  KNVH-DATAB.
  Z1KNVHM-DATBI  =  KNVH-DATBI.
  Z1KNVHM-HKUNNR =  KNVH-HKUNNR.
  Z1KNVHM-HVKORG =  KNVH-HVKORG.
  Z1KNVHM-HVTWEG =  KNVH-HVTWEG.
  Z1KNVHM-HSPART =  KNVH-HSPART.
  Z1KNVHM-GRPNO  =  KNVH-GRPNO.
  Z1KNVHM-BOKRE  =  KNVH-BOKRE.
  Z1KNVHM-PRFRE  =  KNVH-PRFRE.
  Z1KNVHM-HZUOR  =  KNVH-HZUOR.
*
ENDFORM.                                    " FILL_SEGMENT_Z1KNVHM
```

Figure 5-6
ALE-Function Module
for Populating and
Distributing Master
IDOCs

```
FUNCTION ZMASTERIDOC_CREATE_ZDEBHI.
*"_____
*"*"Local interface:
*"      IMPORTING
*"            VALUE(KNVHKEY) LIKE  ZKNVHKEY STRUCTURE  ZKNVHKEY
*"            VALUE(RCVPFC) LIKE    BDALEDC-RCVPFC
*"            VALUE(RCVPRN) LIKE    BDALEDC-RCVPRN
*"            VALUE(RCVPRT) LIKE    BDALEDC-RCVPRT
*"            VALUE(SNDPFC) LIKE    BDALEDC-SNDPFC
*"            VALUE(SNDPRN) LIKE    BDALEDC-SNDPRN
*"            VALUE(SNDPRT) LIKE    BDALEDC-SNDPRT
*"            VALUE(MESSAGE_TYPE) LIKE   TBDME-MESTYP
*"      EXPORTING
*"            VALUE(CREATED_COMM_IDOCS) LIKE   SY-TABIX
*"_____
***********************MODIFICATION****************************
* Programmer     :   Rajeev Kasturi                            *
* This function module is called from the driver FM :          *
```

Figure 5-6
ALE-Function Module
for Populating and
Distributing Master
IDOCs (*Continued*)

```
* "ZMASTERIDOC_CREATE_SMD_ZDEBHI"..                                    *
* The processing is based on the change document object KUNHIER.*
*****************************************************************

    DATA: BEGIN OF F_IDOC_HEADER.
            INCLUDE STRUCTURE EDIDC.
    DATA: END OF F_IDOC_HEADER.
    DATA: BEGIN OF T_IDOC_DATA OCCURS 10.
            INCLUDE STRUCTURE EDIDD.
    DATA: END OF T_IDOC_DATA.
    DATA: BEGIN OF T_IDOC_COMM_CONTROL OCCURS 10.
            INCLUDE STRUCTURE EDIDC.
    DATA: END OF T_IDOC_COMM_CONTROL.
    DATA: ACTIVE_FLAG(1) TYPE C.
    DATA: COMM_CONTROL_LINES LIKE SY-TABIX.
    DATA: IDOC_CIMTYPE LIKE EDIDC-CIMTYP.
    DATA: PARTNER_TYPE LIKE TPAR-NRART.                    "P30K057526
    DATA: COUNTRY_ISO LIKE T005-INTCA.


* initial
    CLEAR T_IDOC_COMM_CONTROL.
    REFRESH T_IDOC_COMM_CONTROL.
    CLEAR T_IDOC_DATA.
    REFRESH T_IDOC_DATA.

    CLEAR IDOC_CIMTYPE.


* fill T_IDOC_DATA for Segment Z1KNVHM with KNVH
    SELECT SINGLE * FROM KNVH
            WHERE HITYP = KNVHKEY-HITYP
              AND KUNNR = KNVHKEY-KUNNR
              AND VKORG = KNVHKEY-VKORG
              AND VTWEG = KNVHKEY-VTWEG
              AND SPART = KNVHKEY-SPART
              AND DATAB = KNVHKEY-DATAB.
    IF SY-SUBRC = 0.
      PERFORM FILL_SEGMENT_Z1KNVHM USING KNVHKEY-MSGFN.
*
      CLEAR T_IDOC_DATA.
      T_IDOC_DATA-SEGNAM = C_SEGNAM_Z1KNVHM.
      T_IDOC_DATA-MANDT  = SY-MANDT.
      T_IDOC_DATA-SDATA  = Z1KNVHM.
*
      APPEND T_IDOC_DATA.
    ENDIF.
```

```
*
* fill IDOC_HEADER
  F_IDOC_HEADER-MESTYP = MESSAGE_TYPE.
  F_IDOC_HEADER-IDOCTP = C_IDOCTP_ZDEBHI.
  F_IDOC_HEADER-CIMTYP = IDOC_CIMTYPE.
  F_IDOC_HEADER-SNDPFC = SNDPFC.
  F_IDOC_HEADER-SNDPRN = SNDPRN.
  F_IDOC_HEADER-SNDPRT = SNDPRT.
  F_IDOC_HEADER-RCVPFC = RCVPFC.
  F_IDOC_HEADER-RCVPRN = RCVPRN.
  F_IDOC_HEADER-RCVPRT = RCVPRT.
  F_IDOC_HEADER-SERIAL = SPACE.
*

*

  CALL FUNCTION 'MASTER_IDOC_DISTRIBUTE'
       EXPORTING
            MASTER_IDOC_CONTROL              = F_IDOC_HEADER
       TABLES
            COMMUNICATION_IDOC_CONTROL       = T_IDOC_COMM_CONTROL
            MASTER_IDOC_DATA                 = T_IDOC_DATA
       EXCEPTIONS
            ERROR_IN_IDOC_CONTROL            = 01
            ERROR_WRITING_IDOC_STATUS        = 02
            ERROR_IN_IDOC_DATA               = 03
            SENDING_LOGICAL_SYSTEM_UNKNOWN = 04.

  IF SY-SUBRC <> 0.
  ENDIF.

  DESCRIBE TABLE T_IDOC_COMM_CONTROL LINES COMM_CONTROL_LINES.
  CREATED_COMM_IDOCS = COMM_CONTROL_LINES.
ENDFUNCTION.
```

Z1KNVHM is moved to EDIDD-SDATA. This complete EDIDD record is then appended to the T_IDOC_DATA internal table. EDIDC information that is available at this point in time—such as message type and IDOC type—is filled, and this structure along with internal table T_IDOC_DATA is passed to SAP™ standard function module MASTER_IDOC_DISTRIBUTE. This standard module determines the sender and receiver information based on the Customer Distribution Model and partner profiles, and distributes the IDOC to the communication layer. See Figure 5-6 for the source code. In essence, this is the processing involved in creating and distributing master data IDOCs.

Figure 5-7

Global Data for the
ALE-Function
Modules

```
FUNCTION-POOL ZDEB.                         "MESSAGE-ID ..
*
*
  DATA: C_MSGFN_I LIKE Z1KNVHM-MSGFN VALUE '009',  "New
        C_MSGFN_U LIKE Z1KNVHM-MSGFN VALUE '004',  "Change
        C_MSGFN_R LIKE Z1KNVHM-MSGFN VALUE '005',  "Refresh
        C_MSGFN_T LIKE Z1KNVHM-MSGFN VALUE '023',  "Synchroniza-
                                                    tion
        C_MSGFN_D LIKE Z1KNVHM-MSGFN VALUE '003',  "Deletion
        C_MSGFN_S LIKE Z1KNVHM-MSGFN VALUE '018'.  "Reissue
  DATA:   C_IDOCS_BEFORE_COMMIT LIKE SY-TABIX VALUE 50.
  DATA:   C_SEGNAM_Z1KNVHM LIKE EDIDD-SEGNAM VALUE 'Z1KNVHM'.
  DATA:   C_IDOCTP_ZCSTHI LIKE BDALEDC-IDOCTP VALUE 'ZKNVHM01'.
  TABLES: KNVH, Z1KNVHM.
```

Activating Change Pointer Generation and Other ALE Configurations

Previously, we learned to create code for the posting of change documents from SAP™ application programs. For purposes of ALE, these change document fields need to be marked for change pointer generation. Furthermore, we have to assign the IDOC fields to the change document fields. As explained earlier, we also need to associate the message type that we created with the appropriate ALE-function module, so that when programs such as RBDMIDOC are executed, they invoke the function modules that we wrote for populating and distributing IDOCs; hence, we need to perform these three configuration tasks:

1. Activate change pointer generation for change document item
2. Assign IDOC field to change document field
3. Allocate function module to message type

To perform these tasks:

■ From transaction **SALE** → Extensions → Master data distribution → Activate change pointer per change document item

■ Enter ZDEBHI for logical message type

■ Make entries in the table as shown in Figure 5-8. Note the additional entry "Key," which represents the key of the object.

■ Save

Note that this step can also be used to deactivate the change pointer generation of certain fields in a message type for the corresponding change document object. By default, all fields of the change document object are active for change pointer generation.

The next step is to associate the IDOC segment fields with the change document fields. This allocation determines the fields for which change pointers are written when a change document is created. To do this:

Figure 5-8

Change Pointer per
Change Document
Item

Table	V_TBD62	Date
Description	Change document items for message type	
Number of entries	17	

Change doc. object	Log.mess.type	Table name	Field name
Client	010		
KUNHIER	ZDEBHI	KNVH	BOKRE
KUNHIER	ZDEBHI	KNVH	DATAB
KUNHIER	ZDEBHI	KNVH	DATBI
KUNHIER	ZDEBHI	KNVH	GRPNO
KUNHIER	ZDEBHI	KNVH	HITYP
KUNHIER	ZDEBHI	KNVH	HKUNNR
KUNHIER	ZDEBHI	KNVH	HSPART
KUNHIER	ZDEBHI	KNVH	HVKORG
KUNHIER	ZDEBHI	KNVH	HVTWEG
KUNHIER	ZDEBHI	KNVH	HZUOR
KUNHIER	ZDEBHI	KNVH	KEY
KUNHIER	ZDEBHI	KNVH	KUNNR
KUNHIER	ZDEBHI	KNVH	MANDT
KUNHIER	ZDEBHI	KNVH	PRFRE
KUNHIER	ZDEBHI	KNVH	SPART
KUNHIER	ZDEBHI	KNVH	VKORG
KUNHIER	ZDEBHI	KNVH	VTWEG

- From transaction **SALE** → Extensions → Master data distribution → Control data for reduction → Assign IDOC field to change document field
- Enter ZDEBHI for logical message type
- Make entries as per Figure 5-9. Note the dummy entry for field "Key"
- Save

The last step is to allocate the function module that we created to the message type (see Figure 5-10). This enables ALE processing programs to invoke the corresponding function module to populate and distribute the IDOCs. Also, remember that we associated the Basic IDOC type that we created with the new message type ZDEBHI in an earlier step. This facilitates the identification of the right IDOC type for that message type and ALE-function module. Follow these steps to complete the configuration:

- From transaction **SALE** → Extensions → Master data distribution → Set up additional data for message types
- Click on NEW ENTRIES
- Enter ZDEBHI for logical message type and Reference message type
- Enter ZMASTERIDOC_CREATE_SMD_ZDEBHI for Editing function module
- Save

As with other ALE interfaces, we need to create a logical system to represent the external system to which these IDOCs are going to be communicated. (Note that you can use an existing logical system as well, if it logically pertains to similar message types.) Configure the Customer Distribution Model to indicate that message type ZDEBHI will flow to this logical system. Define a port with an appropriate file-naming convention, or define a transactional RFC port with a logical RFC destination. Create a partner profile based on the logical system, and maintain its outbound parameters with message type ZDEBHI, Basic IDOC type ZKNVHM01, port, and other processing options as desired. Finally, activate the change pointer generation using transaction **BD50 or SALE** → Distribution scenarios → Master data distribution → Activate change pointer → Activate change pointer for message type. You will have to create a new entry for ZDEBHI and flag it to activate. Ensure that change pointer generation is active at the general level as well.

Figure 5-9
Allocating IDOC
Segment Fields to
Change Document
Fields

| Table | V_TBD22 | | | Date |

Description   Segment field - change document field

Number of entries   16

Segm.type	Field name	Change doc. object	Table name	Field name
Z1KNVHM		KUNHIER	KNVH	KEY
Z1KNVHM	BOKRE	KUNHIER	KNVH	BOKRE
Z1KNVHM	DATAB	KUNHIER	KNVH	DATAB
Z1KNVHM	DATBI	KUNHIER	KNVH	DATBI
Z1KNVHM	GRPNO	KUNHIER	KNVH	GRPNO
Z1KNVHM	HITYP	KUNHIER	KNVH	HITYP
Z1KNVHM	HKUNNR	KUNHIER	KNVH	HKUNNR
Z1KNVHM	HSPART	KUNHIER	KNVH	HSPART
Z1KNVHM	HVKORG	KUNHIER	KNVH	HVKORG
Z1KNVHM	HVTWEG	KUNHIER	KNVH	HVTWEG
Z1KNVHM	HZUOR	KUNHIER	KNVH	HZUOR
Z1KNVHM	KUNNR	KUNHIER	KNVH	KUNNR
Z1KNVHM	PRFRE	KUNHIER	KNVH	PRFRE
Z1KNVHM	SPART	KUNHIER	KNVH	SPART
Z1KNVHM	VKORG	KUNHIER	KNVH	VKORG
Z1KNVHM	VTWEG	KUNHIER	KNVH	VTWEG

We have now completed all the configuration and development of our new functionality for communication of Customer Hierarchy IDOCs. Let us proceed with its testing. The proof of the pudding...

Working the Interface

The objective of this exercise is to check if all the components we built and linked for the Customer Hierarchy interface work in concert to produce IDOCs based on changes to the master data. A new Basic IDOC

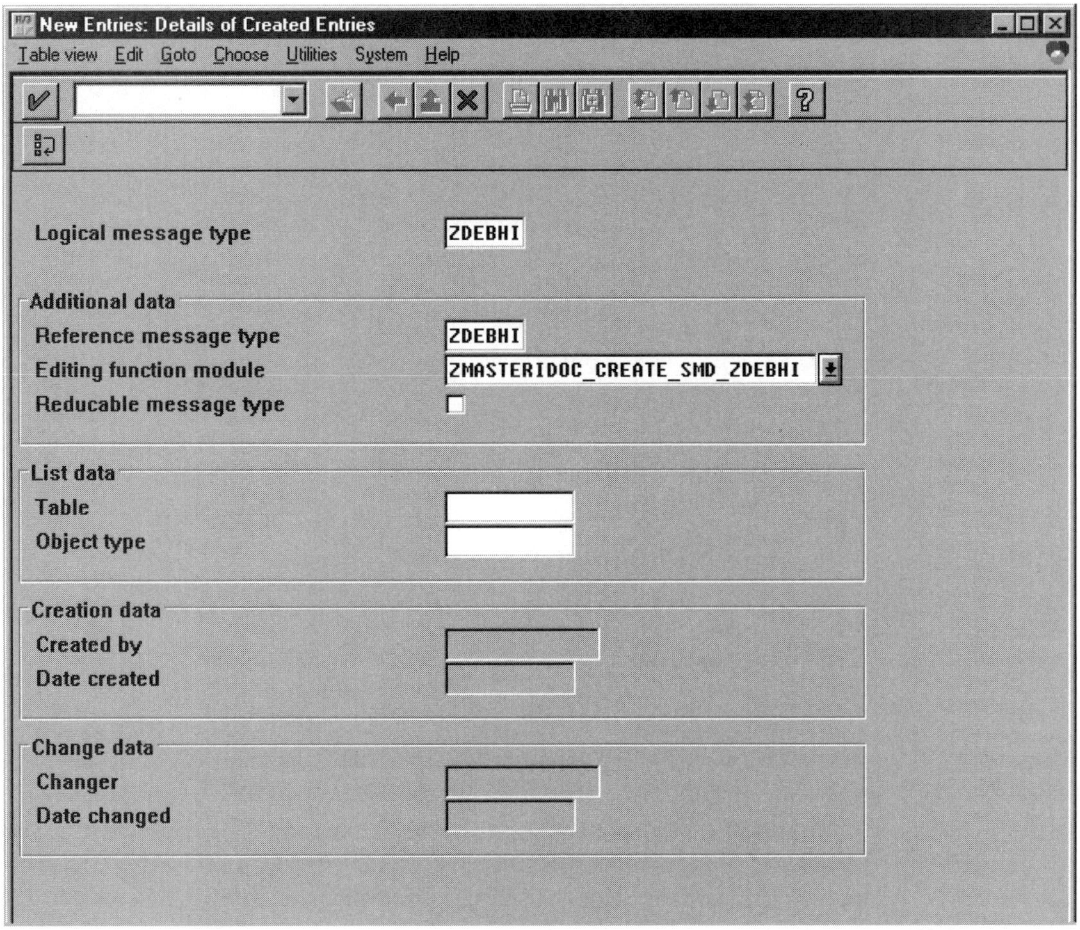

Figure 5-10 Allocating Format Function Module to Message Type

type was created and a new message type was linked to it. Based on an existing change document object, we generated a change document update function module that we incorporated into the SAP™ application program. Two ALE-function modules were written, whose function is to capture the change pointers of the new message type, populate, and distribute the IDOCs. ALE configuration was put in place to activate change pointer generation for the change document fields with corresponding configuration for the IDOC segment fields and the change document fields. We associated the driving ALE-function module with the new message type in order to invoke it upon processing of the change pointers. Finally, we completed the ALE configuration by defining and linking the logical system, Customer Distribution Model, port, partner profile, and change pointer activation.

Let us outline some of the test cases for tracking changes to the Customer Hierarchy. Following are a few of them. Depending on your application configuration and business requirements, there may be more test scenarios; however, the objects and programs that we built should handle all situations with minor enhancements, if at all, to the code we added to program RVKNVH00.

- Assign new hierarchy
- Reassign hierarchy
- Delete hierarchy
- Change hierarchy details, such as validity date
- Assign/Reassign hierarchy node with future effective date
- Assign multiple future hierarchies
- Assign multiple overlapping hierarchies

Using transaction **VDH1**, you can carry out the preceding test scenarios and more. Once you have conducted each change and saved the application data, check the CDHDR and CDPOS tables for change documents reflecting the changes you made. Use object class KUNHIER as a selection parameter. Subsequently, check tables BDCP and BDCPS for corresponding change pointer entries. We are now ready to create the IDOCs. Use transaction **BD21** or execute program RBDMIDOC with parameter message type ZDEBHI. You should receive informational messages indicating the number of communication IDOCs created. Use transaction **WE02** or **WE05** to display the IDOCs created.

The IDOC data should reflect the application data and the message function will indicate the nature of change. For example, in the case of reassigning the hierarchy node to a different node, there will be two IDOCs created, one with message function 004 and the other with 009. The IDOC with 004 (Change) will indicate that the validity of the node's previous assignment has ended. The "valid to" date will be in the past. The IDOC with message function 009 (Create) will reflect the beginning of the new assignment. Your testing will indicate to you that the IDOCs will faithfully record the changes occurring to the Customer Hierarchy data, and will be in a form that should be easily interpreted by the external system.

As you may have realized from reading and applying this chapter, creating new ALE functionality is not a daunting task. If approached in a logical fashion, you can build the various components with ease and link them together with simple configuration. Also, the coding involved is minimal. It is important to note that SAP™ delivers all the tools necessary to construct additional ALE functionality.

Electronic Data
Interchange

Overview

Electronic Data Interchange (EDI) is a technology that gives companies the capability of exchanging business documents with their trading partners such as banks, customers, and vendors. The format of these electronic documents is determined by industrywide EDI standards such as EDIFACT and ANSI X12. EDI greatly enhances business connectivity and provides automated rapid turnaround on business processes. SAP™ R/3™ provides clients with the capability of a full-fledged EDI system that is fully integrated with R/3™ applications. For example, a company can send an EDI invoice to its customers, send and receive purchase/sales orders from vendors/customers, receive dispatch advice from its vendors, and exchange remittance advice with its banks. (For a sample scenario, refer to the introductory chapter.) In fact, it is possible to implement EDI with most, if not all, business documents that are exchanged with a company's trading partners.

The underlying technology of EDI uses the same basis as ALE technology. For example, the IDOC interface is common between EDI and ALE. The IDOC types and structures are the same, whether EDI or ALE. IDOCs in EDI have EDIDC and EDIDD records, as in ALE. In most cases, EDI processing uses the same function modules as used by ALE services. The concepts of partner profiles and port definitions are the same. For EDI, partner profiles (partner agreement numbers) need not have a logical system as their base. The partner types supported are KU for Customer, LI for Vendor, and B for Bank. EDI port definitions are typically file-based ports, whereas ALE ports could be file, transactional RFC, R/2™, or Internet. Note that EDI does not use the ALE concept of distribution models; hence, there are no filter objects that can be used as selection criteria. However, elements such as message types are common to ALE and EDI. As you will realize by reading this chapter, the configuration steps involved in setting up an EDI interface are very similar to those of an ALE interface. An important difference is that while EDI is primarily used for exchanging transactional data/documents, ALE can be used for master data, transactional data, and control data distribution.

In this chapter, we prototype an outbound EDI scenario—sending invoices (ANSI X12 810) to customers. We go through the various configuration steps in setting up the interface and test the creation of invoice IDOCs. We also learn the application configuration needed for generating an output record (NAST table record) that is the basis for creation of outputs in some of the logistics modules. An important component of any EDI or ALE interface is *IDOC mapping and translation.* We learn about mapping and mapping tools in this chapter. The concepts presented in this chapter are applicable to most EDI interfaces, and as mentioned earlier, many techniques are common to both ALE and EDI. As you will learn, the differences in building ALE and EDI interfaces are minor, and the message types available for EDI are a subset of all the message types for ALE interfaces. One should bear in mind that EDI transactions are possible only for the document formats defined by industry standards such as EDIFACT and ANSI X12. It is also possible to enhance the EDI functionality with the same approach that was used for enhancing ALE functionality. If the EDI document exists in the realm of industry-standard EDI, and SAP™ application generates that document even if no message type exists for it, then it is possible to create new EDI functionality to meet this new requirement with an approach discussed in earlier chapters.

Let us proceed with the configuration required for creating invoice IDOCs. *Invoices* are documents sent to a company's customers requesting payments for products or services delivered. The flow of documents is: a sales order is created for a customer for the requested quantity of materials; then a delivery is created in order to deliver the goods to the customer; once the goods have been picked and "post goods issued," a billing document (invoice) is created that requests payments for goods delivered. The message type we use is INVOIC and its corresponding IDOC type is INVOIC01. We will first configure the output determination for billing documents, create a port and partner profile with outbound parameters and message control, and test the creation of invoice IDOCs.

Configuring Output Determination

In SD and MM modules, message (output) determination uses the condition technique in order to generate an output and determine its quality in terms of medium, timing, and type. This output is used for generating output documents based on transactional data in the SD and MM modules. *Configuration* typically involves the setting up of condition tables, access sequence, output type, output determination procedures, and assignment of output procedures. In most cases SAP™-provided condition tables, access sequences, and output types may meet the requirements for generating the desired output records in the NAST table.

However, it is possible to develop new elements to do the same. Following are the steps for configuring output determination.

- **From the** IMG → Sales and Distribution → Basic Functions → Output → Output Determination → Output proposal using condition technique → Maintain Output determination for billing documents → Maintain condition tables **or transaction VOK2** → SD Document → Billing document → Condition table → Create/Change/ Display. **The listed condition tables are 008—Billing document type, 011—Sales organization/Billing type, and 018—Sales organization/Receiving country. Let us choose to use 008, where field Billing document type (FKART) from the catalog is used to build the access sequence.**

- **From VOK2** → SD Document → Billing document → Access sequence. **You will see several access sequences delivered by SAP™. Let us choose to use sequence 0001, based on the billing type.**

- **Let us choose to create a new output type with specific requirements for EDI output. To do this: from VOK2** → SD Document → Billing document → Output types. **Switch to the change view mode by clicking on** DISPLAY<->CHANGE **button. Click on button** NEW ENTRIES. **Enter ZBIL for output type and 0001 for access sequence. In panel** General, **choose** CONDITION ACCESS. **In panel for** Condition Record Proposal, **enter "6" (EDI) for Medium, "PY" (Payer) for Partner Function, and "1" for Time (processing by program RSNAST00). Save. The medium we chose refers to an EDI output, and the partner function PY (payer) indicates that the output should be sent to the Payer of the Customer, as determined by the Customer Master partner functions (table KNVP). See Figure 6-1. Click on button** PROCESSING PROGRAM **on the Output type screen. Create a new entry for output type ZBIL with medium "6" for EDI, program RSNASTED, and form routine EDI_PROCESSING. Save the entry. Back up to the initial screen, and click on button** PARTNER DEFINITION. **Create an entry for output type ZBIL with medium "6" for EDI and partner function "PY" for payer. Save. Note that the partner function can also be defined as BP—Bill-to-party.**

- **The next step is to assign the output type that we created to an output determination procedure. To do this: from VOK2** → SD

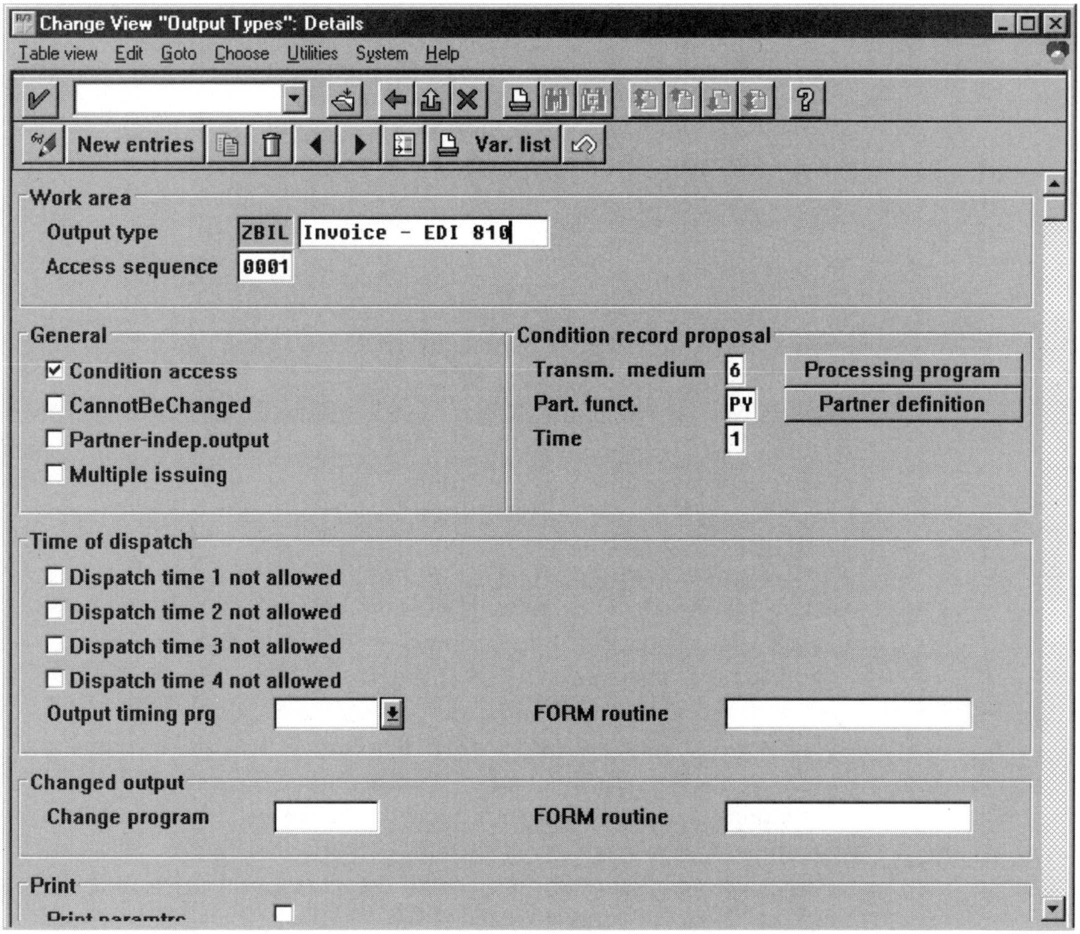

Figure 6-1 Configuring Output Type

Document → Billing document → Output determination procedure. **Pick an output determination procedure that will be assigned to a particular billing type. Include output type ZBIL as one of the steps in the output determination procedure. There is no need to specify a "Requirement," unless the business scenario requires it.**

■ **As the penultimate step to output determination configuration, assign the output procedure to a billing type, say F2. This can be done from VOK2** → SD Document → Billing document → Assign.

■ The final step is to create condition records for the output type we configured. To do this: **From** `SAP main menu` → `Logistics` → `Sales and Distribution` → `Master Data` → `Output` → `Billing Document` → `Create`. **Enter the required data on the screen such as "PY" for partner function, "6" for medium, "1" for time and the appropriate code for language desired. Save the entries.**

Configuring Ports, Partner Profiles

Now that we have completed the output determination (application) configuration, let us proceed with the EDI technical configuration, which includes port definition, partner profile creation, and maintaining entries on the EDPAR table for cross-reference to the external partner number.

■ Let us understand the underlying concepts of communications between the SAP™ port and an EDI subsystem in an outbound scenario. The settings we make in the port definition can indicate to the EDI subsystem through synchronous RFC the time the file was transmitted (created), its location, and file name. Since SAP™ does not append to an existing file of IDOCs, and a file with the same name is *overwritten,* it is better to use dynamic file names. These file names can be created with a particular pattern based on the function module specified in the outbound port definition. When an IDOC is created through the outbound port from SAP™, a field OUTMOD on the control record (EDIDC) is populated based on the settings we make in the processing options of the outbound parameters of the partner profile. See Table 6-1 for values and their descriptions.

■ If OUTMOD is 1 or 3 and the automatic start possible flag has been turned on in the command file settings of the port definition, SAP™ invokes the EDI subsystem through a shell script specified in the settings. The parameters passed are the file's directory and name. The EDI subsystem deletes the file after processing is completed. Also, with an OUTMOD value of 1 or 3, a status value of "18" (triggering EDI subsystem OK) is assigned to the IDOC after the successful invocation of the subsystem. This does not indicate that the EDI subsystem processed the IDOC successfully; that is done through the inbound status file created by the EDI subsystem. For

TABLE 6-1

OUTMOD Values
and Descriptions

OUTMOD	Description
1	One IDOC written to flat file, EDI subsystem activated immediately
2	One IDOC written to flat file, EDI subsystem started on external schedule
3	All IDOCs matching selection criteria written to flat file, EDI subsystem activated immediately
4	All IDOCs matching selection criteria written to flat file, EDI subsystem started as per external schedule

outbound EDI IDOCs, it is possible to determine the status of processing by the EDI subsystem. The subsystem creates a status file, which can then be automatically or programatically imported into SAP™ for status update of the outbound IDOCs. When the status file has been created, the subsystem starts the SAP™ system by calling a C program "startrfc." The status file is then imported into the SAP™ system that updates the IDOC status appropriately. Note that this is done by referencing the key information—DOC-NUM (IDOC number). Once SAP™ completes processing, it deletes the status file. Let us step through the process of creating the port definition. First, we need to create a logical RFC destination for use in the Command File of the port definition in order to trigger the EDI subsystem. Use transaction **SM59** or from the main menu, Tools → Administration → Administration → Network → RFC Destination. Place cursor on TCP/IP connections and click on button CREATE. Enter name of RFC destination, say LRFCEXMPL, type of entry "T" for starting an external program using TCP/IP connection, and a description. Press the ENTER key. This will display Figure 6-8. Enter the directory and program name "rfcexec" ("rfcexec.exe" for Windows NT server). If you wish to run the program on a specific host, click on button EXPLICIT HOST and enter the appropriate name of the server. Save.

■ The next step is to create a port definition. Use transaction **WE21** or WEDI → IDOC → Port Definition. Place cursor on "File" and click on button CREATE. On the following screen, click on button NEW ENTRIES. Enter the name of the port, say EDIPORT, and a description. Click on button COMMAND FILE. Enter the logical destination LRFCEXMPL that we created in the previous step. Enter the directory (path) where the subsystem shell script is placed.

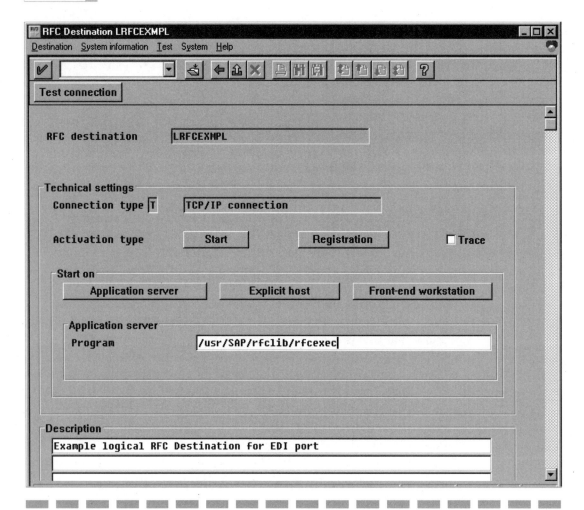

Figure 6-2 RFC Destination—Type TCP/IP

Remember to add the "/" at the end of the path (for Unix servers). Enter the name of the shell script in the appropriate field. This is typically the "sapenq" program supplied by SAP™ for triggering the EDI subsystem. You can choose to mark the check box "Automatic start possible"—this will trigger the EDI subsystem automatically, if the option in the partner profile was set to Start the subsystem. See Figure 6-3. After these entries, click on the button OUTBOUND FILE. Enter the directory (path), a file name, or use a standard function module to create a dynamic file name. The

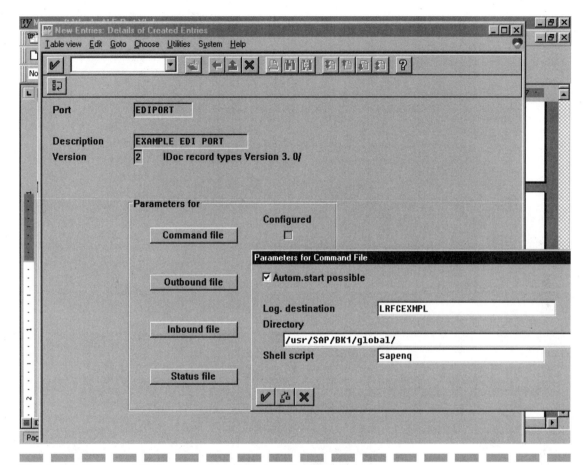

Figure 6-3 Command File Parameters for Outbound Port Definition

function modules are available from the pull-down menu (F4) on the field Function Module.

- It is possible to create such function modules to meet the unique requirements that you might have in terms of file-naming conventions and the batch network architecture. The next step is to specify the parameters for status file. Click on button STATUS FILE and enter the directory (path) where the EDI subsystem creates the status file, file name, or function module.

- Using transaction **WE20** or WEDI → IDOC → Partner Profile, create an entry for the corresponding payer of the customer to whom the invoice is to be sent. The partner type is "KU" for customer. After entering the partner number and partner type, click on the button CREATE. Enter "A" for partner status and enter the appropriate values for fields in the section Receiver of notifications. See Figure 6-4. The person/position/organizational unit entered here will receive workflow items in case of errors in the interface. (See Chapter 8 for more details on workflow.) Save. The basic partner profile has been created. Click on the button OUTBOUND PARAMETERS. On the following screen make the following entries: message type INVOIC, message code 810, partner function PY, port name as configured in port definition (previous step), and

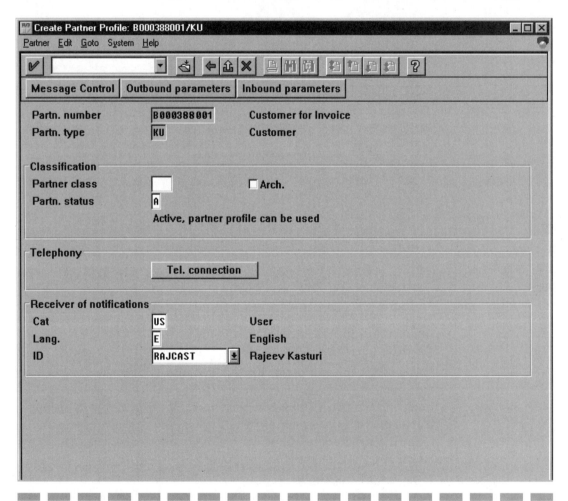

Figure 6-4 Partner Profile General Parameters

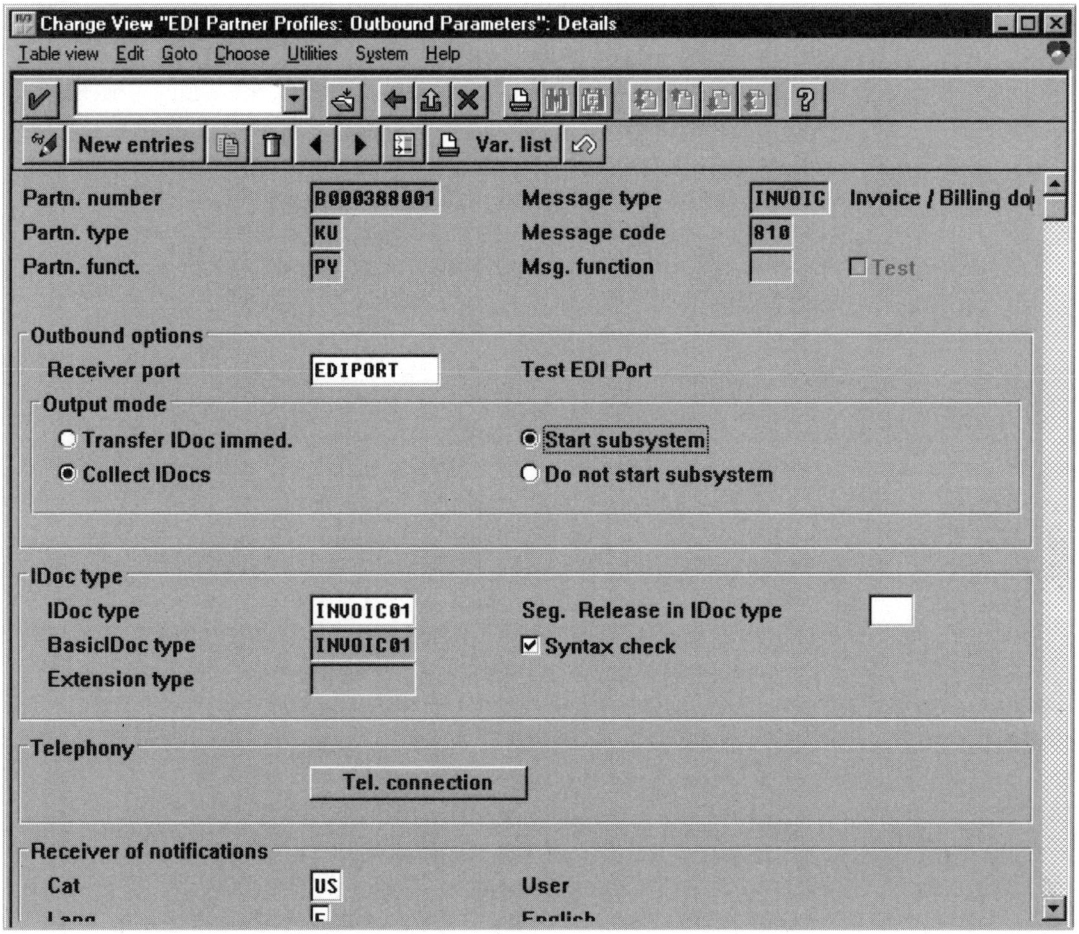

Figure 6-5 Partner Profile Outbound Parameters

IDOC type INVOIC01. See Figure 6-5. Choose the processing option to be `Collect IDOCs`. This option will accumulate IDOCs and the file gets created through the port once you schedule program RSE-OUT00. Choosing the radio-button START SUBSYSTEM enables R/3™ to start the EDI subsystem (translator and LAN/WAN communication network) automatically when the IDOCs are output from the port. To enable this, you have to specify a shell script in the port definition in the command file parameters. Save. Click on the button MESSAGE CONTROL. Enter "V3" for application, "ZBIL" for output type, "INVOIC" for message type, "810" for message code, and "SD09" for process code. Save entries. See Figure 6-6.

■ The next step is to create entries in the EDPAR table for cross-reference to the external system. The EDPAR table stores entries for EDI partners and maps the SAP™ customer number and partner function to the external representation of the customer. In the case of an outbound invoice, the external partner number is used to determine the sender partner number, with a partner type of LI (vendor). Note that if an entry is not found on the EDPAR table for

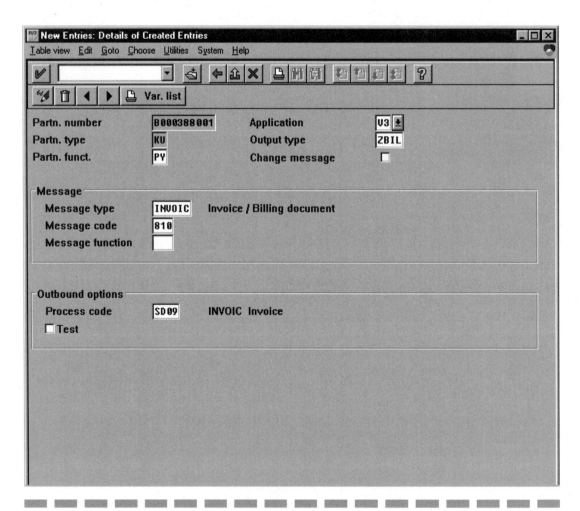

Figure 6-6 Partner Profile Message Control

that SAP™ customer number and partner function PY (payer), then the processing function module checks the field KNVV-EIKTO for a value to populate as the sender partner number. In Customer Master, field KNVV-EIKTO represents `Account at Customer` in the sales screen. Hence, for an outbound invoice, it is important to maintain either of the previously mentioned entries. Note that in case of other message types such as DESADV (Shipping notification—Dispatch Advice), the base logical system is used as the sender partner number, as in ALE outbound interfaces. To maintain the EDPAR table, use transaction **VOED** → `Partner` → `Application` → `Conversion` or from the `IMG` → `Sales and Distribution` → `Electronic Data Interchange` → `EDI Messages` → `Configure EDI partners` → `Partners` → `Application` → `Conversion`. Enter the SAP™ customer number, partner function, external partner number, and internal partner number (usually the same as the SAP™ customer number). Save your entries. Note that the external partner number is used for determining the trading partner by the EDI system.

Working the Interface

Now that we have completed the configuration for an outbound EDI invoice (ANSI X12 "810"), let us test the interface by creating IDOCs and send them to the EDI subsystem. In order to accomplish this, we first create a sales order (transaction **VA01**) for a given customer, and material(s) with certain quantities. As a subsequent function, create a delivery (transaction **VL01**) for the sales order. Complete "picking" of the delivery items and execute function "post goods issue." Execute transaction **VF01** to create a billing document for the delivery number that we created in the previous step. Once the SD document (delivery number) has been "processed" in transaction **VF01,** go to `Header` → `Output` from the main billing document screen. Check if an output record has been created for output type ZBIL that we configured earlier. See Figure 6-7. You should see an entry for output type ZBIL, with medium "6" (EDI), partner function "PY," name of the payer, and the status of the output. The status field has three values: 0, for not yet processed; 1, for processed successfully; and 2, for processed with errors.

As the next step, we have to execute program RSNAST00 to create an IDOC based on the output type generated in the previous step. This is

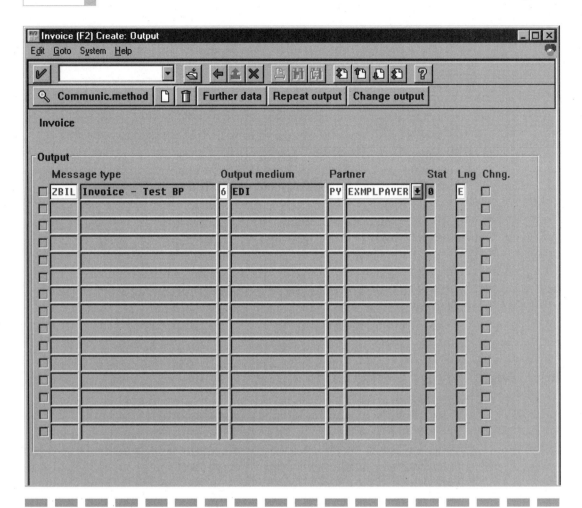

Figure 6-7 Output Record

so because while configuring the output type, we indicated the processing time to be a value of "1," which implies that the output will be processed by the next run of program RSNAST00. Note that a value of "4" would have created the IDOC immediately, although this is a significant overhead on the system. Execute program RSNAST00 from transaction **SE38** or from WEDI → Test → Outbound from NAST. In the selection-parameters, enter "V3" (billing) for application, "ZBIL" for output type, and "6" (EDI) for medium. See Figure 6-8.

Executing this program will create IDOCs of type INVOIC01 for the output records that we created using transaction **VF01** (Billing docu-

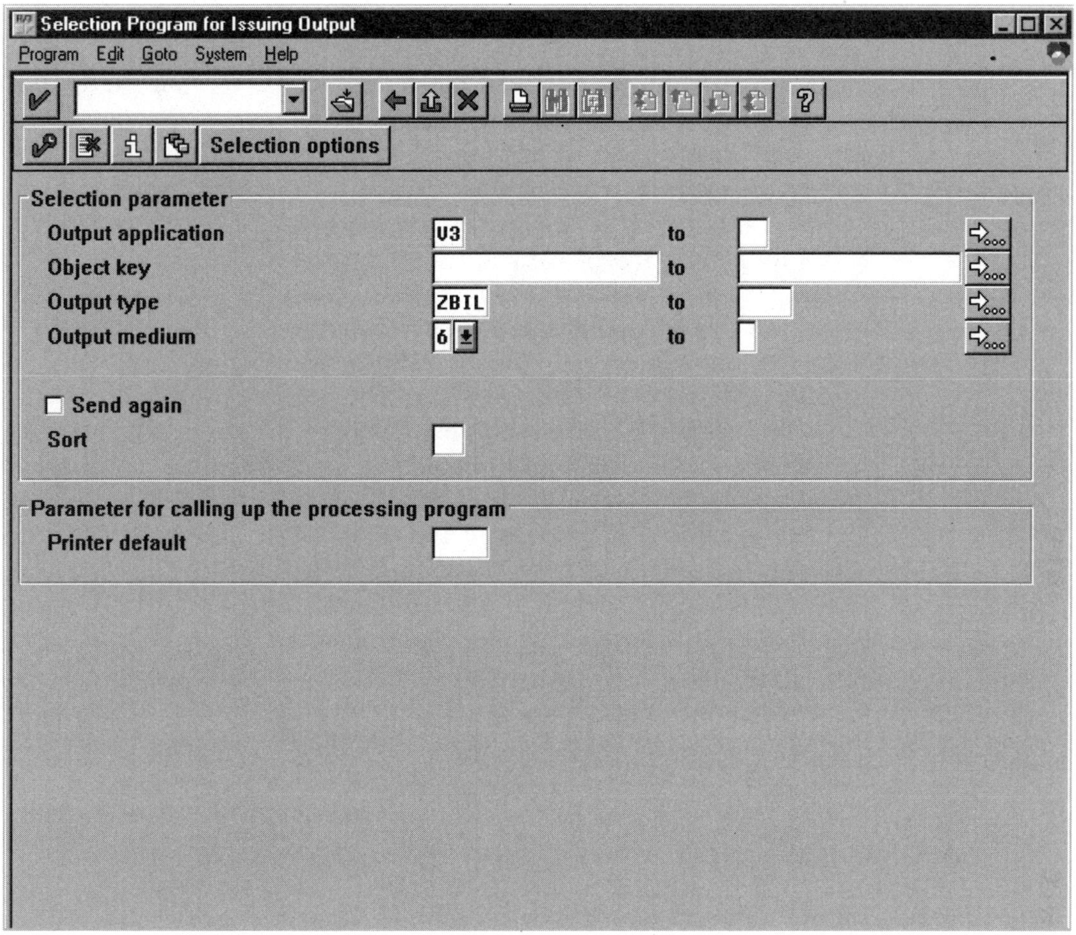

Figure 6-8 Selection Parameters for Program RSNAST00

ments—create). Informational messages will be issued by RSNAST00 indicating the IDOC number(s) that were added. Use transaction **WE05** to view the IDOCs that were created. Ensure that they are in status "30"—IDOC ready for dispatch (ALE service). The next step is to "dispatch" these IDOCs to the EDI subsystem. The IDOCs have been collected for further processing since we chose the processing option to be "Collect IDOCs." Use program RSEOUT00 to dispatch the IDOCs to the EDI subsystem. Enter relevant parameters in the selection screen for program RSEOUT00 (transaction **WE14**) and execute. Informational messages will be issued regarding the number of IDOCs selected for processing. If the processing option selected in the outbound parameters of the partner profile is "Start subsystem" and the flag for "automatic start possible" is turned on in the command file parameters of the port definition, then the EDI subsystem is started automatically with file location and name as parameters. Successful triggering of the EDI subsystem for the IDOCs contained in the file sets the IDOC status to "18" (triggering EDI subsystem OK). However, this status does not imply that the IDOCs were processed correctly by the subsystem.

In order to ensure that the IDOCs were processed successfully by the EDI subsystem, we have to process a status file produced by the subsystem. This file has to be imported into SAP™ and processed to update the status records of the outbound IDOCs. This process can be automated by getting the EDI subsystem to format a status file and starting the SAP™ system automatically by calling C program "startrfc." After this file is processed, SAP™ deletes it from the system. The status file can also be processed in batch by executing program RSESTA00, which can be scheduled periodically or triggered due to the presence of a status file. If an error occurs during the execution of this program, a workflow message is sent to the EDI administrator's inbox, and table EDFI2 is updated with an entry containing the key of the last record processed. If the program is restarted for the same status file, processing resumes from the next record. Use transaction **OYEK** to view table EDFI2.

An outbound EDI IDOC typically goes through the following statuses:

01 IDOC added

30 IDOC ready for dispatch (ALE service)

03 Data passed to port OK

24 Control information of EDI subsystem OK

06 Translation OK

08 Syntax check OK

Note that the preceding statuses *need not* have the same value and sequence for every installation, since both the status value and sequence could change based on the configuration settings and processing options chosen.

For inbound EDI documents, SAP™ has provided several process codes to post the inbound IDOC data to the application. The EDI subsystem receives the EDI document from a trading partner, converts it into the IDOC format, and triggers "sapdeq" and "startrfc" processes on

SAP™ while passing the IDOC into the SAP™ system. Typically, the subsystem maintains a trading partnership database to map and route the documents to the appropriate SAP™ partner number. On SAP™, the configuration involves the setup of the partner profiles for the trading partner (sender) and maintaining the appropriate process code on the inbound parameters screen. The processing can be started immediately or IDOCs can be collected for processing in the background. It is also possible to use program RSEINB00 for importing an IDOC file into SAP™ R/3™.

Mapping and Mapping Tools

A key component of the success of an ALE or EDI interface is the accurate mapping of IDOC structures to the external format (outbound) or external format to IDOC structures (inbound). Data mapping plays a crucial role in the correctness of exchange of data to and from the R/3™ system. (Of course, in the case of R/3™-R/3™ ALE interfaces through tRFC connections, data translation from IDOCs to the application is automatically carried out by SAP's™ ALE-function modules.) In fact, the task of data mapping is an integral part of the development effort and should be incorporated into the prototyping and gap analysis phases of the project.

In order to successfully map the IDOC to the external format, whether it is an EDI document or an external system format, the first step is to understand the structure of the chosen IDOC type and its segments. Extensive documentation on the IDOC's structures and segment fields can be found on the R/3™ system by using transaction WE60. This lists the hierarchy of the segments and a description of its fields including data type, length, and offset. After obtaining a copy of the external system format and the description of its hierarchy and fields, build a spreadsheet relating the IDOC segment and field to the external record structure and field. Note that certain IDOCs use *IDOC qualifiers*—this implies that the same segment can be redefined to convey different sets of values based on the value of the first field, the IDOC qualifier. Also, the IDOC structure usually contains *looping structures* whereby a few segments form a group in the general hierarchy. You will find that certain segments or group of segments are mandatory while others are optional. The occurrence of a segment can be determined by "minimum" and "maximum" fields in the IDOC documentation. Where applicable, the spreadsheet should also detail the starting position, length, and data type of the field. Specify the conversion codes/values of a particular field. It is possible that the date and time format of certain fields in the external system may not be the same as SAP's™ format. In such a case, include the translation between the two formats. Default values may need to be populated in either the IDOC or the external record structure.

With the advent of mapping tools that translate data to and from SAP's™ proprietary IDOC format, data translation and distribution have been made simple and efficient processes providing seamless integration of R/3™ and external systems. There are several third-party vendors that offer interface solutions that complement the R/3™ system. These products vary in capabilities from a basic EDI subsystem to a comprehensive system for all electronic commerce/interface solutions. A few products have been certified by SAP™ for EDI, ALE, and/or BAPI technologies. Considering such complementary software for an interface solution may be a worthwhile proposition since these products reduce or eliminate custom programming, and minimize development and testing efforts. It is also plausible that a middle-ware may be a necessity in lieu of prohibitively expensive homegrown solutions. In making a decision to use such products, one must take into consideration the resources available to learn, implement, and maintain the product and associated hardware.

Some of the companies that are market leaders in providing products for interface solutions are Sterling Commerce Inc. with *Gentran: Server Extension for R/3* and *Connect:Direct,* and TSI International Software Ltd. with *Mercator for R/3.**

Gentran: Server Extension for R/3 is an electronic commerce (EC) product that has been certified by SAP™, and is built on client/server architecture. It is capable of multipartner EC messaging environment with cross-referencing function between Gentran and the R/3™ system for identification of trading partners. Its mapping tool is capable of conditional and boolean logic functions using whichever one can customize the mapping needs of the implementation. The product has a user-friendly graphical interface with audits and controls built in. Gentran can report the status of IDOCs back to the R/3™ system for outbound interfaces. Although Gentran has been primarily popular in implemen-

---

*Gentran: Server Extension for R/3 and Connect:Direct are trademarks or registered trademarks of Sterling Commerce Inc. (www.sterlingcommerce.com). Mercator for R/3 is a registered trademark of TSI International Software Ltd. (www.tsisoft.com).

tations requiring an EDI subsystem, it can handle ALE interfaces as well. Sterling Commerce's product Connect:Direct aids the process of data movement. With ALE, Connect:Direct is capable of IDOC file transfers as opposed to tRFC. To aid the mapping process, Gentran's mapping tool accepts SAP's™ IDOC parser output from transaction `WE63` or program RSEIDOC3. Menu path `WEDI → Documentation → IDOC type parser`.

TSI's Mercator for R/3 is a robust interface product, especially for ALE scenarios. Mercator for R/3 has been certified by SAP™ for both ALE and EDI. The interface technologies it supports are BAPI, ALE, EDI, and both synchronous and asynchronous RFC connections. Mercator can accomplish complex mapping logic with its object-based mapping design, as opposed to the positional mapping approach. The product has an easy-to-use, drag-and-drop user interface for mapping. Mercator is based on an open architecture and it works with flat files, relational databases, application program buffers, and message queuing. Mercator is equipped with an ALE converter/adapter, which enables a direct connection to the R/3™ system for seamless communication of IDOCs that makes the external system seem to be another R/3™ system. In combination with IBM's MQSeries and MQLink* messaging systems, Mercator can achieve near real-time, message-based communications without the problems associated with a file-based architecture. The product has a BAPI importer as well as an IDOC importer that simplify the process of generating maps. The IDOC importer uses SAP's™ output from program RSEIDOC3.

As you might have gathered from the previous chapters, prototyping, developing, and implementing ALE and EDI interfaces can be easily accomplished with a few configuration steps, and little or no custom development. With the aid of third-party tools, it is possible to achieve smoothly functioning interfaces that enhance the productivity of the organization. ALE and EDI technologies can drastically reduce prototyping, design, development, implementation, and maintenance efforts, and companies can enjoy the benefits of SAP's™ strategic interface technologies.

---

*MQSeries and MQLink are registered trademarks or trademarks of IBM Corp. (www.ibm.com).

Periodic Processing

Overview

Having configured and built the ALE/EDI interfaces, you are now ready to implement them in a production environment and maintain the interfaces. SAP™ provides several programs that perform various functions required to execute and maintain ALE and EDI interfaces. These programs can be scheduled as a job to run periodically or, if necessary, be executed online. Note that ALE and EDI programs can be incorporated into an SAP™ job or job stream just like any other SAP™ program, with appropriate variants. This chapter describes several ALE/EDI programs and their uses, categorized by outbound processing, inbound processing, and other functions. Among the "other" programs, there are functions for tRFC/aRFC monitoring, ALE audit, reorganization of certain ALE database tables, IDOC traces, and so forth.

Outbound Processing

The functions provided by SAP™ in ALE/EDI outbound processing are creation of IDOCs, "sending" master data through IDOCs, passing IDOCs to the port, and reprocessing of IDOCs in case of errors.

Program RBDMIDOC is used to create master data IDOCs based on change pointers. It accepts a master data message type as the only parameter. Executing this program for a given message type generates IDOCs based on change pointers for that message type and transports them to the receiving system. As explained earlier, *change pointers* are objects that record a change to certain types of application data on the R/3™ system. The receiving system is identified based on the Customer Distribution Model. The receiving logical system should also have a valid partner profile with correctly defined outbound parameters indicating the message type, port, and a corresponding IDOC type. Note that you can use this program to create IDOCs based on "reduced" message types as well, if you have carried out the IDOC reduction for certain master data message types and activated it. (See IDOC reductions in Chapter 4.) Once the program RBDMIDOC completes the processing of change pointers for that message type, it flags those change pointers as "processed." As you know, this flag is maintained on table BDCPS. The program issues informational messages regarding the number of "master" IDOCs and "communication" IDOCs created. Note that the number of communication IDOCs created could differ from the number of master IDOCs depending on the logical system(s) and filter objects configured for message flow in the Customer Distribution Model. This program can also be executed through transaction BD21. Program RBD-MIDOC can be scheduled periodically to gather all change pointers for that message type and create IDOCs. This is especially useful when it is required to communicate changes to master data to other R/3™ or external systems in order for the systems to be in sync.

Programs RBDSE* can be used to create master data IDOCs. For example, program RBDSEMAT creates material master IDOCs based on the parameters and selection-options specified, and transports them to the receiving system(s) in the ALE layer. The capability of "sending" IDOCs is provided for all master data on the R/3™ system. The program names typically start with RBDSE. The parameters and selection-options for the program vary based on the application, but message type is a mandatory field in most cases. Note that you can use reduced message types in cases where IDOC reduction is supported. You can also specify the logical system you are sending these IDOCs to. A couple of the parameters are for *parallel processing,* a technique that can be used to improve performance and optimize the interface (see Chapter 10, "ALE Optimization"). For these programs to work correctly, all ALE configuration needs to be in place, such as logical systems, distribution model, partner profiles, and ports. If the processing option in the outbound parameters of the partner profile is set to "immediate," then the IDOCs are automatically dispatched to the port, and in case of an RFC destination, tRFC calls are invoked. A few examples of these programs are RBDSEDEB for customer master, RBDSECHR for characteristics, RBDSEBOM for material bill of materials, RBDSECOE for cost elements, and RBDSEGLM for general ledger accounts. This series of programs can be scheduled as batch jobs in order to refresh or sync up the data in the other R/3™ or external systems. It can also be used to load data into the other system's databases during startup.

Program RSNAST00 is used to create IDOCs from the NAST table and message control for transactional data. This program is primarily used for SD and MM applications supported by message control mechanisms. As explained in Chapters 3 and 6, this concept is based on condition technique and output types. This program is applicable only when the timing configured in the output type is a value *other* than 4 ("immediate"). The important parameters for program RSNAST00 are a two-byte output application, output type, and output medium. Ensure that message control parameters such as output type and process code in the partner profile have been maintained appropriately. A successful execution of the program will result in informational messages indicating the IDOC numbers of the IDOCs created. For the program to create the desired results, the entire ALE configuration needs to be in place, such as logical system, distribution model, port, and partner profile. RSNAST00 can be scheduled periodically to capture the transactional data created/changed and create IDOCs in the ALE layer. This program can also be executed through transaction `WE15`.

Program RSEOUT00 is used to "dispatch" the outbound IDOCs in status "30" (IDOC ready for dispatch—ALE service) to its port. When the processing option in the outbound parameters of the partner profile is set to "Collect IDOCs," the IDOCs generated by ALE programs are stored and collected in R/3's™ IDOC databases in status "30." In order to send it to the other R/3™ or external system, you have to execute program RSEOUT00. In case the port defined for these IDOCs and associated in the partner profile is linked to an RFC destination, either tRFC/aRFC calls are automatically generated or the shell script associated with the RFC destination is triggered. Program RSEOUT00 has several parameters and selection-options such as message type, receiver information—port, partner type, partner number, IDOC number, creation date, and so forth. The field "Maximum number of IDOCs to process" merely indicates the number of IDOCs sent out in one sweep of the program, or technically speaking, one *Logical Unit of Work* (LUW). The default is 5000. For example, if it is a file-based port with the file name having a date and time stamp, and there are 7000 IDOCs to be written out, program RSEOUT00 is first going to create a file of 5000 IDOCs and then another file with 2000 IDOCs. Due to certain system settings, such as time limits for program execution or other requirements, this figure may need to be adjusted upward or downward. Program RSEOUT00 can be scheduled periodically to externalize or send the IDOCs out of the system to another R/3™ or external system. Typically, this program is the second step of a two-step job, with the first step being a program to create IDOCs, such as the ones mentioned previously.

Program RBDAGAIN is used for reprocessing IDOCs with errors. This program processes IDOCs with an error status of:

■ 02: Error transmitting data to port

■ 04: Error in EDI subsystem control information

- 05: Error in conversion
- 25: Continue processing despite syntax error (outbound)
- 29: Error in ALE service

Before executing this program, you must determine the cause for the error and rectify the problem. RBDAGAIN reprocesses these IDOCs and puts them in a status of "30," if the partner profile outbound parameter was set to "Collect IDOCs," or a status of "03" (data passed to port) if the partner profile outbound processing option was set to "Transfer IDOC immediately." IDOCs can be selected for reprocessing by program RBDAGAIN's parameters/selection-options such as IDOC number, creation date, time, message type, partner type of receiver, partner function of receiver, and partner number (partner profile name) of receiver. On the main screen for RBDAGAIN, you will also find a checkbox for "Import in Background." If this checkbox is flagged, then the IDOCs selected by the criteria specified are not displayed, and the program attempts to reprocess them in the background. Informational messages are issued indicating the new status of the IDOC. If the checkbox "Import in Background" is unmarked, then the selected IDOCs are presented one after another to the user, who will have the option to edit the IDOC, check for error messages, or process it. You will receive informational messages indicating the results of reprocessing and its new status. Note that in the course of processing, program RBDAGAIN could generate a new IDOC in status "30" or "03" (as the case may be), based on the original IDOC. The *original IDOC* is then placed in a status of "33" (original of an IDOC that was edited), and no further processing is possible, other than archiving it.

Program RBDSYNEO is used for processing IDOCs despite syntax errors. IDOCs with syntax errors have a status of "26." Syntax errors in an outbound IDOC are caused due to incorrect placement of segments in the hierarchy defined by SAP™, missing mandatory segments, incorrect EDIDD key information, and the like. If you want to process IDOCs in status "26" by ignoring the syntax errors, use program RBDSYNEO. IDOCs can be selected by the program's parameters/selection-options such as IDOC number, creation date, creation time, partner type of receiver, partner number of receiver, message type, and so on. The initial panel for this program also has a checkbox for "Import in Background." When this flag is turned on (the default value), the IDOCs that match the selection criteria are processed in the background without being displayed. Informational messages are issued indicating the IDOC number, message type, and new status. If the checkbox is unmarked, the program displays the selected IDOCs one at a time, presenting you with the option of editing, checking for errors, or processing them despite syntax errors. A message is output indicating the IDOC number, message type, and new status. After its successful processing, the IDOC is put in a status of "30" (IDOC ready for dispatch) if the processing option in the outbound parameters of the partner profile was set to "Collect IDOCs," or status "03" (IDOC passed to port OK) if the processing option was set to "Transfer IDOC immediately." This program can also be accessed using transaction **BD88**.

The preceding programs can also be accessed through the **BALE** menu: from **BALE** → Periodic work → ALE Outbound IDOCs. It displays a panel as shown in Figure 7-1.

Inbound Processing

SAP™ provides several programs to facilitate inbound processing that can be executed either online or in a batch mode for periodic processing. The functions include posting IDOCs to the application, reprocessing IDOCs in error status, and processing edited IDOCs.

Program RSEINB00 is used to import files containing IDOCs into the R/3™ system. This program is used only when the inbound IDOCs are contained in a text file. RSEOUT00 has only one parameter for the path- and file name. During the process of importing the IDOCs, the partner number, message type, and all other pertinent control information are gathered from the EDIDC record of the IDOC. Based on the processing option selected in the inbound parameters of the partner profile, background, or immediate processing, the IDOCs are created in a status of "64" if free of syntax errors, or posted to the application immediately. In case of errors, workflow messages are sent to the recipient defined in the partner profile.

Program RBDAPP01 is used to process IDOCs that have not been posted to the application immediately and are in status "64." This program posts the IDOC data to the application. Inbound IDOCs are created in a status of "64" when the IDOCs have been imported into the R/3™ system, have been successfully added to the IDOC database (status "50"), and have passed the syntax check. This status is achieved when the processing option in the inbound parameters of the partner profile has been set to a choice other than "process immediately." The

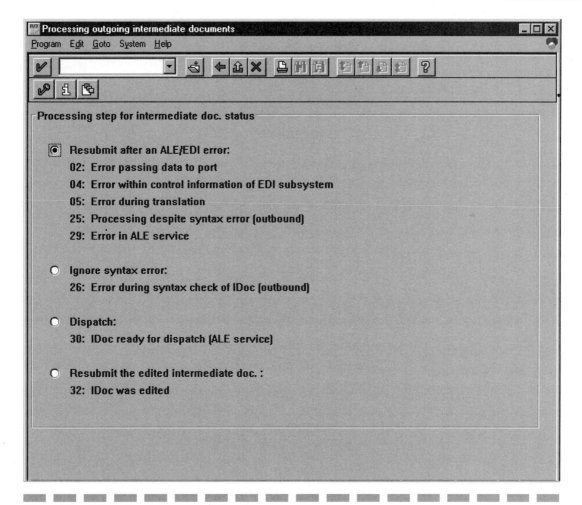

Figure 7-1 ALE Outbound Processing Panel

parameters/selection-options for program RBDAPP01 include IDOC number, creation date and time, message type, partner details of sender such as number (partner profile name) and type. See Figure 7-2.

The program also has parameters for parallel processing, packet size, and server group. These three parameters are used to reduce the processing time of a high volume of IDOCs by enabling parallel processing across multiple application servers. When "parallel booking" is turned on, the program submits a packet of IDOCs, whose size is determined by parameter "Pack. Size" to each application server defined in the server group. This technique greatly reduces processing time and increases

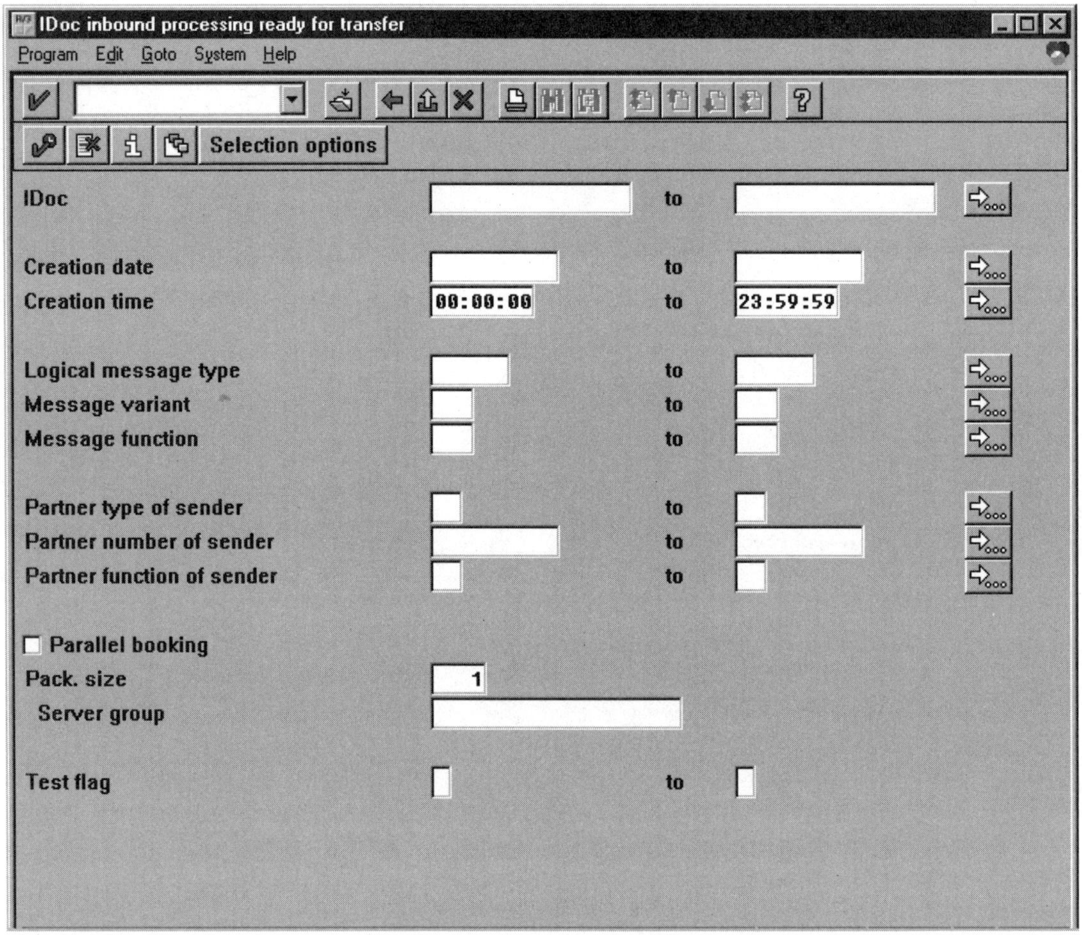

Figure 7-2 Program RBDAPP01 Selection Panel

throughput. We discuss this approach in more detail in Chapter 10, "ALE Optimization." Note that if the requirement is to process the IDOCs in a certain sequence, you should not use parallel processing. Furthermore, you can specify the sequence of IDOCS to be processed by populating the field "SERIAL" on the EDIDC of each IDOC with a sequence number. RBDAPP01 sorts the IDOCs selected in that run and processes them in the sequence specified. This is also known as *serialization*.

Program RBDMANIN is used for reprocessing IDOCs in a status of "51" (application document not posted). This program attempts to post the data to the application. It is useful in situations when IDOCs are rejected by the application modules due to missing or untimely data, or other problems of a temporal nature. Also, based on the error, the data can be rectified and the IDOC can be reprocessed by this program. The parameters/selection-options of RBDMANIN include IDOC number, creation date and time, message type, and details of sender such as partner number and partner type. There is also a flag for the option to "Import in background." If this flag is checked, then all the IDOCs selected are processed in background, without being displayed, and informational messages are issued regarding their new status; if unmarked, IDOCs are displayed one at a time and can be processed individually.

Program RBDAGAI2 is used to reprocess IDOCs with errors. Only IDOCs in the following status can be reprocessed by this program.

- 56: IDOC containing errors added
- 61: Continue processing despite syntax error (inbox)
- 63: Error passing IDOC to the application
- 65: Error in ALE service

The parameters/selection-options for program RBDAGAI2 include IDOC number, creation date and time, message type, and details of sender such as partner number and type. This program also has a flag for "Importing in background," which enables the user to process the IDOCs selected without being displayed. Informational messages are issued giving the new status of the IDOCs processed. If the checkbox is unmarked, IDOCs are displayed for individual processing.

Program RBDSYNEI reprocesses IDOCs despite syntax errors. The IDOCs need to be in status "60" (syntax error in IDOC) for processing by this program. RBDSYNEI ignores the syntax errors and attempts to post the data to the application. The parameters/selection-options for this program include IDOC number, creation date and time, message type, and sender details such as partner number and type. This program also has a checkbox for "Import in background," which enables the user to process these IDOCs in the background without being displayed. If the flag is unmarked, the IDOCs are displayed one at a time and can be processed individually. Informational messages are issued indicating the new status of the IDOCs.

Program RBDAGAIE is used to process edited IDOCs. That is, if the IDOC was added to the database and was subsequently edited (status "69"), this program can be used to process the data and post it to the application. Note that this program will accept IDOCs only with a "permissible" set of previous status values. For example, if an IDOC was in status "60" (syntax error in IDOC), and was subsequently edited (status "69"), then the program will not process it since "60" is not a permissible value. The parameters for this program are IDOC number and direction (1 = outbound, 2 = inbound). As you may have realized, this program is common to both inbound and outbound IDOCs.

The preceding programs can also be accessed via **BALE** → Periodic work → ALE Inbound IDOCs. See Figure 7-3.

Although the above inbound and outbound programs can be executed to process or reprocess IDOCs with errors, it is important to determine

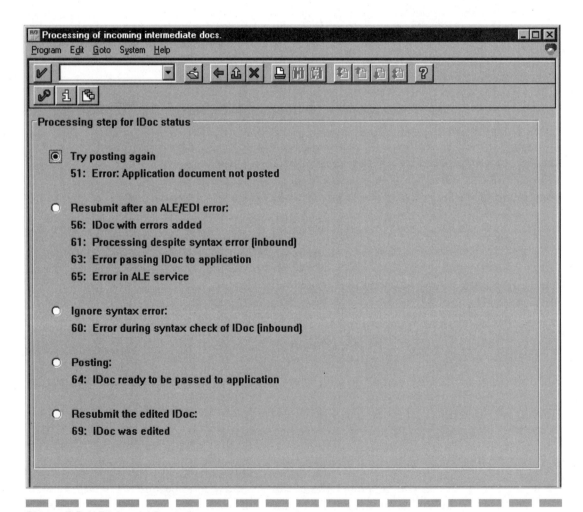

Figure 7-3 ALE Inbound Processing

the cause of those errors and rectify them before resuming the execution of these programs.

Other ALE Programs

Other than programs for inbound and outbound processing of IDOCs, there are several programs that perform various important functions to aid the reporting, monitoring, and organization of ALE processes. These include programs for checking the status of RFC execution, audit confirmation, reorganization of change pointers and audit databases, statistical analysis of ALE audits, cross-system IDOC reporting, and the monitoring of tRFC and aRFC communications. It is important to note that these programs play a vital role in the smooth operation of ALE interfaces in production, and can be scheduled to run periodically to report and confirm ALE processing.

Program RBDMOIND is used to convert the status of IDOCs sent out of the system using RFC to a status confirming successful execution. That is, IDOCs in a status of "03" (data passed to port OK) are checked for successful dispatch to the other system and are updated to a status of "12" (dispatch OK). If the dispatch was not successful, the "03" status is not updated. See Figures 7-4 and 7-5 for a before and after status. The program has two parameters—"IDOC creation date (from)" and "Commit work after...IDOCs." All IDOCs in a status of "03" that were created *from* the date specified are selected for processing by this program. The second parameter specifies the number of IDOCs after which the status for all those IDOCs is updated (committed to the database). This program can be scheduled to run periodically, and its frequency can be determined based on the volume of ALE processing and other considerations such as the resources available to monitor it. Program RBDMOIND can also be accessed from **BALE** → Periodic work → Check IDOC dispatch.

Program RSARFCEX is used to execute RFC calls that have not been executed yet. These suspended calls result from such causes as connection error, gateway to the target system not active, termination, or waiting in the queue for resources to become available for further processing. Under normal circumstances, when RFC calls are not successful, jobs are scheduled automatically to reprocess these calls; this is done in order to ensure the successful delivery of data to the target system. The number and frequency of retries can be controlled by adjusting certain parameters on the RFC destination (more on this in Chapter 10, "ALE

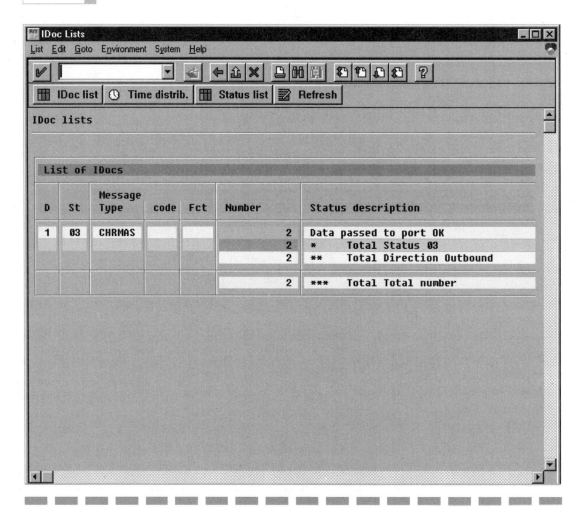

Figure 7-4 RBDMOIND—IDOC before Status Conversion

Optimization"). It is also possible to turn off the automatic reprocessing of these RFC calls—there is a good reason to do so. As mentioned earlier, when RFC calls are unsuccessful, batch jobs are scheduled repeatedly until they are successful or the maximum number of retries has been reached. If there are several communication errors—for instance, gateway server not responding—the result could be that hundreds of batch jobs are created, which could flood the batch processors on the system. This could snowball into more aRFC jobs being created. In order to avoid such a precarious situation, you could turn off automatic processing for the RFC calls and schedule program RSARFCEX instead. This

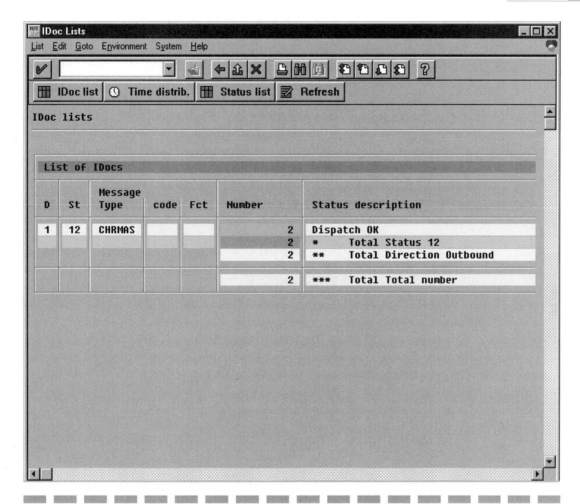

Figure 7-5 RBDMOIND—IDOC after Status Conversion

program could periodically reprocess the pending RFCs. The selection-options available for this program are Date, RFC destination, and User ID. You can also choose the status of the RFC—communication error, not yet processed, termination, and/or currently being processed. Program RSARFCEX can also be accessed from **BALE** → Periodic work → Transactional RFC.

Program RBDSTATE is used for audit confirmation of ALE transactions between two R/3™ systems. By *audit confirmation,* we mean the indication of success or failure of the ALE transaction on the target system. Use of this program reports the status of the transaction on the target system back to the sending system. This process is an interface in itself from the target system to the sender system, facilitated by message type ALEAUD. In this section, we learn the various steps needed to set up ALEAUD and execute program RBDSTATE.

Let us consider two different R/3™ systems with base logical systems BK1CLNT010 (sender system) and BK2CLNT020 (target system). Assume that we are distributing characteristics master, message type CHRMAS from BK1CLNT010 to BK2CLNT020. When we send CHRMAS02 IDOCs from BK1CLNT010, their status is "03" (data passed to port OK), if they were successfully externalized from the sender system. If the IDOCs were received and processed successfully on the target system BK2CLNT020, the status of those IDOCs on the target system is "53" (application data posted). Remember that we had to create a partner profile BK1CLNT010 on the target system BK2CLNT020 in order to receive the CHRMAS messages. The inbound parameters of BK1CLNT010 partner on the target system have CHRMAS as the message type and CHRM as the process code. Now, we need to configure the target system BK2CLNT020 to send ALEAUD messages to BK1CLNT010, the sender system, and we also need to configure BK1CLNT010 to receive those messages in order to update the status of CHRMAS IDOCs sent to the target system. Follow these steps:

- On the target system BK2CLNT020, configure the distribution of message flow of type ALEAUD to logical system BK1CLNT010.

- Create filter object using object type MESTYP with a value of the message type that you need audit confirmation for. This message type must be flowing from the sender, BK1CLNT010 to BK2CLNT020. In this example, the value of the filter object type MESTYP would be CHRMAS, message type for characteristics master. Save the distribution model. Use transaction **BD64** to do this.

- On target system BK2CLNT020, create an RFC destination with name BK1CLNT010. Choose the relevant connection type and enter the logon parameters and password for the R/3™ system on which BK1CLNT010 resides. Use transaction **SM59** to do this.

- On target system BK2CLNT020, generate partner profile and port definition using transaction **SALE** → Communications → Generate partner profile. Specify the customer model as configured above. Check the partner profile to ensure outbound parameter entries for message types ALEAUD and SYNCH.

- On sender system BK1CLNT010, create a logical system for BK2CLNT020. Create a partner profile for logical system

BK2CLNT020 with inbound parameters for message type ALEAUD, with process code AUD1.

▪ Distribution of customer model on BK2CLNT020 to BK1CLNT010 is not necessary.

Now we are ready to test the ALE audit confirmation process. From the sender system BK1CLNT010, send a couple of CHRMAS02 (characteristics master) IDOCs down to the target system BK2CLNT020; ensure that the status of the IDOCs is "03" (data passed to port). Check the target system BK2CLNT020 for receipt of these IDOCs. Ensure that they are in a status of "53" (application data posted). Execute program RBD-STATE with appropriate parameters. Specify BK1CLNT010 for "Confirm to system," CHRMAS for "Message type," and date, if necessary. Upon successful execution, informational messages will be issued indicating the IDOC number and status of the ALEAUD IDOC. (Note that a single ALEAUD audit IDOC can contain audit messages for multiple application IDOCs. This capability reduces the traffic of IDOCs between the two systems, and keeps the overhead of audit confirmations at a minimum.) Check the sender system BK1CLNT010 for the receipt of the ALEAUD message. The status of the CHRMAS IDOCs that we sent to the target system must have changed to "41" (application document created in target system). This completes the test of ALE audit confirmations. See Figures 7-6 and 7-7 for IDOC display of target and sender system.

Audit confirmations can play a significant role in the reporting and monitoring of production systems. You can schedule program RBD-STATE periodically on the target systems to report back to the sender systems. Keep in mind that you need to maintain a sufficient time lag between the sending of application IDOCs to the target system and the execution of this audit program, since the application documents need to be posted on the target system. This program can also be accessed from **BALE** → Periodic work → Audit confirmation.

Program RBDAUD01 is used for obtaining a statistical analysis for the ALE audits that were performed by program RBDSTATE. This program gathers information on the IDOC status as reported based on the message type ALEAUD. In order for this report to function, all the settings for ALEAUD must have been performed as outlined earlier. The report columns are as follows. The receiver system column identifies the receiver logical system. The message type indicates the type of message flow, while "Created on IDOC" gives the date of creation. The column "Last IDOC" shows the time when the last IDOC was dispatched from the system on that particular day. Total IDOCs gives us the sum of IDOCs that were sent, and the columns "Outbound queue" and "Inbound

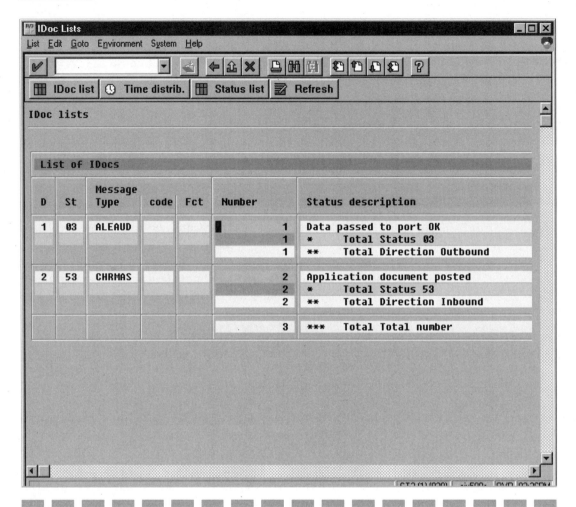

Figure 7-6 Application IDOCs and Audit IDOC on the Target System

queue" indicate the number of IDOCs waiting to be processed in that particular queue. Specifically, the outbound queue shows the number of IDOCs on our own system that are waiting to be dispatched, and the inbound queue indicates the number of IDOCs that have been received by the target system, but not yet processed. Double-clicking on a data line shows another list that indicates the number and status of IDOCs being processed in our own system, and the number and status of IDOCs being processed in the receiver system. On the selection panel of this program there are parameters/selection-options for logical receiver system, message type, and so forth. There is also a flag for "Incomplete

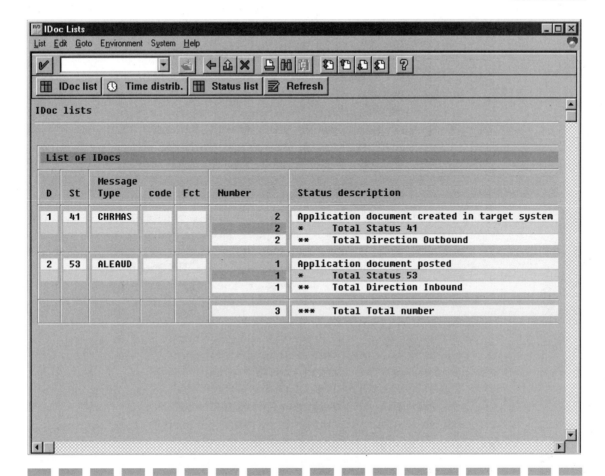

Figure 7-7 Application IDOCs and Audit IDOC on the Sender System

statistics." This means that the report will select either those IDOCs that are not yet processed in the outbound or inbound queue, or if the IDOCs for the current day have not yet all been included in today's statistics. The latter can be identified by the fact that there is an entry in the report column "Last IDOCs" of a time less than 24:00:00, implying that only those IDOCs have been included in the statistic. This report is particularly useful in monitoring the throughput of the interfaces. Program RBDAUD01 can be scheduled periodically to obtain statistics of the ALE audits. This function can also be accessed from BALE → Monitoring → Audit Analysis.

Program RBDAUD02 is used for reorganizing the audit database tables. This program deletes the audit entries from the tables. In test mode, it provides you with a report of entries that will be deleted, but does not actually delete them. Another flag gives you the capability of deleting entries only if the IDOCs have been sent out of the system completely. Date of audit statistics is also a selection-option. This report is useful for maintaining the audit databases, especially when the volume of audit statistics is high. This program can also be accessed from **BALE** → Periodic work → Reorganization → Audit databases.

Program RBDCPCLR is used to reorganize the change pointer databases. As mentioned earlier, change pointers are stored on table BDCP and their status records are stored on table BDCPS. Over a period of time, the number of obsolete or processed change pointers becomes very large, and starts degrading the performance of master data ALE interfaces that are based on change pointer mechanisms. This is so because, whenever master data ALE-function modules are executed in this mode, they access these two tables and also update BDCPS once the processing is complete. In order to improve performance and clear obsolete and processed change pointers, you can use program RBDCPCLR. The program has checkboxes and parameters/selection-options for "Obsolete change pointers" and "Processed change pointers." By obsolete, we mean all change pointers until the date and time specified, whether they have been *processed or not*. Processed change pointers implies only those objects that have been processed; the PROCESS flag on table BDCPS is "X." You can specify a range of selection date and time. There is also a flag for running the program in "test" mode. With this, the program merely selects the change pointers for processing, but does not delete them from the database. This is a good option to confirm the records you are going to delete. Informational messages indicate the number of obsolete and processed change pointers that were selected by the run. Note again that obsolete change pointers selected are deleted regardless of the processing status. This program can be scheduled to run periodically based on the technical and business requirements.

Program RBDMOIN8 is used for cross-system IDOC reporting. It generates a trace of the flow and timings of the IDOCs across R/3™ systems. This is a very useful report, not only to track the performance aspects of IDOC transfers, but also to trace the movement of IDOCs themselves; it gives us a cross-reference of the IDOC number in the sending system and the IDOC number in the receiver system. The parameters and selection-options for the program include message type, receiver details such as partner type and partner number (mandatory), from creation date and time, and to creation date and time. The first level of the report gives us the status of IDOCs in the receiving (target) system, and average, maximum, and minimum transfer times. If you drill down using the push-button SENDIDOC → RCVIDOC, you will see a list with the IDOC numbers on the sending system and receiving system, and date and times, and the delta (difference) between the two times. See Figures 7-8 and 7-9. If you drill down using push-button IDOCS (OWN SYSTEM), a report will be displayed with an overview of status, and you will find push buttons for further drill downs for IDOC LISTS, TIME DISTRIBUTION and STATUS LIST DETAILS. This function can also be accessed from **BALE** → Monitoring → IDOC Trace.

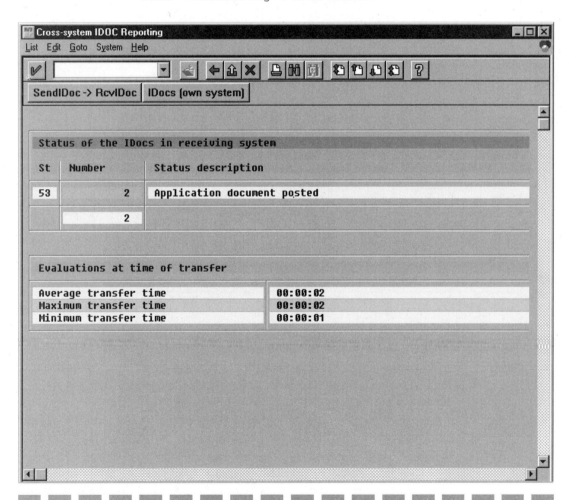

Figure 7-8 IDOC Trace Report Overview

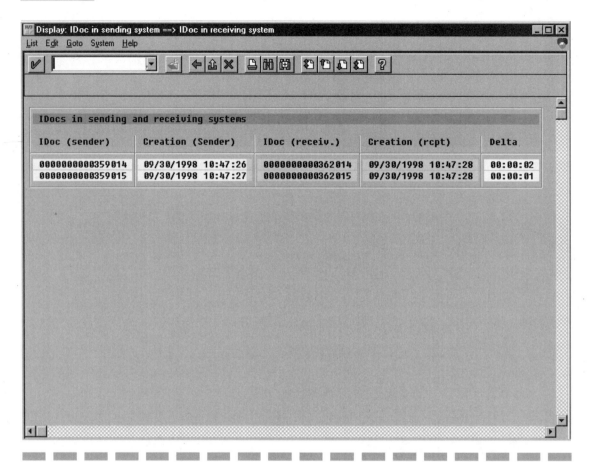

Figure 7-9 Cross-System IDOC Reporting

Program RSARFCRD is used for monitoring RFC activity in the system. This program is the central point for recording of errors in the RFC transactions. The report takes into account only calls that are currently active or RFC calls in error. After the execution of the RFC calls, only those in error remain in its logs. The logs contain brief messages describing the type of error and other temporal statistics along with the RFC call ID. This program can also be accessed from transaction **SM58** or **BALE** → Monitoring → Transactional RFC. We discuss RFCs and their monitoring in detail in Chapter 10, "ALE Optimization."

As we have seen, SAP™ provides us with several programs to facilitate the execution, auditing, reporting, and monitoring of ALE/IDOC interfaces. These tools play an important role in the smooth operation and troubleshooting of interfaces during both the development and production phases of the implementation.

Workflow for ALE and EDI Error Handling

Overview

Having learned the steps involved in setting up ALE and EDI interfaces, and scheduling various processing programs, we now turn our attention to error processing and handling. In ALE and EDI, error handling is facilitated by an SAP™ technology known as *workflow*. SAP's™ *Business Workflow* is a technology that enables the coordination and control of customer-specific business process flows across applications and work areas. This technology is fully integrated with the R/3™ system, and was introduced in version 3.0 in order to enhance the application functionality provided in the standard R/3™ system. For example, a *business* workflow scenario could be the release of a payment to a vendor. Payment blocks can be set up for accounting line items, and this could trigger a series of procedures whereby the payment is presented to the person responsible for approving such items. Once it is approved, the payment is released for further processing. This is a very simple example among the many business workflow scenarios that can be configured in R/3™. Workflow for ALE and EDI error processing is a specific instance of SAP's™ Business Workflow. In this chapter, we focus only on this type of workflow, and learn the various steps involved in setting up workflow for error handling in ALE and EDI interfaces. As we go through the configuration, we will become familiar with workflow concepts and terminology; however, this chapter is not designed to give you an in-depth view of Business Workflow, its concepts, or inner workings.

When an error occurs in an ALE/EDI interface, it triggers an event, known appropriately enough as a *triggering event,* which in turn initiates a specific *task* associated with it. The IDOC in error is linked to the *task container,* and the workflow is presented to the responsible person as a *work item* in his/her *integrated inbox*. This person or group of persons can determine the cause of error, correct the problem, and directly execute the IDOC for posting to the application. A workflow item in the inbox is like an executable email—an email that you can execute in order to cause a change to the application data and/or to trigger a series of processes, which, in a simplistic nutshell, describes the workflow for error handling in ALE and EDI interfaces.

Although it is possible to configure workflow for outbound IDOCs, workflow is typically user-ready for inbound ALE/EDI interfaces. In this chapter, we learn to configure workflow by setting up organizational units, activating triggering events, and the ALE objects. We also learn that based on the type of error—for example, technical or business application—workflow can be directed to the inbox of a certain person, group of persons, or an organizational position/role. This organizational structure can be defined in workflow configuration. As this chapter makes clear, workflow technology uses an object-oriented approach. It is possible to enhance or even create new workflow functionality for ALE and EDI error processing. Some of the ALE/EDI-function modules have customer functions wherein you can enhance the workflow processing.

It should be emphasized that workflow is a powerful technology in SAP™ R/3™ that streamlines the handling and processing of errors in ALE and EDI interfaces. With recent improvements, it is also possible to link workflow to standard email systems such as Microsoft Mail and Lotus Notes.*

Workflow Configuration

Workflow configuration for error processing of ALE/EDI interfaces can be accomplished and activated by following the steps listed below. This configuration supports the basic scenarios for error processing, and should suit the purpose of most applications. There are many *tasks* available for ALE and EDI application scenarios, other than the tasks preset for ALE technical errors. As mentioned earlier, different types of errors resulting in different work items can be routed to separate organizational units/jobs/positions/persons. The example illustrated in this chapter should serve as a template for not only basic scenarios, but also complex error-handling situations. Other than the activation of workflow, most objects and configurations are transportable through the Correction and Transport System, or CTS.

- Create an organizational plan
- Create organizational units
- Create positions/jobs—staff assignments
- Assign holder of positions
- Assign task(s) to positions
- Activate triggering events; event linkage

---

*Microsoft Mail and Lotus Notes are trademarks or registered trademarks of their respective companies.

- Activate workflow generally
- Configure ALE/EDI partner profile parameters for receiver of notifications
- Set ALE/EDI Administrator in the EDI system table

In a nutshell, these steps can be carried out in order to generate workflow items in case of errors in the ALE/EDI interface. We take the example of inbound Goods Movement ALE interface (message type WMM-BXY) to illustrate the steps. Note that other than the assignment of tasks to the position and its event linkage, all configuration steps are independent of the message type or content of the workflow items.

Let us proceed with the configuration steps listed previously.

- *Create an organizational plan and organizational unit(s):*
  An *organizational plan* is a representation of an organizational structure associated with tasks and processes; every plan must contain at least one *organizational unit*. A root organizational unit is an object that is at the highest level, and all other units, jobs, positions, and holders of these jobs and positions are below this root unit. To create a root organizational unit, use transaction **PPOC** or from SAP's™ main menu Tools → Business Engineering → Business Workflow → Organization → Definition Tools → Organization plan → Create. [You can access the Business Workflow (Organization) menu with transaction **SWLW**.] Enter an abbreviation, say DEMO-ORG-001, and a name for the root organizational unit. Choose radio-button OVERALL VIEW. Click on icon CREATE. You are presented with a screen listing the root at the top. Place the cursor on this line and click on icon CREATE to define subunits. Let us create two subunits, ALE/EDI Tech and Applicn Team. The first unit will handle errors of a technical nature, and the second unit will deal with application errors. The tasks will be assigned to these units in a subsequent step. Note that SAP™ assigns internal numbers to organizational units, jobs, and positions automatically. You can choose the view of the structure by using the menu option View → Key On or Abbreviation On, and so forth. See Figure 8-1.
- *Create staff positions/jobs:* To do this, click on button STAFF ASSIGNMENTS. Place the cursor on one of the two subunits created, and click on button POSITION. Enter abbreviation, say ALE-ERR-HNDL for unit ALE/EDI Tech and APP-ERR-HNDL for unit Applicn

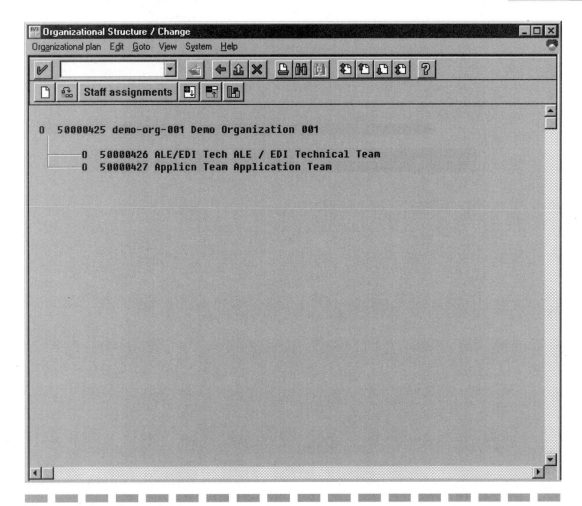

Figure 8-1 Organizational Units

Team, and name of the positions in the lower half of the pop-up
panel. Ignore message "position without a job." We have now created a position for each subunit, and these positions will handle
ALE errors and application errors, respectively. See Figure 8-2.

■ *Assign holder/s (users) to these positions:* After placing the cursor
on the position, click on button ASSIGN HOLDERS. Choose the user ID
of a person who will be responsible for that position. Note that you
can have multiple persons associated with one position. Repeat
this operation for both positions created under the two subunits.
See Figure 8-3.

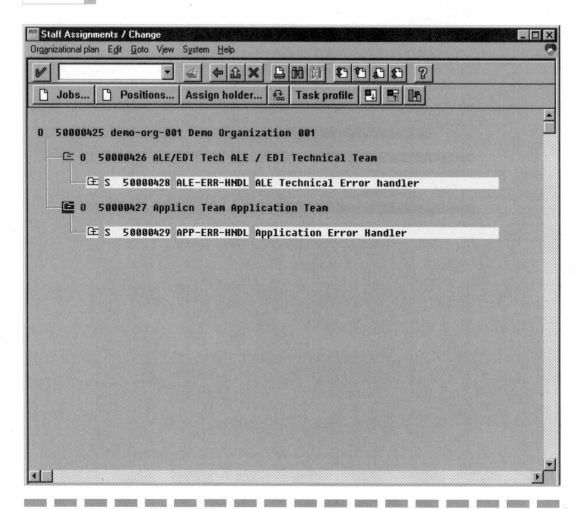

Figure 8-2 Organizational Units and Positions

- *Assign task(s) to positions:* In workflow, a *task* is an activity in which an action is taken on an object via the task container. Tasks are categorized as single-step (*customer/standard tasks*) and multistep (*workflow task/workflow template*). Most ALE/EDI error-handling tasks are single-step standard tasks. There are several tasks that are available for both technical errors and application errors. SAP™ provides us with powerful search mechanisms to identify the right task for the desired activity. In order to associate tasks with the positions we created in an earlier step, place the cursor on the position and click on button TASK PROFILE. In the fol-

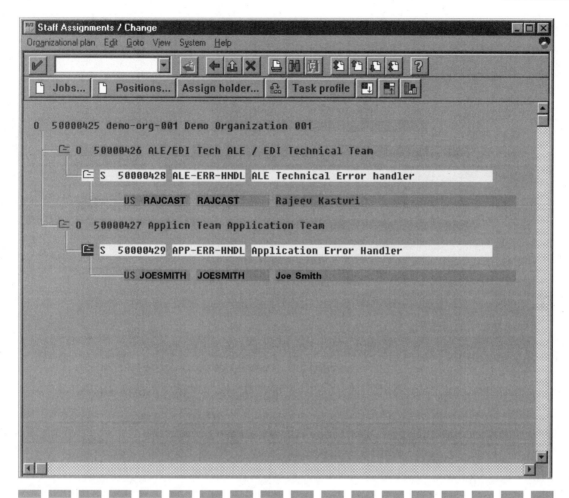

Figure 8-3 Organizational Units, Positions, and Holders

lowing screen, place the cursor on the position and click on button ASSIGN TASK. You will see a pop-up box for search. Choose STRUC-TURE SEARCH. This will display a hierarchical structure of business application components or task catalog. You can toggle between the two views by clicking on the appropriate button on the pop-up panel.

Drill down through Cross Application components → ALE → Tasks. You will find four tasks for error and syntax handling, inbound and outbound. Select these tasks for association with the position ALE-ERR-HNDL. Repeat this operation for position APP-

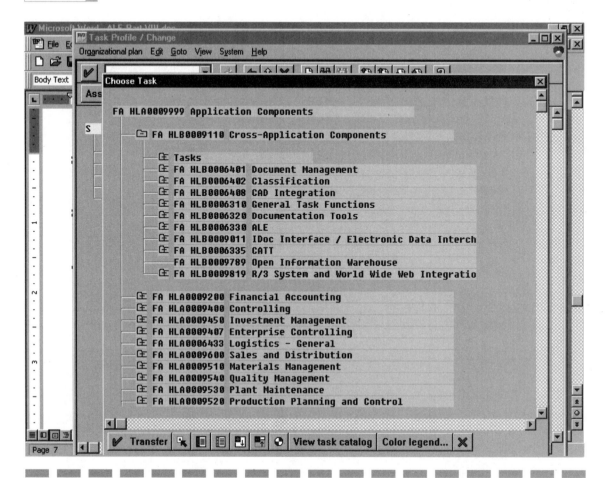

Figure 8-4 Task Search—Business Application Component View

ERR-HNDL. For example, if we need to assign the task for all application errors related to Goods Movements interface, message type, WMMBXY, use the search string to find the task relevant to this message type. Assign this task to the position. See Figures 8-4 and 8-5.

■ *Activate the event linkage:* As mentioned earlier, events known as *triggering events* are triggered whenever a particular activity occurs. This in turn initiates the task associated with it; hence, we need to ensure that the linkage between the triggering event and the task is activated. To accomplish this, double-click on the task on the panel you were at in the previous step; on the subsequent

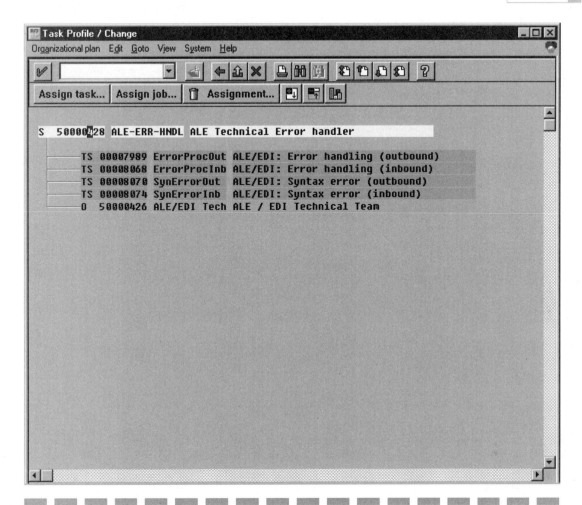

Figure 8-5 Assigning Tasks to Positions

screen, click on button TRIGGERING EVENTS; from the menu `Goto →` `Event Linkage`. A pop-up panel will appear with the task and triggering event. Use the ACTIVATE button to activate this linkage. Note that a status of "activated" is usually the default. See Figure 8-6.

- *Perform basic settings for workflow activation:* This can be done through: `SALE → Basic Configuration → Make basic set-` `tings for workflow`. It is recommended that you use the option AUTOCUSTOMIZING. This procedure will automatically make the set-

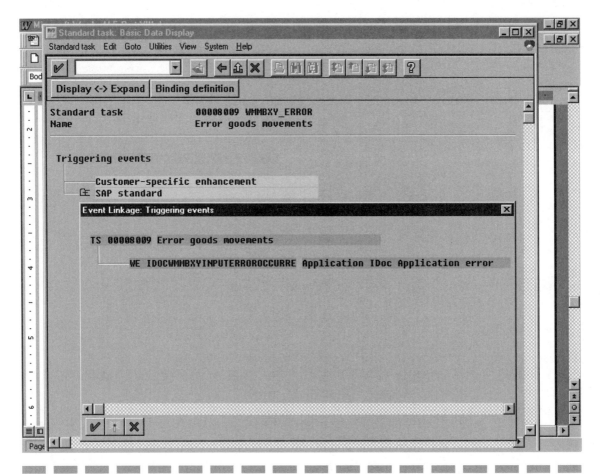

Figure 8-6 Event Linkage

tings for workflow. There are certain authorizations that you need to have before you perform this operation. You may also need to maintain the RFC destination for workflow manually. Do not forget to "test" the RFC destination. Once all the indicators are green, you may proceed with testing the workflow customizing by clicking on VERIFY WORKFLOW. This should result in the creation of workflow items in your integrated inbox. See Figure 8-7.

■ *Configure the ALE/EDI objects in order to direct the workflow items to the appropriate inbox:* This is done, once the workflow has been configured and customized, through settings in the outbound or inbound parameters of the partner profile. Maintain the fields

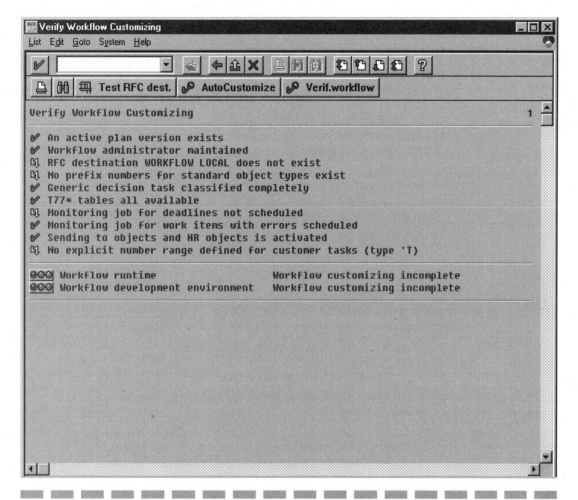

Figure 8-7 Workflow Customizing—Basic Settings

under `Receiver of Notifications`. Enter "S" for position or "US" for user in the field `Category`. Enter the language code in the next field, and name of position or user in field `ID`. For example, if you specify the position `APP-ERR-HNDL` that we created earlier as the receiver of notifications, the person(s) associated with that position would receive workflow items in his/her SAPOffice Inbox in case of application errors. Use transaction **WE20** to do this.

■ *Assign a position or user to the EDI Administrator parameter for ALE/EDI administrative/technical messages:* This is maintained

on table EDADM. To access this function: from WEDI → Control
→ IDOC → Administration. Maintain parameter EDIADMIN. For
parameter value, enter character string "S <position-id>" or
"US<user-id>". We can use the position we created, ALE-ERR-
HNDL, for technical errors as the Administrator ID.

In order to test the workflow that we set up, simulate errors in the
application and/or IDOC layer and check the integrated inbox for workflow items. Choosing the workflow item will display the error messages
[also see ERROR TEXT (button)]. You will also be able to display or even
change, if need be, the IDOC data. Once you correct the error appropriately, you can execute the workflow item for posting the IDOC to the
application. Note that if the workflow item is sent to a group of users—
such as a position, job, or unit—then the item will appear in the inboxes
of all the users; however, the item will disappear from their inboxes as
soon as it is reprocessed or deleted.

Setting up basic workflow for ALE and EDI error handling is essentially a simple process. It is also possible to create new workflow functionality or enhance the existing functionality through configuration
and a minimal amount of coding. Usually, there are customer functions
or user exits that can be used to influence the workflow processing of a
particular ALE/EDI interface. To create new workflow functionality, you
have to define workflow elementary objects and associate appropriate
procedures to them.

Workflow is a powerful technology that enhances business processes
and streamlines flow of processes in an organization. If configured prop-
erly, it can be used effectively to monitor ALE and EDI interfaces.

CHAPTER 9

IDOC Archiving

Overview

During the phases of development and testing, and eventually production, a large number of IDOCs of different message types may get created on the R/3™ databases. Once these IDOCs have been sent to their receiving system in outbound interfaces or processed in your system in the case of inbound interfaces, the utility value of these IDOCs may be little or none. It is also possible that you might need to store these IDOCs for regulatory or reconciliation purposes. In any case, there is a need to take these IDOCs off the R/3™ databases and hold them in other storage systems, or perhaps even delete them from the system permanently. This is possible through an SAP™-delivered mechanism called *archiving,* which is available for most SAP™ objects belonging to various applications such as SD, MM, FI, and so forth. In ALE and EDI, an IDOC is an object that can also be archived. In fact, the archiving object type itself is known as "IDOC." In SAP™, archiving is enabled through the Archiving Development Kit, or ADK. SAP™ provides several programs and function modules that can be used out of the box for archiving of many SAP™ objects such as Sales Orders, Invoices, and so forth. The "archiving class" for IDOCs was first introduced in SAP™ with release 3.0. If need be, one can develop custom programs for archiving using the ADK. It should be noted that in order to delete IDOCs from the system, they have to be archived first. It is also possible to reload IDOCs that have been archived.

In this chapter, we learn the steps involved in configuring the R/3™ system for archiving IDOCs, and familiarize ourselves with the programs available for archiving, reading archives, reloading archived IDOCs, deleting archived IDOCs, and managing the archives. We also learn that these programs can be scheduled to run periodically in order to perform various functions within the realm of IDOC archiving.

Let us take a look at the functions available for archiving of IDOCs. From the central archiving transaction **SARA,** it is possible to schedule *archiving* and *deletion* runs, as well as manage and monitor archived data. In the case of deletion, archiving can be followed by automatic deletion or scheduled later. When we schedule a program to *reload* IDOCs, it is possible to choose them from the set of IDOC archives; and IDOCs in the archives are written to an SAP™ database and assigned a status "reloaded." We can also use the *read* function to view all IDOCs in an archive. Note that archived IDOCs still remain on the SAP™ database until they are deleted.

Preliminary Configuration

In order to execute the archive programs, a couple of parameters need to be set. The first step is to enable certain IDOC status for archiving. This is done so that only IDOCs of a particular set of status codes can be archived. For example, IDOCs with status "64" should be excluded from archiving since they have not yet been posted to the application. This can be accomplished by using transaction WE47 or from WEDI → Control → Status maintenance. Choose a status, say "03," and display it. The subsequent screen has a radio-button for ARCHIVING with choices "possible" or "excluded." Make a choice appropriate to the IDOC status. See Figure 9-1.

The next step is to maintain the physical file path for a logical file name. Most archiving programs use the logical file name ARCHIVE_GLOBAL_PATH_WITH_ARCHIVE_LINK. Designate a physical file path to the logical file name. This can be accomplished by using transaction FILE or SF02. This is the directory in which all the archive files will be created and stored.

Ensure that you have sufficient authorization to perform archiving functions. For your user ID, authorization BATCH_ADMIN_ID should have a value of "Y." In addition, you should have the authorization object S_IDOCCTRL, activity "24" in your security profile.

IDOC Archiving Programs

IDOC archiving functions are accessed through the central archiving transaction SARA. Execute this transaction, enter "IDOC" for Object Name, and ENTER. This will display a refreshed screen with options ARCHIVE, DELETE, RELOAD, ANALYZE, and MANAGEMENT. See Figure 9-2.

Clicking on button ARCHIVE leads you to a screen that requests a variant for the archiving program RSEXARCA. Click on button MAINTAIN, and enter data for selection parameters and options such as DATE OF LAST CHANGE OF IDOC, MESSAGE TYPE, MESSAGE CODE, MESSAGE FUNCTION, DIRECTION, and IDOC NUMBER. After saving the variant, from the previous panel, maintain the start date and spool parameters. Once both panel lights are green, click on the EXECUTE button. This program uses the function module EDI_ARCHIVE_IDOCS of function group EDIA. See Figures 9-3 and 9-4.

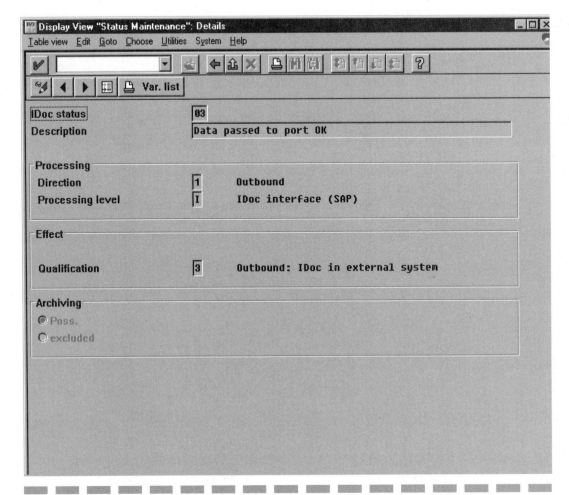

Figure 9-1 Enabling Archiving for IDOC Status

This will schedule background jobs automatically for archiving of IDOCs meeting the selection criteria specified in the variant. Click on JOB OVERVIEW to monitor the job. At the successful completion of the jobs, you will find a spool list containing details of the archiving run. See Figure 9-5 for an example.

The archiving process can be run periodically in batch, and can be scheduled as a background job. To facilitate periodic processing, SAP™ has also delivered program RSEXARCB. In the panel for selection parameters, you can choose the unit of time, the frequency of runs, message type, message function, message code, and direction. This is a very use-

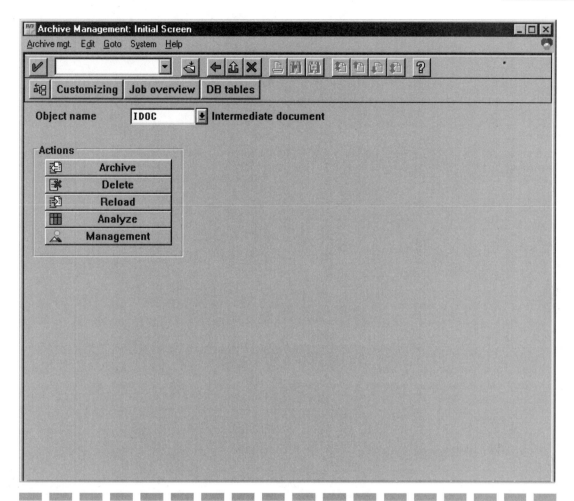

Figure 9-2 SARA—Central Archiving Transaction; Display for Object IDOC

ful program for setting up a production schedule for archiving IDOCs. See Figure 9-6.

The delete program RSEXARCD is used to delete archived IDOCs from the database. Note that the IDOCs must be in "archive" status before you can purge them permanently from the system. The main panel is as shown in Figure 9-7. Clicking the button ARCHIVE SELECTION presents a list of IDOC archives that are candidates for deletion. You also have to maintain the start date and spool parameters. Execution of the program results in the automatic creation and submission of the background job. Button JOB OVERVIEW takes you to a list of jobs. The suc-

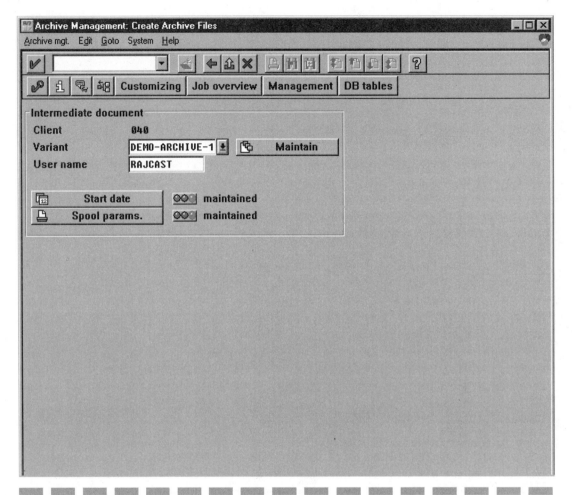

Figure 9-3 Execution Screen for Archiving IDOCs

cessful completion of this job results in the deletion of the archived IDOCs selected, and a spool list with statistics pertaining to the run. This program uses the function module EDI_DELETE_ ARCHIVED_IDOCS.

Note that deletion of IDOCs can be triggered in two ways. The first is to link the deletion process to the archiving program. This can be done through customizing the transaction for archiving: from the IMG → Cross Application components → General task functions → Define control parameters for archiving sessions or transaction SAR3. Choose the entry for object IDOC. You will see a subpanel

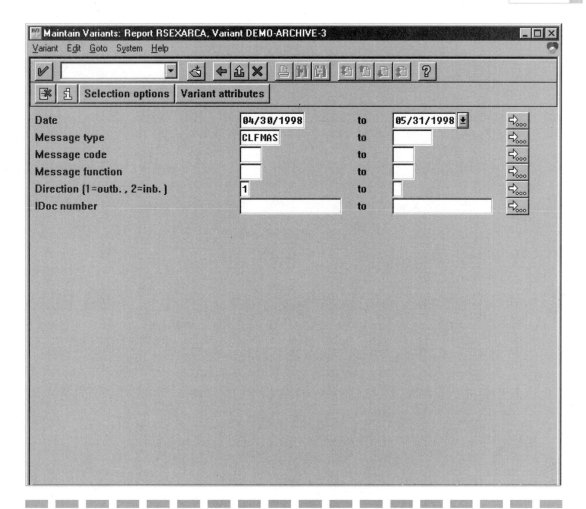

Figure 9-4 Selection Variant Parameters for IDOC Archiving

for SETTINGS FOR DELETE PROGRAM. Mark the checkbox START AUTOMATI-
CALLY. See Figure 9-8. This enables the automatic deletion of IDOCs
with the archive run. The other option is to run program RSEXARCD by
itself through the **SARA** transaction. This program can also be scheduled
to run periodically. Note that deletion of IDOCs from the archives (database) is an irreversible action.

Option RELOAD from the **SARA** main menu for object IDOC gives us the
capability of reloading IDOCs from an archive. This can be accessed by
running program RSEXARCL. The first step is to select the archive
from which you want to reload. This is done by clicking on the button

Figure 9-5
Sample Output of an
IDOC Archiving Run

```
10/08/1998                  List of archived IDocs

|System BK1                        Date 10/08/1998  Time 14:42:02
|
|Archive

| Message type     Code    Function   Status   Date     Time
Direction IDoc number         |

Statistics of archived objects

Archive file: 000047-001IDOC     Number of objects:       5,138
Size in MB:               8.116

| Table       Number      Description
|
|_____
| EDIDC       5,138    Control record (EDI Intermediate Document)
| EDIDD     247,935    Data segment (EDI Intermediate Document)
|
| EDIDS      17,746    Status record (EDI IDoc)
|


Archiving session: 000047 Number of objects:         5,138
Size in MB:               8.116

| Table       Number      Description
|
|_____|
| EDIDC       5,138    Control record (EDI Intermediate Document)
| EDIDD     247,935    Data segment (EDI Intermediate Document)
| EDIDS      17,746    Status record (EDI IDoc)
|_____
| CLFMAS                                03    04/30/1998 10:11:40
Outbound 0000000000226028
| CLFMAS                                03    04/30/1998 10:11:40
Outbound 0000000000226029
| CLFMAS                                03    04/30/1998 10:11:40
Outbound 0000000000226030
| CLFMAS                                03    04/30/1998 10:11:41
Outbound 0000000000226031
| CLFMAS                                03    04/30/1998 10:11:41
Outbound 0000000000226032
| CLFMAS                                03    04/30/1998 10:11:41
```

Figure 9-5
Sample Output of an
IDOC Archiving Run
(*Continued*)

```
Outbound 0000000000226033
| CLFMAS                              03        04/30/1998 10:11:41
Outbound 0000000000226034
| CLFMAS                              03        04/30/1998 10:11:41
Outbound 0000000000226035
| CLFMAS                              03        04/30/1998 10:11:41
Outbound 0000000000226036
| CLFMAS                              03        04/30/1998 10:11:41
Outbound 0000000000226037
```

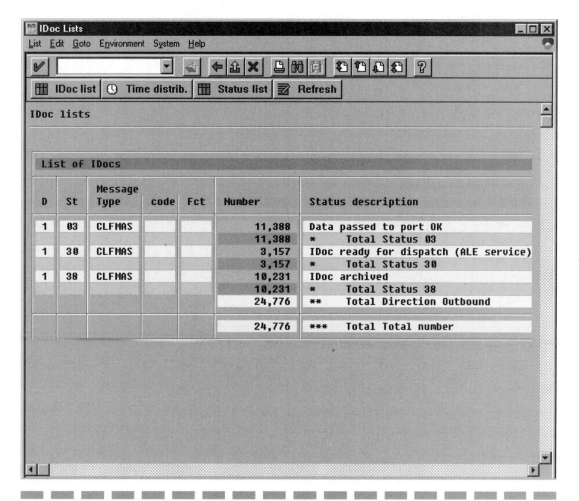

IDoc Lists

List   Edit   Goto   Environment   System   Help

IDoc list   Time distrib.   Status list   Refresh

IDoc lists

List of IDocs

D	St	Message Type	code	Fct	Number	Status description
1	03	CLFMAS			11,388	Data passed to port OK
					11,388	* Total Status 03
1	30	CLFMAS			3,157	IDoc ready for dispatch (ALE service)
					3,157	* Total Status 30
1	38	CLFMAS			10,231	IDoc archived
					10,231	* Total Status 38
					24,776	** Total Direction Outbound
					24,776	*** Total Total number

Figure 9-6 IDOC Lists

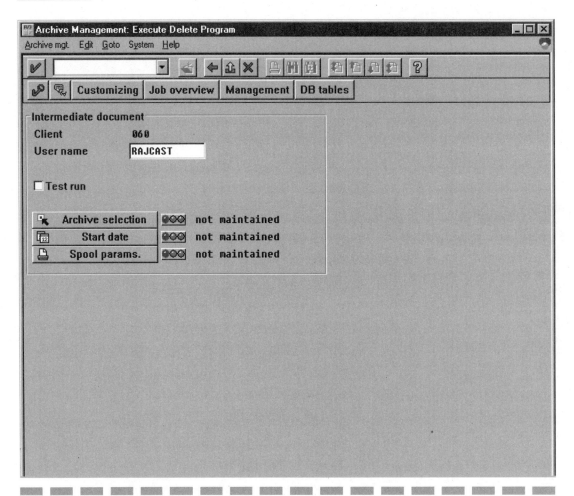

Figure 9-7 Execute Delete Program

ARCHIVE SELECTION that displays a list of archives that are candidates for reloading. You also have to maintain start date and spool parameters for the reload job. Executing this program transfers control to function module EDI_RELOAD_IDOC_ARCHIVE. As one of the first steps, it executes a form IS_RELOADING_POSSIBLE that determines if the current client corresponds to the client from which the data are achived, and also verifies if there is an IDOC in the database with the same IDOC number; this is done in order to avoid conflicts in the IDOC database. IDOCs that have been reloaded have new status records with value "35" for outbound and "71" for inbound. Note that the reload pro-

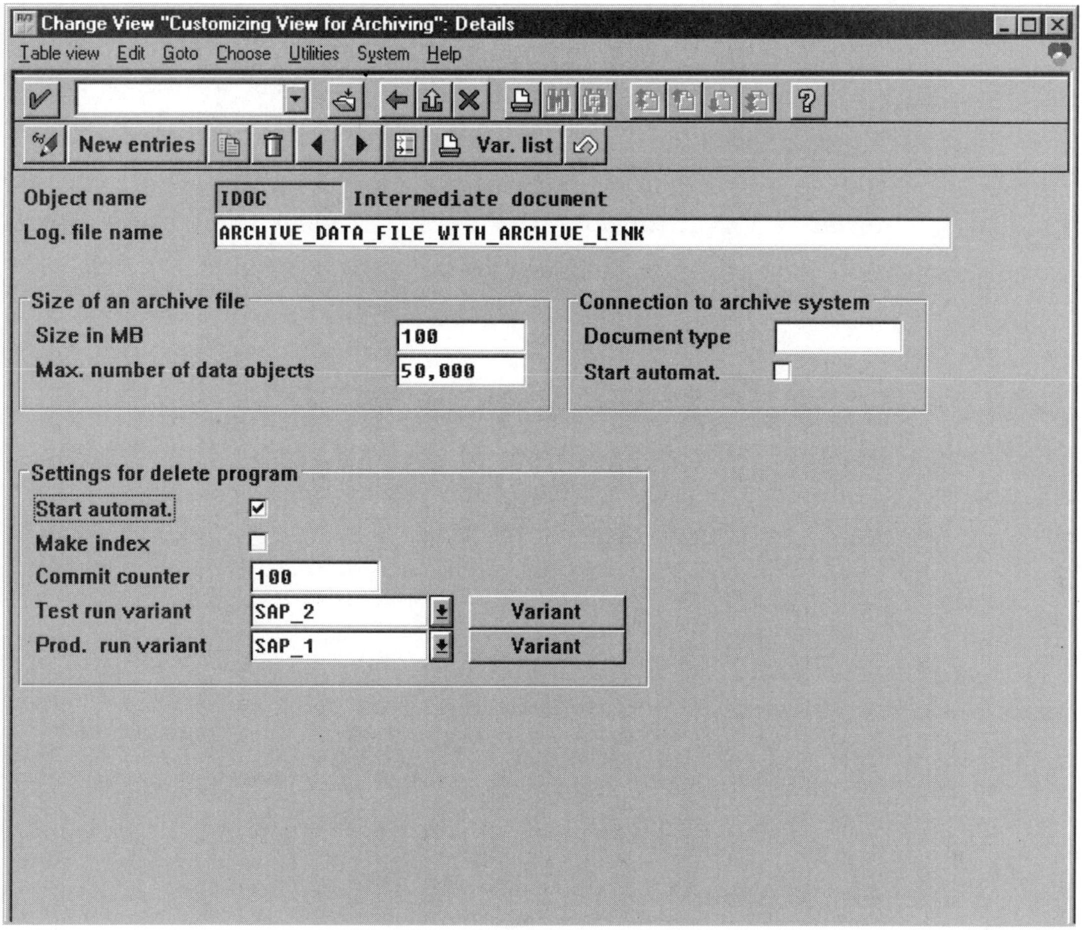

Figure 9-8 Customizing Settings—Automatic Deletion of IDOCs

gram only flags IDOCs as reloaded, and does not mark them so in the archives; hence, it is possible to reload the same archive several times, provided the IDOCs have not been deleted. The successful execution of the program outputs informational messages pertaining to the statistics of the reload.

Program RSEXARCR is used for reading and analyzing archives, and executes function module EDI_READ_IDOC_ARCHIVE. The read program can be accessed directly, and you have the capability of selecting the archive from an archive selection list.

The last option on the **SARA** main panel for object IDOC is MANAGE-MENT. This is a useful tool whereby you can monitor and manage the archives. Clicking on this option displays the list of archives performed to date with its status. It also has additional information such as archive ID. Double-clicking an archive presents a pop-up panel that indicates the file name of that archive, and you also have the choice of entering a short text to further describe the archive run. Note that an archive is marked complete (green light) when the IDOCs have been successfully deleted from the database. See Figure 9-9.

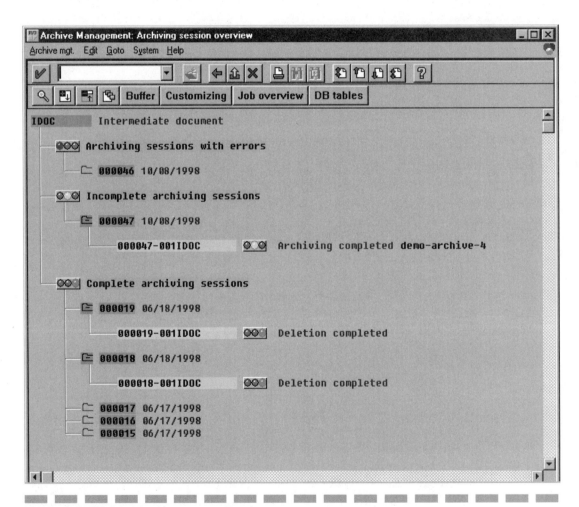

Figure 9-9 IDOC Archive Management Panel

It is important to note that if you have generated IDOCs in SAP™ releases 2.1, 2.2, 3.0A, or 3.0B, a data conversion is necessary before you can upgrade to 4.0. This conversion can be optimized if the IDOCs are archived prior to conversion. For releases 3.0 and 3.1, the archiving programs are already available; however, for releases 2.1 and 2.2, you can execute archiving programs only after the upgrade.

As you may have realized, IDOC archiving is a simple procedure that aids the maintenance of application IDOCs and IDOC databases. In most cases, the programs and procedures delivered by SAP™ suit the purpose. However, the programs can be enhanced or new functionality created using the ADK—Archive Development Kit. Most enhancements are usually limited to IDOC or archive selection parameters.

ALE Optimization

Overview

Having read the previous chapters, you should be prepared to prototype, develop, test, and implement ALE and EDI interfaces. However, to implement these interfaces efficiently greatly depends on performance issues related to their functioning. It is important to note that your efforts to configure and deploy ALE and EDI interfaces with optimum settings will preclude performance problems in production, while maximizing throughput and minimizing resource usage. If proper settings or processing options are not chosen, it is possible that these interfaces could lead to bottlenecks that might impact the normal functioning of the R/3™ system. In this chapter, we explore and learn performance-related issues, and understand optimum parameters, settings, and processing options for the express purpose of implementing smoothly functioning interfaces.

The objective of ALE optimization is threefold:

1. *Maximize throughput:* This indicates the number of application objects (Material Master, Sales Orders, Invoices, etc.) transferred from one system to another within a given period of time—for example, transferring 40,000 Customer Master IDOCs in an hour or less.

2. *Maximize speed:* Transfer of a single application object within a reasonable time period reflecting real-time or near-real-time processing.

3. *Minimize impact on dialog users:* While transferring a large number of application objects, ALE processes can impact normal dialog users by using most, if not all, dialog work processors on an instance. Also, the hardware resources required may not be reasonable; hence, there is a need to fine-tune the settings in order to minimize any negative impact on the system.

The preceding objectives are the most basic reasons to optimize ALE interfaces, but there are likely other business or data-processing requirements that could drive the need for optimization. Research has shown that ALE processes (nonapplication) take approximately 15-20 percent of the total processing time. Although this is true, poorly implemented interfaces could cause undesirable and unacceptable bottlenecks. The purpose of this chapter is to make you aware of options that exist for you to implement better-performing interfaces. Note that there are no exact magic numbers or settings that would tremendously improve performance; however, this chapter sets forth some guidelines and delineates optimum settings.

As a first step, we delve deeper into the communication methods ALE uses to transport application objects through IDOCs. Then we explore the processing modes and options available to us, also taking a look at the monitoring tools available to us. After this, we learn certain techniques to improve communication and processing times. Finally, we summarize the contents of this chapter as guidelines to ALE optimization.

Communications

There are three main steps to ALE processing.

Step 1 is the sender-side processing wherein the application and ALE services create a master IDOC in memory that contains all the data needed for the application object. From this master IDOC, a communication IDOC is created for each receiver defined in ALE configuration, which is stored on the IDOC database. Different receivers may receive a different set of data depending on the filters set in the ALE distribution model. Whereas the application provides master or transactional data in a specific format, ALE-function modules are responsible for storing them in an IDOC format.

Step 2 is the transfer of IDOCs from the sender to the receiver using the network. In this step, ALE determines the receiver of the communication IDOC based on the information stored on the EDIDC record of the IDOC in the IDOC database. Each sender communication IDOC has only one receiver. If there are multiple receivers for a given master IDOC, then there will exist multiple communication IDOCs on the sender. The communication IDOC is sent over the network to the receiver system using TCP/IP and CPI-C communication methods.

Step 3 is the receipt of the IDOC on the target system and subsequent processing. On the receiving side, the communication IDOC is first stored on the IDOC database before further processing. After this, application-function modules are called to post the data to the application databases. The logical transfer is complete only after the application data are successfully posted on the target system. However, from the sender's perspective, the storage of the IDOC on the target system's IDOC database signals the end of a successful transfer. The communication IDOC's status can be now updated appropriately from a communication point of view. As described in Chapter 7, "Periodic

Processing," we can also report the final status of the IDOC on the target system back to the sending system by means of message type ALEAUD (ALE audit messages).

The IDOC database plays an important role in ALE processing. It enables both offline and asynchronous interface processing to other systems irrespective of their availability at that point in time. ALE processes can repeatedly attempt to deliver the IDOCs to the target system, as well as handle errors. As we learned earlier, the IDOC database consists of three main tables: (1) EDIDC for the control record, (2) EDID2 (cluster EDI30C) for the data records (EDIDD records), and (3) EDIDS for the status records. IDOC data are stored in a machine-independent character-based ASCII format.

To refresh our memory, there are three ways of generating IDOCs for communications to the target system. The first method is through change pointers for master data. Program RBDMIDOC can be run to analyze the changes occurring to the master data and create communication IDOCs. The second method is to "directly send" master data using SAP™-delivered ALE programs. The third way is to generate transactional-data IDOCs through application processing such as program RSNAST00, which is based on message control/condition techniques. The ALE layer uses configuration information to determine receivers and filters to create communication IDOCs from master IDOCs. These communication IDOCs are then stored in IDOC databases.

ALE interfaces use one of two communication methods: (1) Transactional Remote Function Calls (tRFCs) or (2) File Transfer Protocol (FTP). The word *transactional* in tRFC implies that one or more function calls are bundled together in a single logical unit of work (LUW), which typically represents a transaction. tRFC methodology ensures transactional integrity between two R/3™ systems. This communication method is generally used for R/3™-R/3™ interfaces. (Note that you can use tRFC to connect to external systems as well.) SAP™ delivers a tRFC library with certain functions. The second method, FTP, is a sequential process and is controlled at the operating-system level; FTP is typically used in EDI interfaces. Let us further explore the two communication methods.

Transactional Remote Function Calls (tRFCs)

In the case of transactional RFC communications, when the process is started on the sender system, a message is written to the tRFC queue.

An item in the tRFC queue is then sent across the network to the target system, which also has a tRFC queue to which this item is written. On the sender system, the tRFC queue consists of tables ARFCSSTATE and ARFCSDATA, and on the receiver system it consists of tables ARFCRSTATE and ARFCRDATA. The STATE tables contain status information of the tRFC call on the sender and receiver system, respectively, while the DATA tables contain the list of function modules to be invoked along with their parameter values.

Following are the six steps that describe the tRFC communication process on the sender and receiver system. See Figure 10-1.

1. On the receiver system, the function module to be executed for inbound processing is INBOUND_IDOC_PROCESS; hence, on the sender system, this RFC function to be invoked—along with its parameters—is written to the tRFC queue (the ARFC tables mentioned earlier). This is invoked by the COMMIT statement in the sender's logical unit of work.

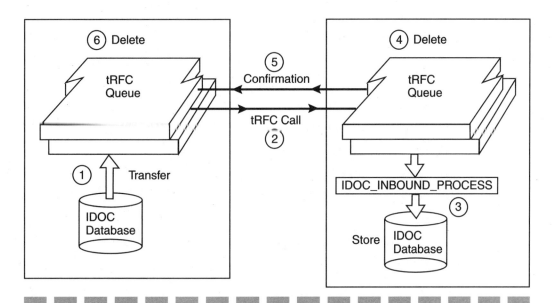

Figure 10-1 tRFC Communications Between Two R/3 Systems

2. On the sending system's instance, a dialog work process executes function ARFC_SHIP to transfer data to the target system over the network. The data are then written to the tRFC queue on the receiver system (ARFC tables).

3. In a dialog work process on the target system, function IDOC_INBOUND_PROCESS is called to store the transferred IDOC in the receiver's IDOC database.

4. A COMMIT statement on the receiver logical unit of work initiates the deletion of the tRFC entries on the receiver system.

5. The target system communicates an acknowledgment to the sender system using function ARFC_DEST_CONFIRM.

6. On the target system, the receipt of this acknowledgment triggers the deletion of the entry from the sender's tRFC queue. This completes the logical unit of work (LUW) on the sender system, and the dialog work processor used for the transfer is released.

When an IDOC is sent out of the sender system, it attains a status of "03"—Data passed to port OK. In order to check if the tRFC was successful, we need to schedule program RBDMOIND as explained in Chapter 7, "Periodic Processing." This program checks the status of the tRFC and adds a status record of value "12"—Dispatch OK, to the IDOC if the tRFC was successful. You can also monitor the tRFC queue by using transaction SM58 or from BALE → Monitoring → Transactional RFC. This only displays entries on the tRFC queue that are yet to be sent or if there was an error in executing the tRFC call. When tRFCs fail, SAP™ has a mechanism whereby batch jobs are automatically scheduled to reprocess the transaction. The batch jobs have an ID in the format "ARFC:[transaction-ID]" and can also be viewed from SM58 by selecting an entry and Information → Display Background Jobs. The attributes and creation of these batch jobs can be controlled from transaction SM59 for that particular RFC destination. From transaction SM59, select an RFC destination → Destination → tRFC Options. You have the option to suppress the background job altogether for that RFC destination or change the number of retries and time interval between two retries. The defaults are: create batch jobs, 30 retries, and 15 minutes between two retries. Remember that you have to schedule program RSARFCEX to reexecute the tRFC calls. Note, too, that this program executes all outstanding RFC calls as opposed to the batch job that executes only failed tRFC. In some cases, the suppression of these background jobs could be useful, since it generates a large number of jobs for failed tRFCs that might flood the work processors—resulting in even more batch jobs being created. Hence, this can be preempted by suppressing the generation of batch jobs for high-volume RFC destinations. See Figure 10-2.

As mentioned earlier, tRFC communications can be used for either an R/3™-to-external system or an external system-to-R/3™ system. In order to improve performance for outbound communications, that is an R/3™-to-external system, it is suggested that the external program be registered with the R/3™ gateway. If the program is not registered, the system requires the program to be started for each data transfer. To register a program, from transaction **SM59**, choose the RFC destination (TCP/IP) and click on button REGISTRATION; enter the required informa-

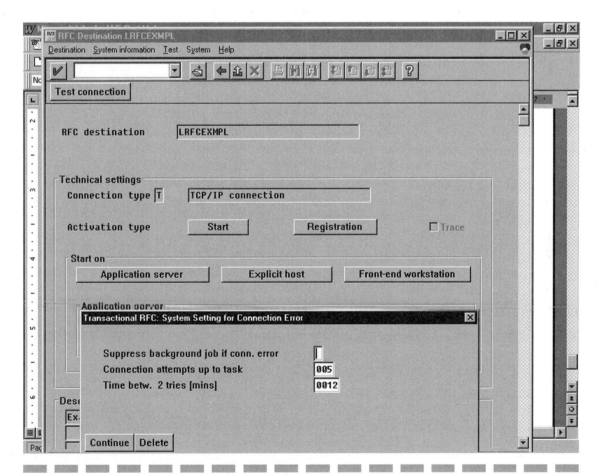

Figure 10-2 Control of Automatic Batch Job Creation for RFC Communications

tion. If an entry is made in "saprfc.ini," the program gets automatically registered at gateway server start-up. It is possible to register the program multiple times to achieve parallel processing, but this option is effective only if the external program is capable of multitasking and record-level locking. IDOC serialization is negated with this form of processing. Note that for communications from an external program to the R/3™ system (inbound), this concept of registration does not apply. If data transfers are frequent, then it may be helpful to keep the connection active after logon and transfer data whenever they arrive. SAP'™s gateway server will ping the external program frequently and will keep the connection open, if available. It is also suggested that the external program send packets of IDOCs rather than single IDOC data transfer. R/3™-to-R/3™ connection programs cannot be registered. This implies that a new logon is attempted for each tRFC call.

There are two methods by which the IDOCs are processed by the application on the receiver system. The first, most widely used method is a call to certain application-function modules that posts data directly to the application database. In this case, there are fewer application checks made as compared to the other approach. With this method, it is also possible to achieve mass update wherein several IDOCs can be processed in one call, a technique that helps significantly reduce overall processing time. Only certain message types are capable of mass updates. To determine this, use transaction **BD51**. The column "Input Type" has three possible values for the inbound function module: 0, for mass processing possible; 1 and 2, for individual input. If a packet of IDOCs is created on the receiver system, and the inbound function module does not support mass processing, then the IDOCs in a packet are processed sequentially within one work processor. The other method of inbound processing is by traditional batch input technique and calling the function "Call Transaction using <transaction code>" for posting the application data. This approach is slower, but all consistency checks are made during processing. This approach is prevalent in very few inbound IDOC function modules.

It should be noted that updates are performed within the work process that executes the inbound function module with the use of the ABAP/4 keyword SET UPDATE TASK LOCAL. This implies that no update work processor is used to accomplish this task.

Let us differentiate between the three types of RFCs used in R/3™. *Synchronous RFCs* call a function on the remote system and wait for a response. This is used only by ALE for configuration integrity checks.

The calling program is aware of the result of the remotely called function. *Asynchronous RFC* (aRFC) is a remote call in which the process does not wait for a response. These aRFCs are used by the sender in case of parallel direct sending of master data, and by the receiving system in case of parallel inbound processing. Asynchronous RFCs are called with the "call function...starting new task" ABAP/4 statement. *Transactional RFCs* from the sender send a group of remote function calls within a logical unit of work (LUW). If any one of the function calls fails, the entire LUW is rolled back. Transactional RFCs are used by ALE only to transfer IDOCs from one system to another, and only one function INBOUND_IDOC_PROCESS is called on the target system. All tRFCs are called with the ABAP/4 statement "Call function...in background task."

File Transfer Protocol (FTP)

The other communication method is File Transfer Protocol. In an outbound scenario, program RSEOUT00 is executed to create a file of the collected IDOCs, on the IDOC database. This results in an ASCII file of IDOCs, which can then be transferred using FTP to the external system. Note that you have to maintain a file-based port definition for this. In case of inbound processing, the file of IDOCs is imported into SAP™ by program RSEINB00, a process that creates IDOCs on the IDOC database; subsequently, the IDOCs are posted to the application by other inbound-function modules. For purposes of testing, it is possible to convert an outbound file of IDOCs into an inbound file by using transaction WE12. As you learned earlier, file-based communications is primarily used by EDI.

IDOC Processing Options

SAP™ provides us with several options for processing IDOCs, both on the outbound as well as the inbound. These options play a significant role in the performance of ALE interfaces. The processing options available to us can be broadly categorized into three variables: (1) Dispatch Control, (2) Processing Mode, and (3) Unit of Transfer. Let us explore these options.

Figure 10-3

Outbound Processing
Options

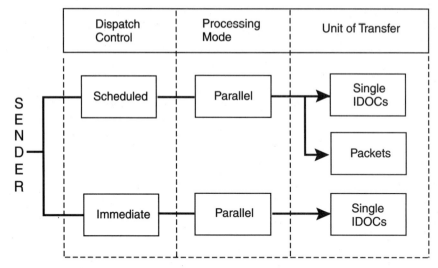

Outbound Processing Options

As can be seen in Figure 10-3, the dispatch of IDOCs can be either immediate or scheduled. Whenever IDOCs are collected and later sent by scheduling program RSEOUT00, no tRFC calls are generated right when those IDOCs are created. The advantage of this is that packets of several IDOCs can be created for improved performance (unit of transfer). The time lag between creation of IDOCs and sending them distributes the workload over time. If the IDOCs are dispatched immediately to the receiving system, the capability of creating packets is lost, which may also result in reduced throughput. It should be noted that the option of sending IDOCs immediately may be a business or data-processing requirement. This option can be set in the outbound parameters of the partner profile.

In case of outbound interfaces, there is no option for the processing mode. Irrespective of immediate or scheduled processing, the IDOCs or IDOC packets will result in the asynchronous creation of tRFC calls.

The unit of transfer option could play an important role in ALE optimization. For outbound IDOCs, it is possible to build packets of several IDOCs while sending them to the receiver system. In this case a single packet of several IDOCs is sent in one tRFC call. The two advantages of this are: (1) on the receiver system, the process has to log on only once for a packet of IDOCs, and (2) the programs processing these IDOCs have to be loaded into memory only once for a packet of IDOCs. This option is possible only in the case of scheduled dispatch of IDOCs. Program RSEOUT00 groups the IDOCs by message type and build packets of the size specified in the outbound parameters of the partner profile. A packet of IDOCs will contain IDOCs of the same IDOC type. RSEOUT00 will dispatch all IDOCs, even if the last packet is smaller than the packet size specified. See Figure 10-4.

As you may have observed, the dispatch control modes are set in the outbound parameters of the partner profile. This mode can be specified

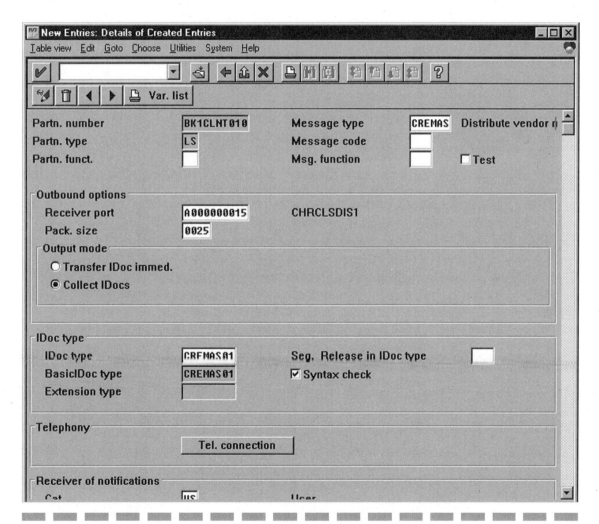

Figure 10-4 Dispatch Control and Packet Size for Outbound IDOCs

for a combination of message type and receiver logical system. Program RSEOUT00 processes one IDOC or IDOC packet sequentially, and the transfer itself is done via tRFC; this implies that no aRFC is used by the process. Also, a new dialog work process is used for processing the tRFC, and once the IDOC or IDOC packet is processed, the next unit is processed by the dialog work process. To a great extent, the time consumed by the tRFC is a function of both the size of the IDOC and the number of IDOCs in a given packet. Throughput improves if the packet size is increased, but huge packets can cause memory shortages, which is an undesirable event. Packet sizes should not be over 1000, and should typically be 30 to 50. As mentioned earlier, there are no magic exact numbers that apply to all situations.

Inbound Processing Options

The inbound processing options that we choose can play a significant role in ALE optimization. As with outbound, there are three types of processing options: (1) Dispatch Control, (2) Processing Mode, and (3) Unit of Transfer. See Figure 10-5.

If on the inbound parameters of the partner profile, the processing option is set to "background," the IDOCs are collected when received from the sending system. These IDOCs have to be processed by program RBDAPP01. In this case, no aRFC calls are generated at the time of receipt of the IDOCs or IDOC packets. The advantages of this option are twofold: since there is a time delay between the receipt of IDOCs and program RBDAPP01, the workload is distributed over time; less dialog work processors are used for processing of IDOCs, making them available to the actual tRFC transfer process. This could preempt the blocking of work processors for the sender system. The other advantage is that you now have the capability of specifying a packet size for processing the IDOCs that have been collected. It is possible to process these IDOCs or IDOC packets in parallel using RFC server group (see next section). As you learned earlier, the status of the IDOC(s) when received from the sender system will be set to "64" if the IDOC was successfully received by the system in the IDOC database.

If the IDOCs processing option is set to "immediate," the function module IDOC_INBOUND_PROCESS invokes the inbound processing immediately after the receipt of the IDOC or IDOC packet. aRFC calls are used to hand over the inbound processing to the work processors.

▬▬ ▬▬ ▬▬ ▬▬

Figure 10-5
Inbound Processing
Options

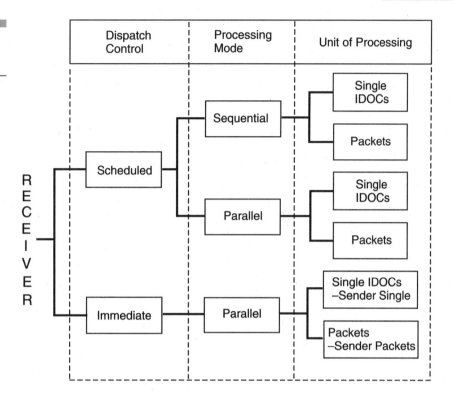

The processing mode of IDOCs can be either *sequential* or *parallel*. The sequential option is possible only with the dispatch mode being "background" (collect IDOCs). The program RBDAPP01 processes the IDOCs or IDOC packets sequentially by default. In this type of processing mode, no aRFC calls are made. All processing is through synchronous RFC by a single dialog work processor. The parallel processing mode is achieved by turning on the flag PARALLEL BOOKING on the RBDAPP01 screen. See Figure 10-6. In this case IDOCs or IDOC packets are processed using aRFC calls by different dialog work processes. This option could improve throughput of IDOCs.

If you specify a packet size in program RBDAPP01, that number of IDOCs is processed in one logical unit of work or logical step. If the inbound-function module is capable of mass processing, all the IDOCs in that packet will be updated in one single step. Even with single update inbound-function modules, the packet is looped through for each IDOC, and the entire packet is processed in one logical step. If this field is set to a value of 1, then the logical step will comprise only a single IDOC at a time.

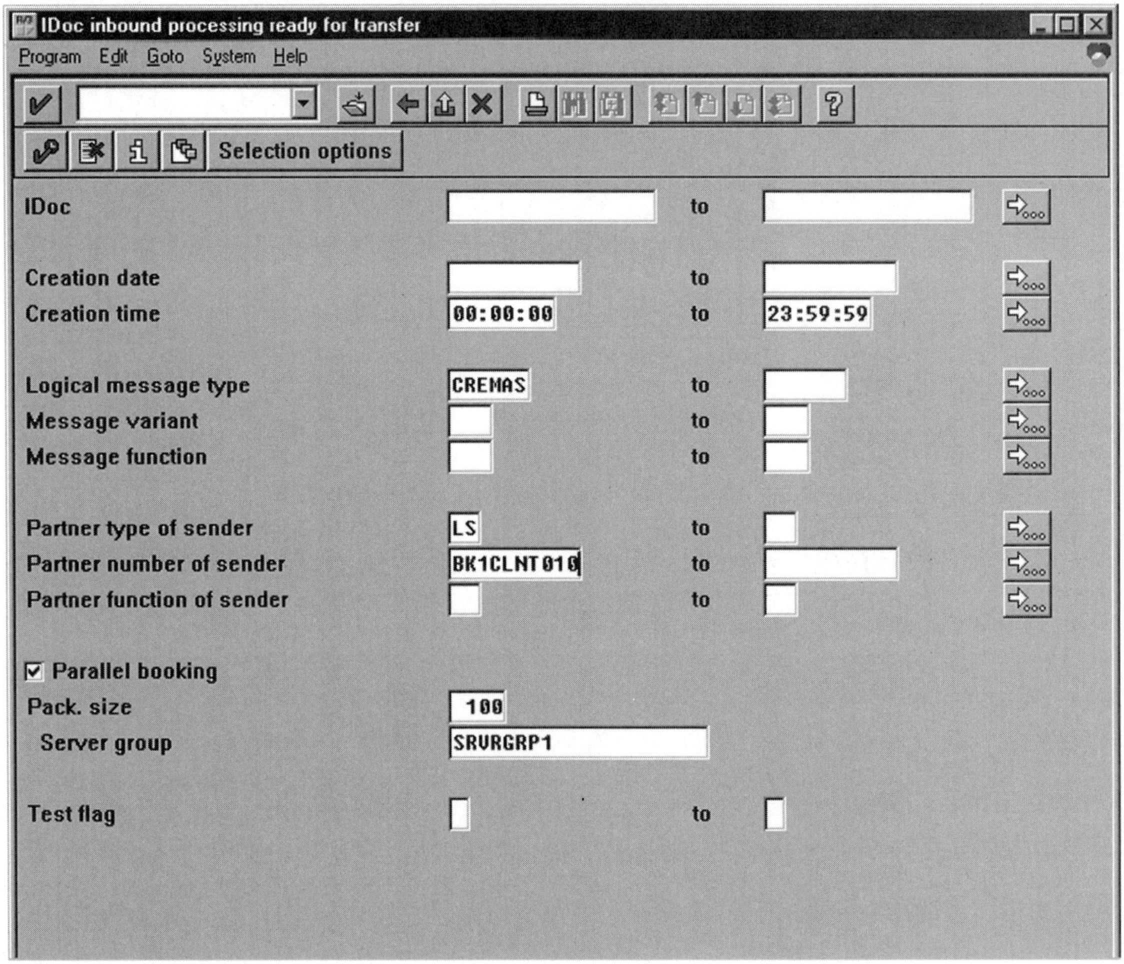

Figure 10-6 Program RBDAPP01—Parallel Processing and Packet Size

RFC Server Groups and Parallel Processing

A *server group* is a collection of application servers used for distributing the workload of a single ALE task. An RFC server group can be used in certain outbound ALE applications and/or inbound IDOC processing. In an outbound scenario, RFC server groups can be used for the distribution of high-volume master data IDOCs. In the case of inbound IDOCs, RFC server groups can be used only if the processing option was set to collect IDOCs ("background" mode in the inbound parameters of the partner profile); subsequent processing is performed through the execution of program RBDAPP01.

To define an RFC server group, use transaction **SM59** → RFC → RFC Group or transaction **RZ12** . Create a group and associate some or all of the application servers available to the group. Contact your Basis Administrator for identifying the servers. Ensure that the load is balanced on the servers and work processors are available for RFC processing.

With master data distribution using ALE, you can specify an RFC server group only in the case of "direct send" of IDOCs from the sender system. For example, with program RBDSEDEB (transaction **BD12**), sending of Customer Master IDOCs, you can specify an RFC group and number of IDOCs (customers) per work process under the section for "parallel processing." When the program is executed, it invokes aRFC calls on multiple work processors of the application servers in the RFC server group. This greatly enhances the throughput of IDOCs on the sender system. See Figure 10-7.

In the case of inbound processing through program RBDAPP01, if an RFC server group is not used, then only work processors of a given server are going to be used for aRFC processing. It is possible that the program could flood all the dialog work processes of that server. For example, if all processes needed to obtain an application object number from the number range tables, the number ranges may need to be loaded into a buffer that needs a work processor. Since this is not available, the processes could deadlock and indefinitely wait on resources. To avoid this performance bottleneck, it is suggested that you use RFC server groups.

Monitoring

In order to successfully carry out optimization measures for ALE interfaces, one must be capable of monitoring the potential problems and performance bottlenecks. SAP™ provides transactions, programs, and tools to monitor ALE processes. Some of the transactions mentioned may be common to other processes on the R/3™ system as well.

Using transaction **WE05** (IDOC Lists), you can display a list of IDOCs that meet the specified criteria. You can obtain a "time distribution" of the creation of IDOCs. This screen gives us an idea about the through-

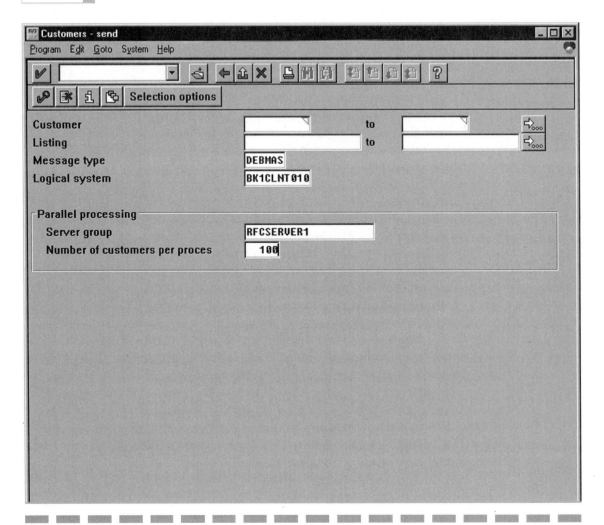

Figure 10-7 Parallel Processing with Direct Send of Master Data

put of IDOCs from the system. You can also generate a graphical representation of this statistic. See Figures 10-8 and 10-9.

The other useful IDOC tool is the *IDOC trace.* This function can be executed from BALE → Monitoring → IDOC Trace or transaction **BDM2**. This display gives us a cross-system IDOC report for specified message type, generation date, and the receiver system. Carefully note the average, maximum, and minimum transfer times. These values are computed based on the time stamps of status records on the sender and receiver systems. This statistic is useful only if the receiver system

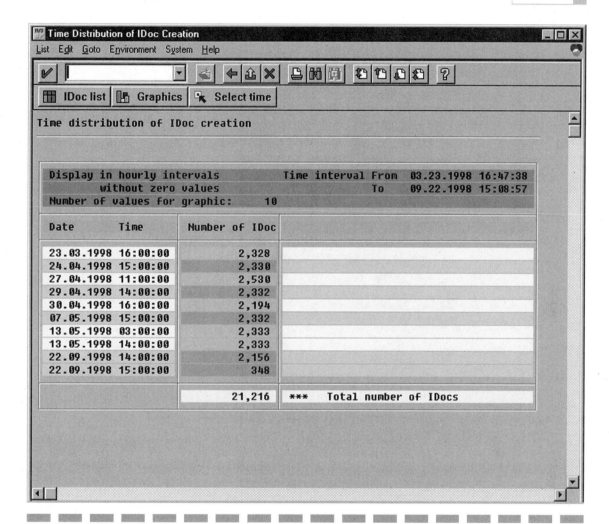

Figure 10-8 Time Distribution of IDOC Creation

processed the IDOCs immediately, which implies that cross-system IDOC reporting is not useful for the scheduled processing mode.

Use transaction **SM58** or BALE → Monitoring → Transactional RFC for monitoring tRFC. The entries in this screen are only those that have not yet been processed or tRFCs in error. Since the workflow system also uses the tRFC method, you may see entries for workflow, too. Every tRFC has a transaction ID, which is unique worldwide and is associated with its IDOC. In the IDOC display/monitor, you can see the

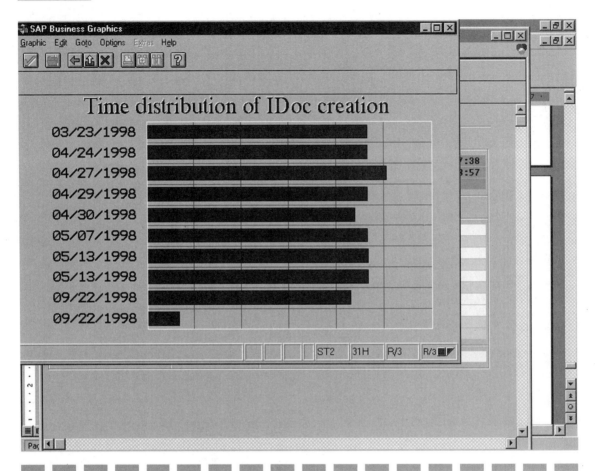

Figure 10-9 Graphic of Time Distribution of IDOC Creation

tRFC transaction ID in the status record message for "03" on the sender system.

Use transactions **SM50** and **SM51** for monitoring of processes on the system. You can identify a tRFC call, on both the sender and receiver systems, by the entry for program SAPLSERFC. aRFC calls on the receiver system can be identified by entries for program SAPLSARFC. Subsequent inbound processing can be detected by the execution entry for their respective modules. If programs RSEOUT00 (for sender) and RBDAPP01 (for receiver) have been scheduled for processing, then entries for batch work processes will appear in the monitor.

Transaction SM37 (Job Overview) can be used to monitor the batch jobs. This job overview could also list the aRFC jobs that are scheduled automatically in case of communication errors.

Summary

Having discussed the various options available for fine-tuning the performance of ALE interfaces, let us summarize the preceding discussion.

- For dispatch control of IDOCs, use scheduled processing instead of immediate processing whenever possible, both on the sender and receiver systems.
- Switch off automatic batch retry for tRFC communication errors.
- Use IDOC packets whenever possible, both for sender and receiver systems.
- In case of SAP™ R/3™-to-external system communications, register the external program. Register it multiple times if multitasking is possible on the external system.
- Based on the activity of batch and dialog processors, schedule transfer/updates of huge volumes of IDOCs during nonpeak times.
- Reorganize the change pointer database regularly using program RBDCPCLR.
- Archive IDOCs periodically.
- Provide a sufficient number of dialog work processors on both the sender system and the receiver system. The number of sender work processes should not be greater than the number of receiver work processes.
- Use parallel processing by implementing RFC server groups for direct send of master data as well as scheduled inbound processing by program RBDAPP01.

The preceding points are a few guidelines to improving and optimizing the performance of ALE interfaces.

SAP™ is constantly enhancing the processes and adding new functionality in the realm of ALE and EDI. With advanced technologies in SAP™ using ALE services as a backbone for communications and application distribution, ALE will continue to play an important and powerful role in ERP implementations. As you might have learned from reading this book, ALE and EDI interfaces can be successfully built and deployed effectively by methodically executing a few steps. It is possible to use these two powerful technologies to synergistically and efficaciously integrate similar or disparate systems.

APPENDIX A

FREQUENTLY USED ALE/EDI TRANSACTIONS

Following is a list of frequently used ALE and EDI transactions. Use the transaction as is from the main menu or use /n from any screen (e.g., /nBALE) or /o to open a new session with the transaction (e.g., /oBD21).

Transaction	Description
SALE	ALE Customizing
BALE	Distribution Administration (ALE)
WEDI	IDOC Type and EDI Basis
BD21	Analyze change pointers—create IDOC from change pointer
BD10	Send Material Master
BD12	Send Customer Master
BD14	Send Vendor Master
BD61	Activate change pointer generally
BD50	Activate change pointer for message type
BD54	Maintain logical systems
BD64	Maintain distribution model
BD71	Distribute customer model
BD87	Process inbound IDOCs
BD88	Process outbound IDOCs
BDM2	Cross-system IDOC reporting
WE02	IDOC Display
WE05	IDOC List
WE20	Maintain partner profile
WE21	Maintain port definition
WE30	Develop IDOC types

Transaction	Description
WE31	Maintain IDOC segment
WE60	IDOC Documentation—IDOC types
WE61	IDOC Documentation—IDOC record types
BDM8	ALE Audit—sending confirmations
BDM7	ALE Audit—statistical analyses
WE12	Inbound processing of outbound file—convert outbound to inbound file
WE14	Process (dispatch) IDOCs through port—RSEOUT00
WE15	Outbound IDOC from NAST—message control
WE16	Inbound file
WE41	Process code outbound
WE42	Process code inbound
SARA	Central IDOC archiving
WE47	Status code maintenance
SAR3	Archiving object customizing
WE63	IDOC type for parser output
WE82	Assign IDOC to message type
SM59	Maintain RFC destinations
SM37	Display batch jobs—job overview
SM50	Process overview
SLG1	Evaluate application log
SM21	System log
SM58	Transactional RFC monitoring
RZ12	RFC Server Group maintenance

APPENDIX B

MESSAGE TYPES

Following is a list of message types available on the R/3™ system.

Table	VEDI_EDMSG
Description	EDI: Logical Message Types
Number of entries	216

Message Type	Description
ABSEN1	Attendance/Absence in KK1
ACCONF	Confirmation of IDOC processing from the application
ACLPAY	Accounting: Inbound invoice
ACLREC	Accounting: Billing document
ACPJMM	Posting in accounting from materials management
ACTIV3	Units in KK3
ACTIV4	Units in KK4
ALEAUD	Acknowledgments about processing status of inbound IDOCS
ALEREQ	General request message
BATCH5	KK5 Batch
BLAOCH	Purchasing contract change
BLAORD	Purchasing contracts
BLAREL	Release order documentation for distributed contracts
BOMDOC	BOMs: Document structure
BOMMAT	BOMs: Material BOM
CHRMAS	Class system: Characteristics master
CLFMAS	Class system: Classification master
CLSMAS	Class system: Classes master

Data contained in this appendix has been obtained from SAP™ Systems' tables of values.

Message Type	Description
CMREQU	Invite TR-CM subsystem to send TR-CM data
CMSEND	TR-CM subsystem sends TR-CM data to central TR-CM
CNPMAS	Configuration profile
COACOR	Core master activity type
COACTV	IDOC for cost center/activity type
COAFET	Request activity type
COAMAS	Master activity type
COCOKA	Control segment CO object/cost element
CODCMT	IDOC for a CO document
COELEM	Cost element master data
COGRP1	Cost center groups
COGRP2	Cost element groups
COGRP5	Activity type groups
COGRP6	Profit center groups
COGRP9	Account groups (Profit Center Accounting)
CONDAT	Control data
CONDBI	Condition index for document changes
COND_A	Conditions: master data for price determination
CONF11	Confirmations in KK1
CONF21	Confirmations in KK2, time events
CONF31	Confirmations in KK3, time events
CONF32	Confirmations in KK3, wage slips
CONF41	Confirmations in KK4, time events
CONF42	Confirmations in KK4, wage slips
CONF51	Confirmations in KK5, run schedules
CONFIG	Configuration for transceiver
COPAGN	Profitability analysis
COPCPA	Costing data CO-PC -> CO-PA
COSCOR	Core master cost center
COSFET	Request cost center
COSMAS	Master cost center

Message Type	Description
COTOTL	IDOC for CO totals records
CPS001	Profitability analysis
CREADV	Credit memo display
CRECOR	Core master vendors
CREFET	Get vendor data
CREMAS	Distribute Vendor Master
DEBADV	Debit display
DEBCOR	Core master Customer Master
DEBFET	Request Customer Master
DEBMAS	Customer Master
DELINS	Delivery schedule/JIT schedule
DESADT	Shipping notification
DESADV	Shipping notification
DIFFE2	Differences in KK2
DIFFE3	Differences in KK3
DIFFE4	Differences in KK4
DIRDEB	Preauthorized withdrawal
DISTU2	Reasons for problems KK2
DOCMAS	Master document
DWLOAD	Download transceiver configuration
EDLNOT	EDL delivery notes
EKSEKS	Purchasing document for Purchasing Info system
EUPEXR	Reference message for electr. signature (for ext. payments)
EXPINV	Export invoice
EXTWA1	External wage type
FIDCCH	Change in FI document
FIDCMT	FI-IDOC to send single items
FIROLL	G/L rollup (GLX)
GLCORE	Master data G/L accounts (CORE IDOC)
GLFETC	Request G/L accounts
GLM000	Test reduction GLMAST

Message Type	Description
GLMAST	Master data G/L accounts (master IDOC)
GLROLL	FI-GLX message type rollup
GSVERF	Cred. memo procedure
HRCPRQ	Personnel Cost Planning—inquiry from CO to HR
HRINW	Time tickets from Logistics
HRMD_A	HR: Master and organizational data (application system)
HRMD_B	HR: Master and organizational data (basis system)
HRPAYP	HR: Transfer FI/CO
HRPRS	Attendances from Logistics
HRTRVL	HR-TRV: Transfer travel expenses FI/CO
INFREC	Purchasing info record
INVCON	Inventory Controlling IDOC
INVOIC	Invoice / Billing document
KNOMAS	Global object dependencies
KOMMOD	Communication module / Transceiver
LCROLL	Legal consolidation
LIP032	Upload infostructure storage loc.stocks (S032)
LIP035	Upload infostructure batch stocks (S035)
LIP039	Distributed IS planning
LIP125	Distributed IS planning
LIS000	LIS external data: sending
LOCAT5	Storage location for run schedules
LOIBOM	Bills of Material
LOICAL	Calendar
LOINUM	IDOC for number of IDOCs sent
LOIPLO	Planned order
LOIPRO	Production order
LOIRNH	Hierarchy/network
LOIROU	Routing
LOIRSH	Run schedule header
LOISTD	Requirements/stock list

Message Type	Description
LOIWCS	Work Center
MALFK5	Reasons for problems, run schedules
MALFU2	Problems in KK2
MATCOR	Core master material
MATFET	Request material
MATMAS	Master material
OPERA2	Operations in KK2
OPERA3	Processes in KK3
OPERA4	Operations in KK4
OPERS2	Operation status in KK2
OPERS3	Workplaces in KK3
OPERS4	Workcenters in KK4
ORDCHG	Purchase order/order change
ORDERS	Purchase order / order
ORDRSP	Purchase order / order confirmation
OSTAT2	Process status CC2
PAYEXT	Extended payment order
PCROLL	Profit center rollup
PEROP2	
PERSO1	Personnel master records in KK1
PERSO2	Personnel master in KK2
PERSO3	Personnel master in KK3
PERSO4	Personnel master in KK4
PICKSD	Picking request
PI_BTC	Data transfer
PKHD5	Kanban closed loops
PKPS5	Kanban container
PKST5	Possible status for Kanban containers
PLANT2	Plants in KK2
PLANT3	KK3: Plant table
PLANT4	KK4: Plant table

Message Type	Description
PRCFET	Request profit center
PRCMAS	Profit center master record
PRODPL	Production plan reporting
QUOTES	Quotation
RCLROL	Reconciliation ledger rollup
RECSHP	Recommended shipments
REMADV	Payment advice
REQOTE	Inquiry
REQUI1	Confirmation request in KK1
REQUI2	Confirmation request in KK2
REQUI3	Confirmation request in KK3
REQUI4	Confirmation request in KK4
REQUI5	Confirmation request in KK5
SDPACK	Packing confirmation
SDPICK	Picking confirmation
SHIPPL	Inbound planned shipments
SHPMNT	Shipping outbound
SISCSO	VIS: Sales order
SISDEL	SIS: Delivery
SISINV	SIS: Billing document
SMMMAN	Master material
SOPGEN	Distributed IS planning
SRCLST	Source List
SRVMAS	Master data service master
STATUS	Message about status information transmission
SYIDOC	Determination of IDOC types
SYNCH	Synchronous communication (e.g., ALE checks)
SYRECD	Determination of IDOC record types
TEST01	Test
TPSDLR	Shipping planning system: Trigger delivery selection
TPSDLS	Shipping planning system: Transfer delivery

Message Type	Description
TPSDST	Status change notification for sales document
TPSLOC	Shipping planning system: Transfer location master data
TPSSHT	Shipping planning system: Transfer planned shipments
TXTRAW	Message for free text in SAPoffice format "RAW"
UNIMA2	Material-specific units of measurement
UNIT2	Units in KK2
UNIT3	Units in KK3
UNIT4	Units in KK4
UPLOAD	Configuration transceiver for upload
VTAMAS	Structure of variant table
VTMMAS	Contents of variant table
WBBDLD	Order book: Product message
WMBBIN	Set Blocking Indicator for Storage Bins
WMCATO	Reversal/Reversal request for transfer order
WMINFO	Information
WMINVE	Inventory count input
WMMBXY	IDOC Report goods movements in IM
WMRREF	Release reference number
WMSUMO	Move storage unit
WMTOCO	Confirm transfer order
WMTORD	Transport request
WMTREQ	Create/Cancel transfer order
WORKC2	Workcenters in KK2
WORKC3	Workcenters in KK3
WORKC4	Workcenters in KK4
WPDCUR	POS interface: Download exchange rates
WPDNAC	POS interface: Download products
WPDSET	POS interface: Download set assignments
WPDTAX	POS interface: Download tax rates
WPDWGR	POS interface: Download material group master
WPUBON	POS interface: Upload sales documents (compressed)

Message Type	Description
WPUERR	POS interface: Upload messages FWWS/POS/SCS
WPUFIB	POS interface: Upload Fin.Acc. interface FWWS/POS
WPUPAE	POS interface: Upload price changes
WPUTAB	POS interface: Upload day-end closing POS
WPUUMS	POS interface: Upload sales data (compressed)
WPUWBW	POS interface: Upload goods movements
WP_EAN	POS interface: Upload/Download EAN assignments
WP_PER	POS interface: Upload/Download person data
WP_PLU	POS interface: Upload/Download article master

Message Types and Assignment to IDOC Types

Table	EDIMSG
Description	EDI: Message Types and Assignment to IDOC Types
Number of entries	241

Message Type	BasIDOC Type	Release
ABSEN1	ABSEN1	30A
ACCONF	ACCONF01	31G
ACLPAY	ACLPAY01	31G
ACLREC	ACLREC01	31G
ACPJMM	ACPJOU01	31G
ACTIV3	ACTIV3	30A
ACTIV4	ACTIV4	30A
ALEAUD	ALEAUD01	30C
ALEREQ	ALEREQ01	30A
BATCH5	BATCH5	30B
BLAOCH	BLAORD01	30B

Message Type	BasIDOC Type	Release
BLAOCH	BLAORD02	30D
BLAORD	BLAORD01	30B
BLAORD	BLAORD02	30D
BLAREL	BLAREL01	30A
BOMDOC	BOMDOC01	31G
BOMMAT	BOMMAT01	31G
CHRMAS	CHRMAS01	30B
CHRMAS	CHRMAS02	31G
CLFMAS	CLFMAS01	30B
CLSMAS	CLSMAS01	30B
CLSMAS	CLSMAS02	31G
CMREQU	CMREQU01	30A
CMSEND	CMSEND01	30A
CNPMAS	CNPMAS01	31G
COACOR	COACOR01	30A
COACTV	COACTV01	30A
COAFET	ALEREQ01	30A
COAMAS	COAMAS01	30A
COCOKA	COCOKA01	30A
CODCMT	CODCMT01	30A
COELEM	COELEM01	30A
COGRP1	COGRP01	31G
COGRP2	COGRP01	31G
COGRP5	COGRP01	31G
COGRP6	COGRP01	31G
COGRP9	COGRP01	31G
CONDAT	CONDAT01	30A
CONDBI	COND_A01	30B
COND_A	COND_A01	30B
CONF11	CONF11	30A
CONF21	CONF21	30A

Message Type	BasIDOC Type	Release
CONF31	CONF31	30A
CONF32	CONF32	30A
CONF41	CONF41	30A
CONF42	CONF42	30A
CONF51	CONF51	30A
CONFIG	DWLOAD	30A
CONFIG	UPLOAD	30A
COPAGN	COPAGN01	30A
COPCPA	COPCPA01	30A
COSCOR	COSCOR01	30A
COSFET	ALEREQ01	30A
COSMAS	COSMAS01	30A
COTOTL	COTOTL01	31G
CPS001	COPAGN01	30A
CREADV	PEXR2001	30A
CRECOR	CRECOR01	30A
CREFET	ALEREQ01	30A
CREMAS	CREMAS01	30A
DEBADV	PEXR2001	30A
DEBCOR	DEBCOR01	30A
DEBFET	ALEREQ01	30A
DEBMAS	DEBMAS01	30A
DEBMAS	DEBMAS02	31G
DEBMAS	DEBMAS02	31H
DEBMAS	DEBMAS02	31H
DELINS	DELFOR01	30A
DESADT	DESADV01	30A
DESADV	DESADV01	30A
DESADV	DESADV01	31H
DESADV	DESADV01	31H
DESADV	DES_ID01	22A

Message Type	BasIDOC Type	Release
DIFFE2	DIFFE2	30A
DIFFE3	DIFFE3	30A
DIFFE4	DIFFE4	30A
DIRDEB	PEXR2001	30D
DISTU2	DISTU2	30A
DOCMAS	DOCMAS01	30C
DOCMAS	DOCMAS02	31G
DWLOAD	DWLOAD	30A
EDLNOT	DESADV01	30A
EKSEKS	EKSEKS01	30A
EUPEXR	IDCREF01	30D
EXPINV	EXPINV01	30A
EXTWA1	EXTWA1	30A
FIDCCH	FIDCCH01	30A
FIDCMT	FIDCMT01	30A
FIROLL	FIDCMT01	30A
GLCORE	GLCORE01	30A
GLFETC	ALEREQ01	30A
GLM000	GLMAST01	30A
GLMAST	GLMAST01	30A
GLROLL	GLDCMT01	30A
GSVERF	GSVERF01	30A
HRCPRQ	SYNCHRON	31G
HRINW	HRPLL40	31G
HRMD_A	HRMD_A01	31G
HRMD_B	HRMD_B01	31G
HRPAYP	HRPAYP01	31G
HRPRS	HRPLL40	31G
HRTRVL	HRTRVL01	31G
INFREC	INFREC01	31G
INVCON	INVCON01	30A

Message Type	BasIDOC Type	Release
INVOIC	INVOIC01	30A
INVOIC	INVOIC01	31H
INVOIC	INV_ID01	21A
KNOMAS	KNOMAS01	31G
LCROLL	GLDCMT01	30A
LIP032	SOPGEN01	30B
LIP035	SOPGEN01	30B
LIP039	SOPGEN01	30A
LIP125	SOPGEN01	30A
LIS000	LIS_EXTR	30D
LOCAT5	LOCAT5	30A
LOIBOM	LOIBOM01	31G
LOICAL	LOICAL01	31G
LOINUM	LOINUM01	31G
LOIPLO	LOIPLO01	31G
LOIPRO	LOIPRO01	31G
LOIRNH	LOIRNH01	31G
LOIROU	LOIROU01	31G
LOIRSH	LOIRSH01	31G
LOISTD	LOISTD01	31G
LOIWCS	LOIWCS01	31G
MALFK5	MALFK5	30A
MATCOR	MATCOR01	30A
MATFET	ALEREQ01	30A
MATMAS	MATMAS01	30A
MATMAS	MATMAS02	30D
MATMAS	MATMAS02	31H
OPERA2	OPERA2	30A
OPERA3	OPERA3	30A
OPERA4	OPERA4	30A
OPERS3	OPERS3	30A

Message Type	BasIDOC Type	Release
OPERS4	OPERS4	30A
ORDCHG	ORDERS01	30A
ORDCHG	ORDERS02	30E
ORDCHG	ORD_ID01	21A
ORDERS	ORDERS01	30A
ORDERS	ORDERS01	31H
ORDERS	ORDERS02	30D
ORDERS	ORD_ID01	21A
ORDRSP	ORDERS01	30A
ORDRSP	ORDERS01	31H
ORDRSP	ORDERS02	30E
ORDRSP	ORD_ID01	21A
OSTAT2	OSTAT2	30A
PAYEXT	PEXR2001	30D
PCROLL	GLDCMT01	31G
PEROP2	PEROP2	30F
PERSO1	PERSO1	30A
PERSO2	PERSO2	30A
PERSO3	PERSO3	30A
PERSO4	PERSO4	30A
PICKSD	SDPIOD01	30A
PI_BTC	BTC_ID01	30A
PI_BTC	BTC_ID02	30A
PI_BTC	BTC_ID03	30A
PKHD5	PKHD5	30A
PKPS5	PKPS5	30A
PKST5	PKST5	30A
PLANT3	PLANT3	30A
PLANT4	PLANT4	30A
PRCFET	ALEREQ01	31G
PRCMAS	PRCMAS01	31G

Message Type	BasIDOC Type	Release
PRODPL	SYNCHRON	30B
QUOTES	ORD_ID01	21A
RCLROL	GLDCMT01	30A
RECSHP	ORDERS02	31G
REMADV	PEXR2001	30A
REQOTE	ORDERS02	30E
REQOTE	ORD_ID01	21A
REQUI1	REQUI1	30A
REQUI2	REQUI2	30A
REQUI3	REQUI3	30A
REQUI4	REQUI4	30A
REQUI5	REQUI5	30A
SDPACK	SDPAID01	30A
SDPICK	SDPIID01	30A
SHIPPL	TPSSHT01	31G
SHPMNT	SHPMNT01	31G
SISCSO	SISCSO01	30A
SISDEL	SISDEL01	30A
SISINV	SISINV01	30A
SMMMAN	MATMAS02	30D
SOPGEN	SOPGEN01	30A
SRCLST	SRCLST01	31G
SRVMAS	SRVMAS01	31G
STATUS	SYSTAT01	31G
SYIDOC	SYIDOC01	31A
SYNCH	SYNCHRON	30B
SYRECD	SYRECD01	31A
TEST01	MATMAS01	30A
TEST01	MATMAS02	30D
TPSDLR	TPSDLR01	31G
TPSDLS	TPSDLS01	31G

Message Type	BasIDOC Type	Release
TPSLOC	TPSLOC01	31G
TPSSHT	TPSSHT01	31G
TXTRAW	TXTRAW01	30A
UNIMA2	UNIMA2	30C
UNIT2	UNIT2	30A
UNIT3	UNIT3	30A
UNIT4	UNIT4	30A
UPLOAD	UPLOAD	30A
VTAMAS	VTAMAS01	31G
VTMMAS	VTMMAS01	31G
WBBDLD	WBB_ID01	30A
WMBBIN	WMBIID01	30A
WMCATO	WMCAID01	30A
WMINFO	WMINID01	30A
WMINVE	WMIVID01	30A
WMMBXY	WMMBID01	30A
WMRREF	WMRRID01	30A
WMSUMO	WMSUID01	30A
WMTOCO	WMTCID01	30A
WMTORD	WMTOID01	30A
WMTREQ	WMTRID01	30A
WORKC2	WORKC2	30A
WORKC3	WORKC3	30A
WORKC4	WORKC4	30A
WPDCUR	WPDCUR01	30A
WPDNAC	WPDNAC01	30A
WPDSET	WPDSET01	30A
WPDTAX	WPDTAX01	30A
WPDWGR	WPDWGR01	30A
WPUBON	WPUBON01	30A
WPUERR	WPUERR01	30A

Message Type	BasIDOC Type	Release
WPUFIB	WPUFIB01	30A
WPUPAE	WPUPAE01	30A
WPUTAB	WPUTAB01	30A
WPUUMS	WPUUMS01	30A
WPUWBW	WPUWBW01	30A
WP_EAN	WP_EAN01	30A
WP_PER	WP_PER01	30A
WP_PLU	WP_PLU01	30A

APPENDIX C

STATUS CODES

Following is a list of status codes with descriptions.

Direction: 1 = Outbound, 2 = Inbound

Processing Level: A = SAP™ Application

I = IDOC Interface

S = External system/EDI Subsystem

IDOC Status	Direction	Processing Level	Description
00	1	I	Not used, only R/2™
01	1	I	IDOC created
02	1	I	Error passing data to port
03	1	I	Data passed to port OK
04	1	S	Error within control information of EDI subsystem
05	1	S	Error during translation
06	1	S	Translation OK
07	1	S	Error during syntax check
08	1	S	Syntax check OK
09	1	S	Error during interchange handling
10	1	S	Interchange handling OK
11	1	S	Error during dispatch
12	1	S	Dispatch OK
13	1	S	Retransmission OK
14	1	S	Interchange Acknowledgment positive
15	1	S	Interchange Acknowledgment negative
16	1	S	Functional Acknowledgment positive

Data contained in this appendix has been obtained from SAP™ Systems' tables of values.

IDOC Status	Direction	Processing Level	Description
17	1	S	Functional Acknowledgment negative
18	1	I	Triggering EDI subsystem OK
19	1	I	Data transfer for test OK
20	1	I	Error triggering EDI subsystem
21	1	I	Error passing data for test
22	1	S	Dispatch OK, acknowledgment still due
23	1	S	Error during retransmission
24	1	S	Control information of EDI subsystem OK
25	1	I	Processing despite syntax error (outbound)
26	1	I	Error during syntax check of IDOC (outbound)
27	1	I	Error in dispatch level (ALE service)
28	1	I	Not used
29	1	I	Error in ALE service
30	1	I	IDOC ready for dispatch (ALE service)
31	1	I	Error—no further processing
32	1	I	IDOC was edited
33	1	I	Original of an IDOC which was edited
34	1	I	Error in control record of IDOC
35	1	I	IDOC reloaded from archive
36	1	S	Electronic signature not performed (timeout)
37	1	I	IDOC added incorrectly
38	1	I	IDOC archived
39	1	I	Receipt confirmed by target system
40	1	I	Application document not created in target system
41	1	I	Application document created in target system
50	2	I	IDOC added
51	2	A	Error: Application document not posted
52	2	A	Application document not fully posted
53	2	A	Application document posted
54	2	A	Error during formal application check

IDOC Status	Direction	Processing Level	Description
55	2	A	Formal application check OK
56	2	I	IDOC with errors added
57	2	A	Test IDOC: Error during application check
58	2	I	Not used
59	2	I	Not used
60	2	I	Error during syntax check of IDOC (inbound)
61	2	I	Processing despite syntax error (inbound)
62	2	I	IDOC passed to application
63	2	I	Error passing IDOC to application
64	2	I	IDoc ready to be passed to application
65	2	I	Error in ALE service
66	2	I	Not used
67	2	I	Not used
68	2	I	Error—no further processing
69	2	I	IDOC was edited
70	2	I	Original of an IDOC which was edited
71	2	I	IDOC reloaded from archive
72	2	I	Not used, only R/2
73	2	I	IDOC archived

APPENDIX D

AUTHORIZATION (SECURITY) OBJECTS FOR ALE AND EDI

Following is a list of some of the authorization objects used for carrying out ALE and EDI development. Contact your Basis Administrator to set up your user-ID for ALE and EDI functions.

Object   ALE/EDI: Maintaining logical systems

Authorization   B_ALE_LS_ALL

Field values

Logical system

   *

Object   ALE/EDI: Distributing master data

Authorization   B_ALE_MA_ALL

Field values

Logical message type

   *

Object   ALE/EDI: Maintaining Customer Distribution Model

Authorization   B_ALE_MO_ALL

Field values

Activity

   *

Customer Distribution Model

   *

Data contained in this appendix has been obtained from SAP™ Systems' tables of values.

251

Object   ALE/EDI: Receiving IDOCs via RFC
Authorization   B_ALE_RC_ALL

Field values

Logical message type

   *

Object   ALE/EDI: Generating messages (e.g., reduction)
Authorization   B_ALE_RE_ALL

Field values

Logical message type

   *

Reference message type

   *

Object   WFEDI: S_IDOCCTRL—General access to IDOC Functions
Authorization   S_IDCCTR_DIC

Field values

Activity

   03

Transaction code

   WE40-WE47

Authorization   S_IDCCTR_IMO

Field values

Activity

   16

Transaction code

   WE12

Authorization   S_IDCCTR_IOI

Field values
Activity
16
Transaction code
WE16

Authorization	S_IDCCTR_MPC

Field values
Activity
02-03
Transaction code
WE40-WE42

Authorization	S_IDCCTR_OID

Field values
Activity
16
Transaction code
WE14

Authorization	S_IDCCTR_ONA

Field values
Activity
16
Transaction code
WE15

Authorization	S_IDCCTR_SHW

Field values
Activity
03

Transaction code

    WE05, WE07, WE55

Authorization   S_IDOC_SHOW

Field values

Activity

    03

Transaction code

    WE05, WE07-WE08, WE40-WE47

Object   WFEDI: S_IDOCDEFT—Access to IDOC Development
Authorization   S_IDCDFT_ALL

Field values

Activity

    *

Name of extension type

    *

IDOC type

    *

Transaction code

    *

Authorization   S_IDOC_SHOW

Field values

Activity

    03

Name of extension type

    *

IDOC type

    *

Transaction code

    WE30-WE33, WE60-WE63

Object   WFEDI: S_IDOCMONI—Access to IDOC Monitoring

Authorization   S_IDCMON_ALL

Field values

Activity

   *

Direction

   *

Logical message type

   *

Partner number

   *

Partner type

   *

Transaction code

   *

Authorization   S_IDOC_SHOW

Field values

Activity

   03

Direction

   *

Logical message type

   *

Partner number

   *

Partner type

   *

Transaction code

   WE02

Object   WFEDI: S_IDOCPART—Access to partner profile (IDOC)

Authorization   S_IDCPRN_ALL

Field values

Activity

*

Partner number

*

Partner type

*

Transaction code

*

Authorization   S_IDOC_SHOW

Field values

Activity

03

Partner number

*

Partner type

*

Transaction code

WE20

Object   WFEDI: S_IDOCPORT—Access to port description (IDOC)

Authorization   S_IDCPOR_ALL

Field values

Activity

*

Port type

*

Transaction code

*

Authorization   S_IDCPOR_DIS

Field values
Activity
03
Port type
*
Transaction code
WE21

Authorization   S_IDOC_SHOW

Field values
Activity
03
Port type
*
Transaction code
WE21

Object   WFEDI: S_IDOCCTRL—General access to IDOC Functions

Field values
Activity
01, 02, 03, 16
Transaction code
WE18, WE19, WE46, WE47, WE56, WE57

Object   Batch Processing: Batch Administrator
Authorization   S_BTCH_ADM

Field values
Batch administrator ID
Y

Object   WFEDI: S_IDOCCTRL—General access to IDOC Functions
Authorization   WFEDI_IDOC–IDOC Archiving

Field values
Activity
24
Transaction code
*

APPENDIX E

CONTROL, DATA, AND STATUS RECORDS

Control Record

Use: The table EDI_DC comprises the control records of the EDI Intermediate Documents. It contains control information on outgoing EDI Intermediate Documents and the processing of incoming EDI Intermediate Documents. Maintenance: The primary key of this table consists of the data elements MANDT and DOCNUM. The table EDI_DC can be maintained only through function modules.

Control Record Structure

- TABNAM: **Name of table structure**
  Internal data type: CHAR
  Internal length: 000010
  Position in structure: Offset: 0000. External length: 000010

- MANDT: **Client**
  Internal data type: CLNT
  Internal length: 000003
  Position in structure: Offset: 0010. External length: 000003

- DOCNUM: **IDoc number**
  Internal data type: CHAR
  Internal length: 000016
  Position in structure: Offset: 0013. External length: 000016

- DOCREL: **SAP™ Release of IDoc**
  Internal data type: CHAR
  Internal length: 000004
  Position in structure: Offset: 0029. External length: 000004

- STATUS: **Status of IDoc**
  Internal data type: CHAR

Data contained in this appendix has been obtained from SAP™ Systems' tables of values.

Internal length: 000002
Position in structure: Offset: 0033. External length: 000002

- DOCTYP: **IDoc type**
Internal data type: CHAR
Internal length: 000008
Position in structure: Offset: 0035. External length: 000008

- DIRECT: **Direction**
Internal data type: CHAR
Internal length: 000001
Position in structure: Offset: 0043. External length: 000001

- RCVPOR: **Receiver port (SAP™ System, EDI subsystem)**
Internal data type: CHAR
Internal length: 000010
Position in structure: Offset: 0044. External length: 000010

- RCVPRT: **Partner type of receiver**
Internal data type: CHAR
Internal length: 000002
Position in structure: Offset: 0054. External length: 000002

- RCVPRN: **Partner number of receiver**
Internal data type: CHAR
Internal length: 000010
Position in structure: Offset: 0056. External length: 000010

- RCVSAD: **EDI: SADR fields in total**
Internal data type: CHAR
Internal length: 000021
Position in structure: Offset: 0066. External length: 000021

- RCVLAD: **Logical address of receiver**
Internal data type: CHAR
Internal length: 000070
Position in structure: Offset: 0087. External length: 000070

- STD: **EDI standard**
Internal data type: CHAR
Internal length: 000001
Position in structure: Offset: 0157. External length: 000001

- STDVRS: **Version of EDI standard**
Internal data type: CHAR
Internal length: 000006
Position in structure: Offset: 0158. External length: 000006

- STDMES: **EDI message type**
Internal data type: CHAR

Internal length: 000006
Position in structure: Offset: 0164. External length: 000006

- MESCOD: **Logical message code**
Internal data type: CHAR
Internal length: 000003
Position in structure: Offset: 0170. External length: 000003

- MESFCT: **Logical message function**
Internal data type: CHAR
Internal length: 000003
Position in structure: Offset: 0173. External length: 000003

- OUTMOD: **Output mode**
Internal data type: CHAR
Internal length: 000001
Position in structure: Offset: 0176. External length: 000001

- TEST: **Test flag**
Internal data type: CHAR
Internal length: 000001
Position in structure: Offset: 0177. External length: 000001

- SNDPOR: **Sender port (SAP™ System, EDI subsystem)**
Internal data type: CHAR
Internal length: 000010
Position in structure: Offset: 0178. External length: 000010

- SNDPRT: **Partner type of sender**
Internal data type: CHAR
Internal length: 000002
Position in structure: Offset: 0188. External length: 000002

- SNDPRN: **Partner number of sender**
Internal data type: CHAR
Internal length: 000010
Position in structure: Offset: 0190. External length: 000010

- SNDSAD: **EDI: SADR fields in total**
Internal data type: CHAR
Internal length: 000021
Position in structure: Offset: 0200. External length: 000021

- SNDLAD: **Logical address of sender**
Internal data type: CHAR
Internal length: 000070
Position in structure: Offset: 0221. External length: 000070

- REFINT: **Reference to interchange file**
Internal data type: CHAR

Internal length: 000014
Position in structure: Offset: 0291. External length: 000014

- REFGRP: **Reference to message group**
  Internal data type: CHAR
  Internal length: 000014
  Position in structure: Offset: 0305. External length: 000014

- REFMES: **Reference to message**
  Internal data type: CHAR
  Internal length: 000014
  Position in structure: Offset: 0319. External length: 000014

- ARCKEY: **EDI archive key**
  Internal data type: CHAR
  Internal length: 000070
  Position in structure: Offset: 0333. External length: 000070

- CREDAT: **Date IDoc was created**
  Internal data type: DATS
  Internal length: 000008
  Position in structure: Offset: 0403. External length: 000008

- CRETIM: **Time IDoc was created**
  Internal data type: TIMS
  Internal length: 000006
  Position in structure: Offset: 0411. External length: 000006

- MESTYP: **Logical message type**
  Internal data type: CHAR
  Internal length: 000006
  Position in structure: Offset: 0417. External length: 000006

- IDOCTYP: **Name of basic IDoc type**
  Internal data type: CHAR
  Internal length: 000008
  Position in structure: Offset: 0423. External length: 000008

- CIMTYP: **Name of extension type**
  Internal data type: CHAR
  Internal length: 000008
  Position in structure: Offset: 0431. External length: 000008

- RCVPFC: **Partner function of receiver**
  Internal data type: CHAR
  Internal length: 000002
  Position in structure: Offset: 0439. External length: 000002

- SNDPFC: **Partner function of sender**
  Internal data type: CHAR

Internal length: 000002
Position in structure: Offset: 0441. External length: 000002

- SERIAL: **EDI/ALE: Serialization field**
Internal data type: CHAR
Internal length: 000020
Position in structure: Offset: 0443. External length: 000020

- EXPRSS: **Overriding in inbound processing**
Internal data type: CHAR
Internal length: 000001
Position in structure: Offset: 0463. External length: 000001

Control Record Documentation

- TABNAM: **Name of table structure**
General: This field contains the name of the underlying table structure. Assignments are made as follows: EDI_DC for the control record; Segment name for the data records (contents of field SEGNAM); EDI_DS for the status records.

- MANDT: **Client**
Definition: A legally and organizationally independent unit that uses the system.

- DOCNUM: **IDoc number**
General: This field identifies the IDoc. The number of the IDoc is client-dependent and is determined using the internal number assignment. Applications: No action required. IDoc interface: The interface determines the unique identification (internal number assignment) of the IDocs. EDI subsystem: Outbound IDocs: The subsystem must store the IDoc number and write it to this IDoc's status records which are to be transferred later. This IDoc number makes it possible for SAP™ to assign the status records to an IDoc. Inbound IDocs: This field is blank and is filled by interface.

- DOCREL: **SAP™ Release of IDoc**
General: Contains the SAP™ Release of the IDoc. Applications: No action required. IDoc interface: Outbound IDocs: The release provides information for the EDI subsystem. It defines from which SAP™ Release the EDI subsystem receives data. The field DOCREL is filled in the function module EDI_DOCUMENT_OPEN_FOR_ CREATE with the value of the field SY-SAPRL. Inbound IDocs: If the field was filled by the EDI subsystem, it is checked against the SAP™ field SY-SAPRL. If the

field is blank, it is filled with the contents of SY-SAPRL. EDI subsystem DOCREL is an optional field. It identifies the version level of the IDoc. Outbound IDocs: In the outbound processing of IDocs, DOCREL should support the EDI subsystem in determining the version level of the IDoc to be processed. Inbound IDocs: The EDI subsystem can fill DOCREL. If DOCREL is filled, its contents are checked against the SAP™ field SY-SAPRL and set to incorrect if the IDocs differ.

- STATUS: **Status of IDoc**
  General: This field contains the current status of the IDoc. These values are provided to monitor the processing and are required during the entire translation procedure for further processing. It is important that both the SAP™ application and the EDI subsystem provide this field with the appropriate values. The status values for outbound IDocs are between "01" and "49," while the status values for inbound IDocs begin with "50." Applications: Outbound IDocs: No action required. Inbound IDocs: During the processing of the IDoc, the status is set explicitly by the application programs via the function module EDI_DOCUMENT_STATUS_SET. IDoc interface: When an IDoc is created, the status is set in the function module EDI_DOCUMENT_CLOSE_CREATE. All other status changes are made explicitly via the function module EDI_DOCUMENT_STATUS_SET. EDI subsystem: Outbound IDocs: The EDI subsystem writes the status changes to a status file (record type EDI_DS), which is then read by the appropriate SAP™ program. The status values of the various processing stages are recorded in the value list. Inbound IDocs: No action required. Input values:

Outbox
00 IDoc interface (SAP™): Not used, only R/2™
01 IDoc interface (SAP™): IDoc created
02 IDoc interface (SAP™): Error passing data to port
03 IDoc interface (SAP™): Data passed to port OK
04 External system/EDI subsystem: Error within control information of EDI subsystem
05 External system/EDI subsystem: Error during translation
06 External system/EDI subsystem: Translation OK
07 External system/EDI subsystem: Error during syntax check
08 External system/EDI subsystem: Syntax check OK
09 External system/EDI subsystem: Error during interchange handling
10 External system/EDI subsystem: Interchange handling OK

11 External system/EDI subsystem: Error during dispatch

12 External system/EDI subsystem: Dispatch OK

13 External system/EDI subsystem: Retransmission OK

14 External system/EDI subsystem: Interchange Acknowledgment positive

15 External system/EDI subsystem: Interchange Acknowledgment negative

16 External system/EDI subsystem: Functional Acknowledgment positive

17 External system/EDI subsystem: Functional Acknowledgment negative

18 IDoc interface (SAP™): Triggering EDI subsystem OK

19 IDoc interface (SAP™): Data transfer for test OK

20 IDoc interface (SAP™): Error triggering EDI subsystem

21 IDoc interface (SAP™): Error passing data for test

22 External system/EDI subsystem: Dispatch OK, acknowledgment still due

23 External system/EDI subsystem: Error during retransmission

24 External system/EDI subsystem: Control information of EDI subsystem OK

25 IDoc interface (SAP™): Processing despite syntax error (outbound)

26 IDoc interface (SAP™): Error during syntax check of IDoc (outbound)

27 IDoc interface (SAP™): Error in dispatch level (ALE service)

28 IDoc interface (SAP™): Not used

29 IDoc interface (SAP™): Error in ALE service

30 IDoc interface (SAP™): IDoc ready for dispatch (ALE service)

31 IDoc interface (SAP™): Error—no further processing

32 IDoc interface (SAP™): IDoc was edited

33 IDoc interface (SAP™): Original of an IDoc that was edited

34 IDoc interface (SAP™): Error in control record of IDoc

35 IDoc interface (SAP™): IDoc reloaded from archive

36 External system/EDI subsystem: Electronic signature not performed (timeout)

37 IDoc interface (SAP™): IDoc added incorrectly

38 IDoc interface (SAP™): IDoc archived

39 IDoc interface (SAP™): Receipt confirmed by target system

40 IDoc interface (SAP™): Application document not created in target system

41 IDoc interface (SAP™): Application document created in target system

50 IDoc interface (SAP™): IDoc added

Inbox

51 SAP™ application: Error: Application document not posted
52 SAP™ application: Application document not fully posted
53 SAP™ application: Application document posted
54 SAP™ application: Error during formal application check
55 SAP™ application: Formal application check OK
56 IDoc interface (SAP™): IDoc with errors added
57 SAP™ application: Test IDoc: Error during application check
58 IDoc interface (SAP™): Not used
59 IDoc interface (SAP™): Not used
60 IDoc interface (SAP™): Error during syntax check of IDoc (inbound)
61 IDoc interface (SAP™): Processing despite syntax error (inbound)
62 IDoc interface (SAP™): IDoc passed to application
63 IDoc interface (SAP™): Error passing IDoc to application
64 IDoc interface (SAP™): IDoc ready to be passed to application
65 IDoc interface (SAP™): Error in ALE service
66 IDoc interface (SAP™): Not used
67 IDoc interface (SAP™): Not used
68 IDoc interface (SAP™): Error—no further processing
69 IDoc interface (SAP™): IDoc was edited
70 IDoc interface (SAP™): Original of an IDoc that was edited
71 IDoc interface (SAP™): IDoc reloaded from archive
72 IDoc interface (SAP™): Not used, only R/2™
73 IDoc interface (SAP™): IDoc archived

- DOCTYP: **IDoc type**
  General: The IDoc type is defined by the applications. They define the sequence of SAP™ segments. The field DOCTYP is linked uniquely with the field tuple IDOCTYP and CIMTYP. DOCTYP is a mandatory field. Applications: Outbound IDocs: The selection module of the application fills the field from the parameter PARTOUT (partner profile). Inbound IDocs: No action required. IDoc interface: It checks whether the specified IDoc type exists. EDI subsystem: Outbound IDocs: DOCTYP, together with DOCREL, uniquely defines the segment structure of the IDoc to be processed. Inbound IDocs: The EDI subsystem determines DOCTYP from the partner profile and fills the field. Input values.

- DIRECT: **Direction**
  General: The field defines the direction of the IDoc transmission. The field DIRECT is mandatory. Applications: Outbound IDocs: The field must be filled with the value "1." Inbound IDocs: No action required, DIRECT is assigned the value "2." IDoc interface:

The field is checked to ensure that it is filled according to the direction. EDI subsystem: Outbound IDocs: No action required, the value is "1." Inbound IDocs: The EDI subsystem fills the field with the value "2." Input values:

"1" Outbound
"2" Inbound

- RCVPOR: **Receiver port (SAP™ System, EDI subsystem)**
  General: This field defines which system receives the IDoc. RCVPOR is a mandatory field. The receiving system can be either an EDI subsystem or another SAP™ system (R/2™ from 5.0F, R/3™ from 2.1). Applications: Outbound IDocs: The application selection module receives the data via the parameter PARTOUT (partner profile). Inbound IDocs: No action required. IDoc interface: It checks whether the specified receiver port exists. EDI subsystem: Outbound IDocs: No action required. Inbound EDI IDocs: The receiving system is always an SAP™ System. The EDI subsystem must determine the system ID and write it to the field in the form SAP™ (e.g., SAPC11).

- RCVPRT: **Partner type of receiver**
  General: This field contains the partner type of the receiver, which defines the commercial relationship between the receiver and sender. The partner types possible are listed in table TEDST. RCVPRT is a mandatory field. RCVPRT and RCVPRN together uniquely identify the receiver. Applications: Outbound IDocs: The application selection module receives the data via the parameter PARTOUT (partner profile). Inbound IDocs: No action required. IDoc interface: It checks whether the field is filled and the value exists. EDI subsystem: Outbound IDocs: The field is part of the identification of the partner profile of the subsystem. Inbound IDocs: The EDI subsystem must fill the field RCVPRT from the information on the receiver ID in the interchange file. This includes, for example, the receiver address, routing address, and so forth. The SAP™ application is identified in this field by its abbreviation (e.g., MM, SD).

- RCVPRN: **Partner number of receiver**
  General: This field contains the partner number of the receiver. The partner number and partner type uniquely identify the receiver. The partner number can be alphanumeric and is a mandatory field. Applications: Outbound IDocs: The application selection module receives the data via the parameter PARTOUT (partner profile). Inbound IDocs: No action required. IDoc interface: It checks whether the field is filled and the specified partner

exists. EDI subsystem: Outbound IDocs: The field is part of the identification of the partner profile of the subsystem. Inbound IDocs: The EDI subsystem must determine the value of the field RCVPRN from the information on the receiver ID in the interchange file. This includes, for example, the receiver address, routing address, and so forth. The SAP™ application is identified in this field by its organizational structure (e.g., sales organization "0001").

- RCVSAD: **EDI: SADR fields in total**
  General: This field can contain a string that is used as a key in an internal SAP™ address directory. This field is not currently used in the R/2™ or R/3™ System in inbound or outbound processing. It is intended for future developments and should therefore be left empty.

- RCVLAD: **Logical address of receiver**
  General: The logical addresses must be defined between the EDI partners. They are used to route IDocs within the SAP™ application system. Applications: Outbound IDocs: If the target system is also an SAP™ System, the logical receiver address is used for routing in the target system. Inbound IDocs: The logical address is assigned to the internal organization via the EDI interface, table EDILOGADR. IDoc interface: No action required. EDI subsystem: Outbound IDocs: No action required. Inbound IDocs: The EDI subsystem determines the logical receiver address from the receiver information in the interchange file and fills the field. Example: In the case of the EDI standard EDIFACT, the logical address can be a combination of the receiver address in the header segment UNB and the routing address in the UNG segment. In the case of the EDI standard ANSI X12, the logical address can be derived from the segments ISA and GS.

- STD: **EDI standard**
  General: This field contains the identification code of the EDI standard. It is a mandatory field. Examples: E EDIFACT X ANSI X.12 Applications: Outbound IDocs: The application selection program receives the data via the parameter PARTOUT (partner profile). Inbound IDocs: No action required. IDoc interface: No action required. EDI subsystem: Outbound IDocs: Control information for the EDI subsystem. Inbound IDocs: For documentation purposes, the field must be filled with the code of the standard used.

- STDVRS: **Version of EDI standard**
  General: This field contains the version and release of the EDI message type in the standard directory. The representation is free,

the field is mandatory. Applications: Outbound IDocs: The application selection module receives the data via the parameter PARTOUT (partner profile). Inbound IDocs: No action required. IDoc interface: No action required. EDI subsystem: Outbound IDocs: Control information for the EDI subsystem. Inbound IDocs: For documentation purposes, the field must be filled with the version and release of the message type used.

- STDMES: **EDI message type**
  General: This field contains the EDI message type. It is a mandatory field. Example: EDIFACT INVOIC ANSI X.12 850. Applications: Outbound IDocs: The application selection program receives the data via the parameter PARTOUT (partner profile). Inbound IDocs: No action required. IDoc interface: No action required. EDI subsystem: Outbound IDocs: Control information for the EDI subsystem. Inbound IDocs: For documentation purposes, this field must be filled with the message type used.

- MESCOD: **Logical message code**
  General: This field is not subject to any standards. It contains a code which is derived from the message code of an EDI message. This field is optional. Applications: Outbound IDocs: The application selection module can fill MESCOD. Inbound IDocs: No action required. IDoc interface: Outbound IDocs: No action required. Inbound IDocs: The field is used to find the inbound partner profile. EDI subsystem: Outbound IDocs: Control information for the EDI subsystem. Inbound IDocs: The field must be filled to determine the partner profile in SAP™.

- MESFCT: **Logical message function**
  General: This field is not subject to any standards. It contains a code which is derived from the message function of an EDI message. It is optional. Applications: Outbound IDocs: The application selection program can fill MESFCT. Inbound IDocs: No action required. IDoc interface: Outbound IDocs: No action required. Inbound IDocs: The field is used to determine the partner profile for inbound processing. EDI subsystem: Outbound IDocs: Control information for the EDI subsystem. Inbound IDocs: This field must be filled to determine the partner profile in the SAP™ System.

- OUTMOD: **Output mode**
  General: This field defines the transfer mode for the IDoc from SAP™ to the EDI subsystem. The field must be filled for outbound IDocs, it must be blank for inbound IDocs. Applications: Outbound IDocs: The application selection module receives the data via the parameter PARTOUT (partner profile). The value can be over-

written so that it is possible to determine in which mode the IDocs are to be transferred. Inbound IDocs: No action required. IDoc interface: Outbound IDocs: The field OUTMOD is used to control the flow of the outbound data. Inbound IDocs: No action required. EDI subsystem: No action required. Input values:

"1" Transfer IDoc immediately and start EDI subsystem
"2" Transfer IDoc immediately
"3" Collect IDocs and start EDI subsystem when transferring
"4" Collect IDocs

- TEST: **Test flag**
General: This field contains a flag indicating whether the EDI message corresponding to the Intermediate Document is a test message. Applications: Outbound Intermediate Documents: The application selection module receives the data via the parameter PARTOUT (partner profile). Inbound Intermediate Documents: The application posting module must check whether an Intermediate Document contains the test flag. If it does, a "productive" posting must not be carried out. IDoc interface: Outbound Intermediate Documents: No action required. Inbound Intermediate Documents: The field is used to find the inbound partner profile. EDI subsystem: Outbound Intermediate Documents: The EDI subsystem must make sure that the EDI message generated is flagged as a test or productive message depending on the field. Inbound Intermediate Documents: The EDI subsystem must identify test messages by an "x" in the field. The field must be filled to determine the partner profile in the SAP™ System. Input values:

"   IDoc contains a productive message
"X" IDoc contains a test message

- SNDPOR: **Sender port (SAP™ System, EDI subsystem)**
General: This field defines which system has sent the IDoc. SNDPOR is a mandatory field. The sending system can be an EDI subsystem or another SAP™ System (R/2™ from 5.0F, R/3™ from 2.1). Applications: No action required. IDoc interface: Outbound IDocs: The sending system is always an SAP™ System. The EDI interface must determine the system ID and write it to the field in the form SAP™ (e.g., SAPC11). Inbound IDocs: It checks whether the specified sender port exists. EDI subsystem: Outbound IDocs: No action required. Inbound IDocs: The specified ID of the sending system must be written to the field SNDPOR.

- SNDPRT: **Partner type of sender**
General: This field contains the partner type of the sender, which defines the commercial relationship between the sender and

receiver. The partner types possible can be found in table TEDST. SNDPRT is a mandatory field. SNDPRT and SNDPRN identify the sender uniquely. Applications: Outbound IDocs: The application is identified in this field by its application code (e.g., MM, SD, etc.). Inbound IDocs: The field contains the partner type of the business partner. IDoc interface: It checks whether the field is filled and the value exists. EDI subsystem: Outbound IDocs: The field is part of the ID of the partner profile of the subsystem. Inbound IDocs: The EDI subsystem must fill the field SNDPRT. It uses the information on the sender ID in the interchange file. This includes, for example, the sender address, the routing address, and so forth. The field must be filled to determine the partner profile in the SAP™ System.

- SNDPRN: **Partner number of sender**
General: The field contains the partner number of the sender. The partner number and the partner type uniquely identify the sender. The partner number can be alphanumeric and is a mandatory field. Applications: Outbound IDocs: The application is identified in this field by its organizational structure (e.g., sales organization "0001"). Inbound IDocs: The field contains the partner number of the business partner. IDoc interface: Outbound IDocs: No action required. Inbound IDocs: The field is used to determine the partner profile. EDI subsystem: Outbound IDocs: The field is part of the identification of the partner profile of the subsystem. Inbound IDocs: The EDI subsystem must fill the field SNDPRN from the information on the sender ID in the interchange file. This includes, for example, the sender address, routing address, and so forth. The field must be filled to determine the partner profile in the SAP™ System.

- SNDSAD: **EDI: SADR fields in total**
General: This field can contain a string which is used as a key in an internal SAP™ address directory. This field is not currently used in the R/2™ or R/3™ System in inbound or outbound processing. It is intended for future developments and should therefore be left empty.

- SNDLAD: **Logical address of sender**
General: The logical addresses must be defined between the EDI partners. They are used to forward IDocs within the SAP™ application system. Applications: Outbound IDocs: No action required. Inbound IDocs: The logical sender address can be used for acknowledgment messages between SAP™ Systems. The logical address is assigned to the internal organization via the EDI interface, table EDILOGADR. IDoc interface: No action required. EDI subsystem:

Outbound IDocs: No action required. Inbound IDocs: The EDI subsystem determines the logical address from the sender information in the interchange file and fills the field. Example: For the EDI standard EDIFACT, the logical address can be a combination of the sender address in the header segment UNB and the routing address in the UNG segment. In the case of the EDI standard ANSI X.12, the logical address can be derived from the segments ISA and GS.

- REFINT: **Reference to interchange file**
  General: This field contains the reference number of the interchange file in which the EDI message was transmitted. Applications: No action required. IDoc interface: Outbound IDocs: The reference number in the control record is updated when the respective status record has been received. References which may have been saved beforehand are overwritten with the last value. Inbound IDocs: No action required. EDI subsystem: Outbound IDocs: The reference number is blank. It is passed to the SAP™ System via the status records of the IDoc. Inbound IDocs: The field must be filled with the reference number of the relevant interchange file.

- REFGRP: **Reference to message group**
  General: This field contains the reference number of the message group in which the EDI message was transmitted. This field should only be filled if message groups are used. Applications: No action required. IDoc interface: Outbound IDocs: The reference number in the control record is updated when the respective status record has been received. References that may have been saved beforehand are overwritten with the last value. Inbound IDocs: No action required. EDI subsystem: Outbound IDocs: The reference number is blank. It is passed to the SAP™ System via the status records of the IDoc. Inbound IDocs: The field must be filled with the reference number of the relevant message group. If a message group is not used, it remains blank.

- REFMES: **Reference to message**
  General: This field contains the reference number of the EDI message. Applications: No action required. IDoc interface: Outbound IDocs: The reference number in the control record is updated when the respective status record has been received. References that may have been saved beforehand are overwritten with the last value. Inbound IDocs: No action required. EDI subsystem: Outbound IDocs: The reference number is blank. It is passed to the SAP™ System via the status records of the IDoc. Inbound IDoc type: The field must be filled with the reference number of the EDI message.

- ARCKEY: **EDI archive key**
  General: This field contains the unique object key of the EDI subsystem for the archive in which the EDI messages are stored in original format. Applications: No action required. IDoc interface: Outbound IDocs: The archive reference in the control record is updated when the respective status record has been received. References that may have been saved beforehand are overwritten with the last value. Inbound IDocs: No action required. EDI subsystem: Outbound IDocs: The archive reference is blank. It is passed to the SAP™ System via the status records of the IDoc. Inbound IDocs: The field must be filled with the archive reference of the EDI subsystem.

- CREDAT: **Date IDoc was created**
  General: Date on which the IDoc was created. Applications: No action required. IDoc interface: The EDI interface ensures that the creation date is set. EDI subsystem: No action required.

- CRETIM: **Time IDoc was created**
  General: Time at which the IDoc was created. Applications: No action required. IDoc interface: The EDI interface ensures that the creation time is set. EDI subsystem: No action required.

- MESTYP: **Logical message type**
  General: This field contains the logical name of a message. It is not subject to any standards. Logical messages are assigned to individual IDoc types by SAP™. Example: the logical message ORDERS identifies purchase orders (outbound) and sales orders (inbound). Applications: Outbound IDocs: The selection module of the application must fill MESTYP. Inbound IDocs: No action required. IDoc interface: Outbound IDocs: If the field is not filled, it is assigned the value of the field STDMES. Inbound IDocs: The field is used to determine the inbound partner profile. If the field is not filled, it is assigned the value of the field STDMES. EDI subsystem: Outbound IDocs: Control information for the EDI subsystem. Inbound IDocs: The field must be filled in order to be able to determine the partner profile in SAP™. If the field is not assigned a value (e.g., control record length—release 2.1), the value of the field STDMES is used. Input values.

- IDOCTYP: **Name of basic IDoc type**
  General: The IDoc type is defined by the applications. They define the sequence of SAP™ segments. The IDoc types delivered by SAP™ in the standard version, as well as those created by the customer, are identified via the field IDOCTYP. The contents of the field DOCTYP are then the same as those of the field IDOCTYP. Applications: Outbound IDocs: The selection module of the applica-

tion fills the field from the parameter PARTOUT (partner profile). Inbound IDocs: No action required. IDoc interface: Checks whether the specified IDoc type exists. EDI subsystem: No action required.

- CIMTYP: **Name of extension type**
General: The IDoc type is defined by the applications. They define the sequence of SAP™ segments. If IDoc types from the SAP™ standard version are extended by the customer, these extensions are identified via the field CIMTYP. The contents of the field DOC-TYP are then different from those of the field IDOCTYP. The contents of the fields IDOCTYP and CIMTYP are assigned uniquely to the contents of the field DOCTYP. Applications: Outbound IDocs: The selection module of the application fills the field from the parameter PARTOUT (partner profile). Inbound IDocs: No action required. IDoc interface: Checks whether the specified IDoc type exists. EDI subsystem: No action required.

- RCVPFC: **Partner function of receiver**
General: This field contains the partner function of the receiver, which defines the function of the receiver for the sender. Applications: Outbound IDocs: The selection module of the application receives the data via the parameter PARTOUT (partner profile). Inbound IDocs: No action required. IDoc interface: No action required. EDI subsystem: Outbound IDocs: The field is part of the identification of the partner profile of the subsystem. Inbound IDocs: The EDI subsystem can fill the field RCVPFC. To do this, the information on the receiver ID in the interchange file is used. This includes, for example, receiver address, routing address, and so forth. Input values.

- SNDPFC: **Partner function of sender**
General: This field contains the partner function of the sender, which defines the function of the sender for the receiver. Applications: Outbound IDocs: No action required. Inbound IDocs: The field contains the partner function of the business partner. IDoc interface: Outbound IDocs: No action required. Inbound IDocs: The field is used to determine the partner profile. EDI subsystem: Outbound IDocs: The field is part of the identification of the partner profile of the subsystem. Inbound IDocs: The EDI subsystem must fill the field SNDPFC. To do this, the information on the sender ID in the interchange file is used. This includes, for example, the sender address, routing address, and so forth. The field must be filled in order to be able to determine the partner profile in SAP™. Input values.

- SERIAL: **EDI/ALE: Serialization field**
General: Used for serialization purposes by the ALE level. The

information here allows the IDoc types to be placed in the correct order in the target system if this order was changed during transmission. Applications: No action required. IDoc interface: No action required. EDI subsystem: No action required.

■ EXPRSS: **Overriding in inbound processing**
General: This field determines for ALE whether a time schedule is to be deactivated for inbound processing and replaced by immediate processing. Applications: No action required. IDoc interface: No action required. EDI subsystem: No action required. Input values:

" No overriding
"X" Overriding

Data Record

Use: The data record has the structure EDI_DD. Each Intermediate Document is formed by a control record, which is followed by several data records. The data record contains organizational information in the first few fields, which places the data records in a sequence and assigns them to an Intermediate Document, and structural information on the application data. The field SDATA contains the application data (up to 1000 bytes). It is interpreted via the segment field by field. The segment is specified in the fields TABNAM and SEGNAM. Maintenance: The data records can be accessed only via a function module API.

Data Record Structure

■ TABNAM: **Name of table structure**
Internal data type: CHAR
Internal length: 000010
Position in structure: Offset: 0000. External length: 000010

■ MANDT: **Client**
Internal data type: CLNT
Internal length: 000003
Position in structure: Offset: 0010. External length: 000003

■ DOCNUM: **IDoc number**
Internal data type: CHAR
Internal length: 000016
Position in structure: Offset: 0013. External length: 000016

■ SEGNUM: **Number of SAP™ segment**
Internal data type: CHAR
Internal length: 000006
Position in structure: Offset: 0029. External length: 000006

■ SEGNAM: **Name of SAP™ segment**
Internal data type: CHAR
Internal length: 000010
Position in structure: Offset: 0035. External length: 000010

■ PSGNUM: **Number of the higher-level SAP™ segment**
Internal data type: CHAR
Internal length: 000006
Position in structure: Offset: 0045. External length: 000006

■ HLEVEL: **Hierarchy level of SAP™ segment**
Internal data type: CHAR
Internal length: 000002
Position in structure: Offset: 0051. External length: 000002

■ DTINT2: **Blank field for EDI_DD**
Internal data type: CHAR
Internal length: 000002
Position in structure: Offset: 0053. External length: 000002

■ SDATA: **Application data**
Internal data type: LCHR
Internal length: 001000
Position in structure: Offset: 0055. External length: 001000

Data Record Documentation

■ TABNAM: **Name of table structure**
General: This field contains the name of the underlying table
structure. Assignments are made as follows: EDI_DC for the control record; Segment name for the data records (contents of field
SEGNAM); EDI_DS for the status records.

■ MANDT: **Client**
Definition: A legally and organizationally independent unit that
uses the system.

■ DOCNUM: **IDoc number**
General: This field identifies the IDoc. The number of the IDoc is
client-dependent and is determined using the internal number
assignment. Applications: No action required. IDoc interface: The

interface determines the unique identification (internal number assignment) of the IDocs. EDI subsystem: Outbound IDocs: The subsystem must store the IDoc number and write it to this IDoc's status records, which are to be transferred later. This IDoc number makes it possible for SAP™ to assign the status records to an IDoc. Inbound IDocs: This field is blank and is filled by interface.

- SEGNUM: **Number of SAP™ segment**
  General: This field contains the sequential number of an SAP™ segment within an IDoc. The numbering is carried out in increments of 1 starting at 1. Applications: No action required. IDoc interface: it checks whether the segment number is filled in increments of 1 (in ascending order) starting from 1. If a segment number does not exist, it is assigned by the EDI interface. EDI subsystem: Outbound IDocs: No action required. Inbound IDocs: The field must be filled in increments of 1 (in ascending order) starting from 1.

- SEGNAM: **Name of SAP™ segment**
  General: This field contains the ten-character SAP™ segment name. It is a mandatory field. Applications: Outbound IDocs: When an IDoc is created, the field must be filled with the segment type. Inbound IDocs: The field identifies the segment for the application data by the segment type. IDoc interface: The field is used for a formal check against the table EDISYN. Outbound IDocs: The SAP™-internal segment type is converted to the external segment name. The external segment name is converted to the SAP™-internal segment type. EDI subsystem: Outbound IDocs: The field is filled with the same contents as the field TABNAM of the same data record. It identifies the segment structure of the application data which is stored in the field SDATA. Inbound IDocs: The field must be filled with the same contents as the field TABNAM of the same data record.

- PSGNUM: **Number of the higher-level SAP™ segment**
  General: This field contains the sequential number of the parent segment to which the segment is hierarchically subordinate. Applications: Outbound IDocs: If the field is blank, the EDI interface determines a value for the field from the table EDISYN; otherwise the value is checked via the table EDISYN. Inbound IDocs: No action required. IDoc interface: The EDI interface determines a value for the field from the table EDISYN; otherwise the value is checked. EDI subsystem: Outbound IDocs: No action required. Inbound IDocs: The EDI interface determines a value for the field

if it is blank. If a value is passed by the EDI subsystem, this value is checked in the EDI interface.

■ HLEVEL: **Hierarchy level of SAP™ segment**
General: This field describes which hierarchy level the segment is assigned to. A segment can be used on only one hierarchy level per IDoc type. The hierarchy level can be calculated as follows: Segments that do not have a higher-level parent segment, whose maximum repetition is 1, and which do not start a segment group have the hierarchy level 1. Segments that do not have a higher-level parent segment but whose maximum repetition is greater than 1 or which start a segment group have the hierarchy level 2. Segments that have a higher-level parent segment have a hierarchy level that is 1 greater than that of the parent segment. The highest hierarchy level for a segment is 99. Applications: No action required. IDoc interface: The EDI interface determines a value for the field from table EDISYN if the field is blank; otherwise the value is checked. EDI subsystem: No action required.

■ DTINT2: **Blank field for EDI_DD**
General: This field is used internally by SAP™ Basis. It must not be filled or processed. Applications: No action required. IDoc interface: No action required. EDI subsystem: No action required.

■ SDATA: **Application data**
General: This field contains the application data of an SAP™ segment. It is a mandatory field. Applications: Outbound IDocs: The application selection module fills this field with the application data for an SAP™ segment. Inbound IDocs: The application update module receives the application data from an SAP™ segment in this field. IDoc interface: No action required. EDI subsystem: Outbound IDocs: The field SDATA contains the application data which are to be converted to an EDI message. An EDI message consists of several data records, each of which contains a field SDATA. Inbound IDocs: The EDI subsystem assigns an EDI message to several data records, each of which contains a field SDATA.

Status Record

Use: The status record has the structure EDI_DS. It contains all status information on an Intermediate Document. Maintenance: The status records can be accessed only via a function module API.

Status Record Structure

■ TABNAM: **Name of table structure**
Internal data type: CHAR
Internal length: 000010
Position in structure: Offset: 0000. External length: 000010

■ MANDT: **Client**
Internal data type: CLNT
Internal length: 000003
Position in structure: Offset: 0010. External length: 000003

■ DOCNUM: **IDoc number**
Internal data type: CHAR
Internal length: 000016
Position in structure: Offset: 0013. External length: 000016

■ LOGDAT: **Date of status information**
Internal data type: DATS
Internal length: 000008
Position in structure: Offset: 0029. External length: 000008

■ LOGTIM: **Time of status information**
Internal data type: TIMS
Internal length: 000006
Position in structure: Offset: 0037. External length: 000006

■ STATUS: **Status of IDoc**
Internal data type: CHAR
Internal length: 000002
Position in structure: Offset: 0043. External length: 000002

■ UNAME: **User name**
Internal data type: CHAR
Internal length: 000012
Position in structure: Offset: 0045. External length: 000012

■ REPID: **Program name**
Internal data type: CHAR
Internal length: 000008
Position in structure: Offset: 0057. External length: 000008

■ ROUTID: **Name of subroutine (routine, function module)**
Internal data type: CHAR
Internal length: 000030
Position in structure: Offset: 0065. External length: 000030

■ STACOD: **Status code**
Internal data type: CHAR

Internal length: 000008
Position in structure: Offset: 0095. External length: 000008

- STATXT: **Text for status code**
Internal data type: CHAR
Internal length: 000070
Position in structure: Offset: 0103. External length: 000070

- SEGNUM: **Number of SAP™ segment**
Internal data type: CHAR
Internal length: 000006
Position in structure: Offset: 0173. External length: 000006

- SEGFLD: **Field name in SAP™ segment**
Internal data type: CHAR
Internal length: 000010
Position in structure: Offset: 0179. External length: 000010

- STAPA1: **Parameter 1**
Internal data type: CHAR
Internal length: 000020
Position in structure: Offset: 0189. External length: 000020

- STAPA2: **Parameter 2**
Internal data type: CHAR
Internal length: 000020
Position in structure: Offset: 0209. External length: 000020

- STAPA3: **Parameter 3**
Internal data type: CHAR
Internal length: 000020
Position in structure: Offset: 0229. External length: 000020

- STAPA4: **Parameter 4**
Internal data type: CHAR
Internal length: 000020
Position in structure: Offset: 0249. External length: 000020

- REFINT: **Reference to interchange file**
Internal data type: CHAR
Internal length: 000014
Position in structure: Offset: 0269. External length: 000014

- REFGRP: **Reference to message group**
Internal data type: CHAR
Internal length: 000014
Position in structure: Offset: 0283. External length: 000014

- REFMES: **Reference to message**
Internal data type: CHAR

Internal length: 000014
Position in structure: Offset: 0297. External length: 000014

■ ARCKEY: **EDI archive key**
Internal data type: CHAR
Internal length: 000070
Position in structure: Offset: 0311. External length: 000070

■ STATYP: **EDI: Type of system error message (A, W, E, S, I)**
Internal data type: CHAR
Internal length: 000001
Position in structure: Offset: 0381. External length: 000001

Status Record Documentation

■ TABNAM: **Name of table structure**
General: This field contains the name of the underlying table structure. Assignments are made as follows: EDI_DC for the control record; Segment name for the data records (contents of field SEGNAM); EDI_DS for the status records.

■ MANDT: **Client**
Definition: A legally and organizationally independent unit that uses the system.

■ DOCNUM: **IDoc number**
General: This field identifies the IDoc. The number of the IDoc is client-dependent and is determined using the internal number assignment. Applications: No action required. IDoc interface: The interface determines the unique identification (internal number assignment) of the IDocs. EDI subsystem: Outbound IDocs: The subsystem must store the IDoc number and write it to this IDoc's status records, which are to be transferred later. This IDoc number makes it possible for SAP™ to assign the status records to an IDoc. Inbound IDocs: This field is blank and is filled by interface.

■ LOGDAT: **Date of status information**
General: This field contains the date on which a status change (success or error) occurred. It has the following format: YYYYMMDD. It is a mandatory field. Applications: Outbound IDocs: No action required. Inbound IDocs: The application must fill the field with SY-DATUM when a status record is added. IDoc interface: No action required. EDI subsystem: Outbound IDocs: The EDI subsystem fills the field with the system date of the status change. Inbound IDocs: No action required.

■ LOGTIM: **Time of status information**
General: This field contains the time at which a status change (success or error) occurred. It has the following format: HHMMSS. It is a mandatory field. Applications: Outbound IDocs: No action required. Inbound IDocs: The application must fill the field with SY-UZEIT when a status record is added. IDoc interface: No action required. EDI subsystem: Outbound IDocs: The EDI subsystem fills the field with the system time of the status change. Inbound IDocs: No action required.

■ STATUS: **Status of IDoc**
General: This field contains the current status of the IDoc. These values are provided to monitor the processing and are required during the entire translation procedure for further processing. It is important that both the SAP™ application and the EDI subsystem provide this field with the appropriate values. The status values for outbound IDocs are between "01" and "49," while the status values for inbound IDocs begin with "50." Applications: Outbound IDocs: No action requied. Inbound IDocs: During the processing of the IDoc, the status is set explicitly by the application programs via the function module EDI_DOCUMENT_STATUS_SET. IDoc interface: When an IDoc is created, the status is set in the function module EDI_DOCUMENT_CLOSE_CREATE. All other status changes are made explicitly via the function module EDI_ DOCUMENT_ STATUS_SET. EDI subsystem: Outbound IDocs: The EDI subsystem writes the status changes to a status file (record type EDI_DS), which is then read by the appropriate SAP™ program. The status values of the various processing stages are recorded in the value list. Inbound IDocs: No action required. Input values:

Outbox
00   IDoc interface (SAP™): Not used, only R/2™
01   IDoc interface (SAP™): IDoc created
02   IDoc interface (SAP™): Error passing data to port
03   IDoc interface (SAP™): Data passed to port OK
04   External system/EDI subsystem: Error within control information of EDI subsystem
05   External system/EDI subsystem: Error during translation
06   External system/EDI subsystem: Translation OK
07   External system/EDI subsystem: Error during syntax check
08   External system/EDI subsystem: Syntax check OK
09   External system/EDI subsystem: Error during interchange handling
10   External system/EDI subsystem: Interchange handling OK

11	External system/EDI subsystem: Error during dispatch
12	External system/EDI subsystem: Dispatch OK
13	External system/EDI subsystem: Retransmission OK
14	External system/EDI subsystem: Interchange Acknowledgment positive
15	External system/EDI subsystem: Interchange Acknowledgment negative
16	External system/EDI subsystem: Functional Acknowledgment positive
17	External system/EDI subsystem: Functional Acknowledgment negative
18	IDoc interface (SAP™): Triggering EDI subsystem OK
19	IDoc interface (SAP™): Data transfer for test OK
20	IDoc interface (SAP™): Error triggering EDI subsystem
21	IDoc interface (SAP™): Error passing data for test
22	External system/EDI subsystem: Dispatch OK, acknowledgment still due
23	External system/EDI subsystem: Error during retransmission
24	External system/EDI subsystem: Control information of EDI subsystem OK
25	IDoc interface (SAP™): Processing despite syntax error (outbound)
26	IDoc interface (SAP™): Error during syntax check of IDoc (outbound)
27	IDoc interface (SAP™): Error in dispatch level (ALE service)
28	IDoc interface (SAP™): Not used
29	IDoc interface (SAP™): Error in ALE service
30	IDoc interface (SAP™): IDoc ready for dispatch (ALE service)
31	IDoc interface (SAP™): Error—no further processing
32	IDoc interface (SAP™): IDoc was edited
33	IDoc interface (SAP™): Original of an IDoc which was edited
34	IDoc interface (SAP™): Error in control record of IDoc
35	IDoc interface (SAP™): IDoc reloaded from archive
36	External system/EDI subsystem: Electronic signature not performed (timeout)
37	IDoc interface (SAP™): IDoc added incorrectly
38	IDoc interface (SAP™): IDoc archived
39	IDoc interface (SAP™): Receipt confirmed by target system
40	IDoc interface (SAP™): Application document not created in target system
41	IDoc interface (SAP™): Application document created in target system
50	IDoc interface (SAP™): IDoc added

Inbox

51   SAP™ application: Error: Application document not posted
52   SAP™ application: Application document not fully posted
53   SAP™ application: Application document posted
54   SAP™ application: Error during formal application check
55   SAP™ application: Formal application check OK
56   IDoc interface (SAP™): IDoc with errors added
57   SAP™ application: Test IDoc: Error during application check
58   IDoc interface (SAP™): Not used
59   IDoc interface (SAP™): Not used
60   IDoc interface (SAP™): Error during syntax check of IDoc (inbound)
61   IDoc interface (SAP™): Processing despite syntax error (inbound)
62   IDoc interface (SAP™): IDoc passed to application
63   IDoc interface (SAP™): Error passing IDoc to application
64   IDoc interface (SAP™): IDoc ready to be passed to application
65   IDoc interface (SAP™): Error in ALE service
66   IDoc interface (SAP™): Not used
67   IDoc interface (SAP™): Not used
68   IDoc interface (SAP™): Error—no further processing
69   IDoc interface (SAP™): IDoc was edited
70   IDoc interface (SAP™): Original of an IDoc which was edited
71   IDoc interface (SAP™): IDoc reloaded from archive
72   IDoc interface (SAP™): Not used, only R/2™
73   IDoc interface (SAP™): IDoc archived

- UNAME: **User name**
  General: This field contains the name of the user active when the status information is provided. It is an optional field. Applications: If the field is blank, it is filled in the interface with SY-UNAME. IDoc interface: If the field is blank, it is filled with the field SY-UNAME. EDI subsystem: Outbound IDocs: The EDI subsystem can pass the name of a user in the field. Inbound IDocs: No action required.

- REPID: **Program name**
  General: This field contains the name of the program that caused the status change. It is an optional field. Applications: The field can be filled with the name of the program that caused the status change. IDoc interface: No action required. EDI subsystem: Outbound IDocs: The EDI subsystem can pass the name of a program in the field. Inbound IDocs: No action required.

- ROUTID: **Name of subroutine (routine, function module)**
  General: This field contains the name of the subroutine that

caused the status change. It is an optional field. Applications: The field can be filled with the name of the subroutine that caused the status change. IDoc interface: No action required. EDI subsystem: Outbound IDocs: The EDI subsystem can pass the name of a subroutine in the field. Inbound IDocs: No action required.

■ STACOD: **Status code**
General: This field contains a code that specifies the field STATUS more precisely. The code either refers to table T100 in the SAP™ System or to codes of the EDI subsystem. The field is intended to be used, in particular, to describe error situations, but can also be used for success messages. Applications: For errors in the SAP™ System, the status code must be set up as follows: Bytes 1–3: "SAP™"; Bytes 4–5: Message ID from T100; Bytes 6–8: Message number from T100. IDoc interface: For errors in the SAP™ System, the status code must be set up as follows: Bytes 1–3: "SAP™"; Bytes 4–5: Message ID from T100; Bytes 6–8: Message number from T100. EDI subsystem: Outbound IDocs: Codes of the EDI subsystem that describe a status change or an error more precisely can be passed. Even if the value of the field STATUS is not changed, several status records can be passed to the SAP™ System, which contain different codes or error messages for the IDoc. A subsystem-specific display of the status records within the SAP™ System can be controlled via table TEDE3 if a different prefix to "SAP™" is used for the first 3 bytes of the code. Inbound IDocs: No action required.

■ STATXT: **Text for status code**
General: This field contains the text on the field STACOD. It is either a text from table T100 in SAP™ or a text of the EDI subsystem. The text can contain up to four "&" symbols, which can later be replaced by the values in the fields STAPA1, STAPA2, STAPA3, and STAPA4. Applications: The text can be added to the message through the status record. The text can still contain the variable symbols. They are replaced by the values in the fields STAPA1 to STAPA4 when the message is displayed. IDoc interface: No action required. EDI subsystem: Outbound IDocs: A text of the EDI subsystem describing the field STACOD can be passed. Even if the value of the field STATUS is not changed, several status records can be passed to the SAP™ System, which contain different information or error messages for the IDoc. Inbound IDocs: No action required.

■ SEGNUM: **Number of SAP™ segment**
General: This field contains the sequential number of the SAP™ segment in which the error occurred. The field within the segment can be specified in the field SEGFLD. Applications: The application

update module writes the number of the segment, during the processing of which the error occurred, to the field. IDoc interface: No action required. EDI subsystem: Outbound IDocs: The EDI subsystem writes the number of the SAP™ segment, during the translation of which an error occurred, to the field. Inbound IDocs: No action required.

- SEGFLD: **Field name in SAP™ segment**
  General: This field contains the name of the field within a segment in which the error occurred. The segment itself is specified by its number in the field SEGNUM. Applications: The application update module writes the name of the field, during the processing of which the error occurred, to the field. IDoc interface: No action required. EDI subsystem: Outbound IDocs: The EDI subsystem writes the name of the field, during the translation of which the error occurred, to the field. Inbound IDocs: No action required.

- STAPA1: **Parameter 1**
  General: This field contains the value determined at runtime with which the first variable symbol is replaced in the field STATXT. Applications: If an error message containing "&" symbols is passed, the value for the variable symbol must be transferred in the correct position. IDoc interface: No action required. EDI subsystem: Outbound IDocs: The EDI subsystem can use the SAP™ concept. Inbound IDocs: No action required.

- STAPA2: **Parameter 2**
  General: This field contains the value determined at runtime with which the second variable symbol is replaced in the field STATXT. Applications: If an error message containing "&" symbols is passed, the value for the variable symbol must be transferred in the correct position. IDoc interface: No action required. EDI subsystem: Outbound IDocs: The EDI subsystem can use the SAP™ concept. Inbound IDocs: No action required.

- STAPA3: **Parameter 3**
  General: This field contains the value determined at runtime with which the third variable symbol is replaced in the field STATXT. Applications: If an error message containing "&" symbols is passed, the value for the variable symbol must be transferred in the correct position. IDoc interface: No action required. EDI subsystem: Outbound IDocs: The EDI subsystem can use the SAP™ concept. Inbound IDocs: No action required.

- STAPA4: **Parameter 4**
  General: This field contains the value determined at runtime with which the fourth variable symbol is replaced in the field STATXT.

Applications: If an error message containing "&" symbols is passed, the value for the variable symbol must be transferred in the correct position. IDoc interface: No action required. EDI subsystem: Outbound IDocs: The EDI subsystem can use the SAP™ concept. Inbound IDocs: No action required.

■ REFINT: **Reference to interchange file**
General: This field contains the reference number of the interchange file in which the EDI message was transmitted. Applications: No action required. IDoc interface: Outbound IDocs: The reference number in the control record is updated when the respective status record has been received. References that may have been saved beforehand are overwritten with the last value. Inbound IDocs: No action required. EDI subsystem: Outbound IDocs: The reference number is passed to the SAP™ System with one of the status records. Only the last reference number is stored with the IDoc. Inbound IDocs: No action required.

■ REFGRP: **Reference to message group**
General: This field contains the reference number of the message group in which the EDI message was transmitted. This field should be filled only if message groups are used. Applications: No action required. IDoc interface: Outbound IDocs: The reference number in the control record is updated when the respective status record has been received. References that may have been saved beforehand are overwritten with the last value. Inbound IDocs: No action required. EDI subsystem: Outbound IDocs: The reference number is passed to the SAP™ System with one of the status records. The last reference is always stored with the IDoc. Inbound IDocs: No action required.

■ REFMES: **Reference to message**
General: This field contains the reference number of the EDI message. Applications: No action required. IDoc interface: Outbound IDocs: The reference number in the control record is updated when the respective status record has been received. References that may have been saved beforehand are overwritten with the last value. Inbound IDocs: No action required. EDI subsystem: Outbound IDocs: The reference number is passed to the SAP™ System with one of the status records. The last reference number is always stored with the IDoc. Inbound IDocs: No action required.

■ ARCKEY: **EDI archive key**
General: This field contains the unique object key of the EDI subsystem for the archive in which the EDI messages are stored in their original format. Applications: No action required. IDoc inter-

face: Outbound IDocs: The archive number in the control record is updated when the respective status record has been received. Inbound IDocs: No action required. EDI subsystem: Outbound IDocs: The archive number of an outbound IDoc is passed to the SAP™ System via the status records. The last reference is always stored with the IDoc. Inbound IDocs: No action required.

■ STATYP: **EDI: Type of system error message (A, W, E, S, I)**
General: This field contains the type of status information: "A," termination message; "E," error message; "W," warning; "I," information; "S," success message. Applications: The field can be filled with the value from SY-MSGTY. IDoc interface: No action required. EDI subsystem: Outbound IDocs: The EDI subsystem can specify the status type in this field. Inbound IDocs: No action required. Values:

"A"   Abnormal termination (evening)
"W"   Warning
"E"   Error
"S"   Success message
"I"   Information

IDOC Type Structure of ALEAUD01

Acknowledgments About Processing Status of Inbound IDocs

- **E1ADHDR: Confirmed message type**
  Status: Mandatory
  Min. number: 1, max. number: 9999999999
  - **E1STATE: Processing information and application object for an IDoc**
    Status: Mandatory
    Min. number: 1, max. number: 99999
  - **E1PRTOB: IDoc number and application object in receiving system**
    Status: Optional
    Min. number: 1, max. number: 1

List of Segment Structures

E1ADHDR: Confirmed Message Type
Segment Release 30C

1. MESTYP: **Logical message type**
   Internal data type: CHAR
   Internal length: 000006
   Position in structure: Offset: 0055. External length: 000006

2. MESCOD: **Logical message code**
   Internal data type: CHAR

Data contained in this appendix has been obtained from SAP™ Systems' tables of values.

Internal length: 000003
Position in structure: Offset: 0061. External length: 000003

3. MESFCT: **Logical message function**
Internal data type: CHAR
Internal length: 000003
Position in structure: Offset: 0064. External Length: 000003

E1STATE: Processing Information and Application Object for an IDoc
Segment Release 30E

1. DOCNUM: **IDoc number**
Internal data type: NUMC
Internal length: 000016
Position in structure: Offset: 0055. External length: 000016

2. STATUS: **Status of IDoc**
Internal data type: CHAR
Internal length: 000002
Position in structure: Offset: 0071. External length: 000002

3. STACOD: **Status code**
Internal data type: CHAR
Internal length: 000008
Position in structure: Offset: 0073. External length: 000008

4. STATXT: **Text for status code**
Internal data type: CHAR
Internal length: 000070
Position in structure: Offset: 0081. External length: 000070

5. STAPA1: **Parameter 1**
Internal data type: CHAR
Internal length: 000020
Position in structure: Offset: 0151. External length: 000020

6. STAPA2: **Parameter 2**
Internal data type: CHAR
Internal length: 000020
Position in structure: Offset: 0171. External length: 000020

7. STAPA3: **Parameter 3**
Internal data type: CHAR
Internal length: 000020
Position in structure: Offset: 0191. External length: 000020

8. STAPA4: **Parameter 4**
   Internal data type: CHAR
   Internal length: 000020
   Position in structure: Offset: 0211. External length: 000020

E1PRTOB: IDoc Number and Application Object in Receiving System
Segment Release 30C

1. DOCNUM: **IDoc number**
   Internal data type: NUMC
   Internal length: 000016
   Position in structure: Offset: 0055. External length: 000016

2. LOGSYS: **Logical system**
   Internal data type: CHAR
   Internal length: 000010
   Position in structure: Offset: 0071. External length: 000010

3. OBJTYPE: **Object type**
   Internal data type: CHAR
   Internal length: 000010
   Position in structure: Offset: 0081. External length: 000010

4. OBJKEY: **Object key**
   Internal data type: CHAR
   Internal length: 000070
   Position in structure: Offset: 0091. External length: 000070

List of Segment Documentation

E1ADHDR: Confirmed Message Type

1. MESTYP: **Logical message type**
   General: This field contains the logical name of a message. It is not
   subject to any standards. Logical messages are assigned to individual IDoc types by SAP™. Example: the logical message ORDERS
   identifies purchase orders (outbound) and sales orders (inbound).
   Applications: Outbound IDocs: The selection module of the application must fill MESTYP. Inbound IDocs: No action required. IDoc
   interface: Outbound IDocs: If the field is not filled, it is assigned
   the value of the field STDMES. Inbound IDocs: The field is used to

determine the inbound partner profile. If the field is not filled, it is assigned the value of the field STDMES. EDI subsystem: Outbound IDocs: Control information for the EDI subsystem. Inbound IDocs: The field must be filled in order to be able to determine the partner profile in SAP™. If the field is not assigned a value (e.g., in control record length—release 2.1), the value of the field STDMES is used. Input values.

2. MESCOD: **Logical message code**
   General: This field is not subject to any standards. It contains a code derived from the message code of an EDI message. This field is optional. Applications: Outbound IDocs: The application selection module can fill MESCOD. Inbound IDocs: No action required. IDoc interface: Outbound IDocs: No action required. Inbound IDocs: The field is used to find the inbound partner profile. EDI subsystem: Outbound IDocs: Control information for the EDI subsystem. Inbound IDocs: The field must be filled to determine the partner profile in SAP™.

3. MESFCT: **Logical message function**
   General: This field is not subject to any standards. It contains a code derived from the message function of an EDI message. It is optional. Applications: Outbound IDocs: The application selection program can fill MESFCT. Inbound IDocs: No action required. IDoc interface: Outbound IDocs: No action required. Inbound IDocs: The field is used to determine the partner profile for inbound processing. EDI subsystem: Outbound IDocs: Control information for the EDI subsystem. Inbound IDocs: This field must be filled to determine the partner profile in the SAP™ System.

E1STATE: Processing Information and Application Object for an IDoc

1. DOCNUM: **IDoc number**
   General: Identifies the IDoc. It is considered a mandatory field. Applications: No action required. IDoc interface: The number range of the IDoc is client-dependent. The IDoc number is determined using the internal number assignment in the function module after the IDoc has been created. EDI subsystem: The EDI subsystem must not fill DOCNUM when the IDoc is being created. This number is assigned by SAP™. In the case of outbound IDocs, however, the EDI subsystem must maintain DOCNUM for later status messages to the SAP™ System.

2. STATUS: **Status of IDoc**

   General: This field contains the current status of the IDoc. These values are provided to monitor the processing and are required during the entire translation procedure for further processing. It is important that both the SAP application and the EDI subsystem provide this field with the appropriate values. The status values for outbound IDocs are between "01" and "49," while the status values for inbound IDocs begin with "50." Applications: Outbound IDocs: No action requied. Inbound IDocs: During the processing of the IDoc, the status is set explicitly by the application programs via the function module EDI_DOCUMENT_STATUS_SET. IDoc interface: When an IDoc is created, the status is set in the function module EDI_DOCUMENT_CLOSE_CREATE. All other status changes are made explicitly via the function module EDI_DOCU-MENT_STATUS_SET. EDI subsystem: Outbound IDocs: The EDI subsystem writes the status changes to a status file (record type EDI_DS), which is then read by the appropriate SAP™ program. The status values of the various processing stages are recorded in the value list. Inbound IDocs: No action required. Input values:

   Outbox
   00 IDoc interface (SAP™): Not used, only R/2
   01 IDoc interface (SAP™): IDoc created
   02 IDoc interface (SAP™): Error passing data to port
   03 IDoc interface (SAP™): Data passed to port OK
   04 External system/EDI subsystem: Error within control information of EDI subsystem
   05 External system/EDI subsystem: Error during translation
   06 External system/EDI subsystem: Translation OK
   07 External system/EDI subsystem: Error during syntax check
   08 External system/EDI subsystem: Syntax check OK
   09 External system/EDI subsystem: Error during interchange handling
   10 External system/EDI subsystem: Interchange handling OK
   11 External system/EDI subsystem: Error during dispatch
   12 External system/EDI subsystem: Dispatch OK
   13 External system/EDI subsystem: Retransmission OK
   14 External system/EDI subsystem: Interchange Acknowledgment positive
   15 External system/EDI subsystem: Interchange Acknowledgment negative

16 External system/EDI subsystem: Functional Acknowledgment positive

17 External system/EDI subsystem: Functional Acknowledgment negative

18 IDoc interface (SAP™): Triggering EDI subsystem OK

19 IDoc interface (SAP™): Data transfer for test OK

20 IDoc interface (SAP™): Error triggering EDI subsystem

21 IDoc interface (SAP™): Error passing data for test

22 External system/EDI subsystem: Dispatch OK, acknowledgment still due

23 External system/EDI subsystem: Error during retransmission

24 External system/EDI subsystem: Control information of EDI subsystem OK

25 IDoc interface (SAP™): Processing despite syntax error (outbound)

26 IDoc interface (SAP™): Error during syntax check of IDoc (outbound)

27 IDoc interface (SAP™): Error in dispatch level (ALE service)

28 IDoc interface (SAP™): Not used

29 IDoc interface (SAP™): Error in ALE service

30 IDoc interface (SAP™): IDoc ready for dispatch (ALE service)

31 IDoc interface (SAP™): Error—no further processing

32 IDoc interface (SAP™): IDoc was edited

33 IDoc interface (SAP™): Original of an IDoc that was edited

34 IDoc interface (SAP™): Error in control record of IDoc

35 IDoc interface (SAP™): IDoc reloaded from archive

36 External system/EDI subsystem: Electronic signature not performed (timeout)

37 IDoc interface (SAP™): IDoc added incorrectly

38 IDoc interface (SAP™): IDoc archived

39 IDoc interface (SAP™): Receipt confirmed by target system

40 IDoc interface (SAP™): Application document not created in target system

41 IDoc interface (SAP™): Application document created in target system

50 IDoc interface (SAP™): IDoc added

Inbox

51 SAP™ application: Error: Application document not posted

52 SAP™ application: Application document not fully posted

53 SAP™ application: Application document posted

54 SAP™ application: Error during formal application check

55 SAP™ application: Formal application check OK

56 IDoc interface (SAP™): IDoc with errors added

57 SAP™ application: Test IDoc: Error during application check

58 IDoc interface (SAP™): Not used

59 IDoc interface (SAP™): Not used

60 IDoc interface (SAP™): Error during syntax check of IDoc (inbound)

61 IDoc interface (SAP™): Processing despite syntax error (inbound)

62 IDoc interface (SAP™): IDoc passed to application

63 IDoc interface (SAP™): Error passing IDoc to application

64 IDoc interface (SAP™): IDoc ready to be passed to application

65 IDoc interface (SAP™): Error in ALE service

66 IDoc interface (SAP™): Not used

67 IDoc interface (SAP™): Not used

68 IDoc interface (SAP™): Error—no further processing

69 IDoc interface (SAP™): IDoc was edited

70 IDoc interface (SAP™): Original of an IDoc that was edited

71 IDoc interface (SAP™): IDoc reloaded from archive

72 IDoc interface (SAP™): Not used, only R/2

73 IDoc interface (SAP™): IDoc archived

3. STACOD: **Status code**

General: This field contains a code that specifies the field STATUS more precisely. The code either refers to table T100 in the SAP™ System or to codes of the EDI subsystem. The field is intended to be used, in particular, to describe error situations, but can also be used for success messages. Applications: For errors in the SAP™ System, the status code must be set up as follows: Bytes 1–3: "SAP™"; Bytes 4–5: Message ID from T100; Bytes 6–8: Message number from T100. IDoc interface: For errors in the SAP™ System, the status code must be set up as follows: Bytes 1–3: SAP™; Bytes 4–5: Message ID from T100; Bytes 6–8: Message number from T100. EDI subsystem: Outbound IDocs: Codes of the EDI subsystem that describe a status change or an error more precisely can be passed. Even if the value of the field STATUS is not changed, several status records can be passed to the SAP™ System, which contain different codes or error messages for the IDoc. A subsystem-specific display of the status records within the SAP™ System can be controlled via table TEDE3 if a different prefix to "SAP™" is used for the first 3 bytes of the code. Inbound IDocs: No action required.

4. STATXT: **Text for status code**
   General: This field contains the text on the field STACOD. It is either a text from table T100 in SAP™ or a text of the EDI subsystem. The text can contain up to four "&" symbols, which can later be replaced by the values in the fields STAPA1, STAPA2, STAPA3, and STAPA4. Applications: The text can be added to the message through the status record. The text can still contain the variable symbols. They are replaced by the values in the fields STAPA1 to STAPA4 when the message is displayed. IDoc interface: No action required. EDI subsystem: Outbound IDocs: A text of the EDI subsystem describing the field STACOD can be passed. Even if the value of the field STATUS is not changed, several status records can be passed to the SAP™ System, which contain different information or error messages for the IDoc. Inbound IDocs: No action required.

5. STAPA1: **Parameter 1**
   General: This field contains the value determined at runtime with which the first variable symbol is replaced in the field STATXT. Applications: If an error message containing "&" symbols is passed, the value for the variable symbol must be transferred in the correct position. IDoc interface: No action required. EDI subsystem: Outbound IDocs: The EDI subsystem can use the SAP™ concept. Inbound IDocs: No action required.

6. STAPA2: **Parameter 2**
   General: This field contains the value determined at runtime with which the second variable symbol is replaced in the field STATXT. Applications: If an error message containing "&" symbols is passed, the value for the variable symbol must be transferred in the correct position. IDoc interface: No action required. EDI subsystem: Outbound IDocs: The EDI subsystem can use the SAP™ concept. Inbound IDocs: No action required.

7. STAPA3: **Parameter 3**
   General: This field contains the value determined at runtime with which the third variable symbol is replaced in the field STATXT. Applications: If an error message containing "&" symbols is passed, the value for the variable symbol must be transferred in the correct position. IDoc interface: No action required. EDI sub-

system: Outbound IDocs: The EDI subsystem can use the SAP™ concept. Inbound IDocs: No action required.

8. STAPA4: **Parameter 4**
General: This field contains the value determined at runtime with which the fourth variable symbol is replaced in the field STATXT. Applications: If an error message containing "&" symbols is passed, the value for the variable symbol must be transferred in the correct position. IDoc interface: No action required. EDI subsystem: Outbound IDocs: The EDI subsystem can use the SAP™ concept. Inbound IDocs: No action required.

E1PRTOB: IDoc Number and Application Object in Receiving System

1. DOCNUM: **IDoc number**
General: Identifies the IDoc. It is considered a mandatory field. Applications: No action required. IDoc interface: The number range of the IDoc is client-dependent. The IDoc number is determined using the internal number assignment in the function module after the IDoc has been created. EDI subsystem: The EDI subsystem must not fill DOCNUM when the IDoc is being created. This number is assigned by SAP™. In the case of outbound IDocs, however, the EDI subsystem must maintain DOCNUM for later status messages to the SAP™ System.

2. LOGSYS: **Logical system**
Definition: System in which applications run integrated on a common data basis. According to SAP™ standards, a client corresponds to a logical system. You can specify a client's logical system when defining the client. The logical system is relevant in the following SAP™ areas: ALE, general: two or more logical systems communicate together. ALE, distribution scenarios (e.g., Cost Center Accounting): definition of a system where a specific application runs. For example, changes to master data can be made only in this system. Workflow objects: the logical system, in which the object is located, is always included in an object's key. When maintaining the logical system note the following: The logical system must be unique companywide. It must not be used by any other ALE system group. In a productive system, the logical system cannot be changed if a value other than zero has already been entered. If a noninitial logical system is changed in retrospect, you

might not be able to find documents in your own system any longer. If the logical system of a document reference does not match with your own, the system assumes the document is located in a different system.

3. OBJTYPE: **Object type**
Definition: An object type is a generic description of an object. In the object type definition, objects are described by specifying their components. An object type is described by: Basic data (e.g., name, creator); Key fields, for uniquely identifying an object; Attributes, as characteristics of an object; Methods, with parameters and exceptions as permitted activites on an object; Events, for describing status changes; Implementation, in program code.

4. OBJKEY: **Object key**

IDoc Type Structure of WMMBID01

Goods Movements for Mobile Data Entry

- **E1MBXYH: Goods movements for mobile data entry (header data)**
  Status: Mandatory
  Min. number: 1, max. number: 1
- **E1MBXY1: Goods movements for mobile data entry (items)**

  Status: Mandatory
  Min. number: 1, max. number: 9999

List of Segment Structures

E1MBXYH: Goods Movements for Mobile Data Entry (Header Data)
Segment Release 30A

1. BLDAT: **Date of the document**
   Internal data type: DATS
   Internal length: 000008
   Position in structure: Offset: 0055. External length: 000008

2. BUDAT: **Posting date in the document**
Internal data type: DATS
Internal length: 000008
Position in structure: Offset: 0063. External length: 000008

3. XBLNR: **Reference document number**
Internal data type: CHAR
Internal length: 000016
Position in structure: Offset: 0071. External length: 0000016

4. BKTXT: **Document header text**
Internal data type: CHAR
Internal length: 000025
Position in structure: Offset: 087. External length: 000025

5. FRBNR: **Number of bill of lading at time of goods receipt**
Internal data type: CHAR
Internal length: 000016
Position in structure: Offset: 0128. External length: 000016

6. XABLN: **Goods receipt/issue slip number**
Internal data type: CHAR
Internal length: 000010
Position in structure: Offset: 0128. External length: 000010

7. TCODE: **Session: Current transaction code**
Internal data type: CHAR
Internal length: 000004
Position in structure: Offset: 0138. External length: 000004

E1MBXYI: Goods Movements for Mobile Data Entry (Items)
Segment Release 30A

1. BEAKZ: **Indicator: line already edited**
Internal data type: CHAR
Internal length: 000001
Position in structure: Offset: 0055. External length: 00001

2. XSTOB: **Flag: Reverse posting**
Internal data type: CHAR
Internal length: 000001
Position in structure: Offset: 0056. External length: 000001

3. MATNR: **Material**
Internal data type: CHAR

Internal length: 000018
Position in structure: Offset: 0057. External length: 000018

4. WERKS: **Plant**
Internal data type: CHAR
Internal length: 000004
Position in structure: Offset: 0075. External length: 000004

5. LGORT: **Storage location**
Internal data type: CHAR
Internal length: 000004
Position in structure: Offset: 0083. External length: 000004

6. CHARG: **Batch number**
Internal data type: CHAR
Internal length: 000010
Position in structure: Offset: 0083. External length: 000010

7. BWART: **Movement type (inventory management)**
Internal data type: CHAR
Internal length: 000003
Position in structure: Offset: 0096. External length: 000003

8. INSMK: **Stock type**
Internal data type: CHAR
Internal length: 000001
Position in structure: Offset: 0096. External length: 000001

9. SOBKZ: **Special stock indicator**
Internal data type: CHAR
Internal length: 000001
Position in structure: Offset: 0097. External length: 000001

10. BZVBR: **Indicator: consumption posting**
Internal data type: CHAR
Internal length: 000001
Position in structure: Offset: 0098. External length: 00001

11. LIFNR: **Vendor (creditor) account number**
Internal data type: CHAR
Internal length: 000010
Position in structure: Offset: 0099. External length: 000010

12. KUNNR: **Customer number**
Internal data type: CHAR
Internal length: 000010
Position in structure: Offset: 0109. External length: 000010

13. KDAUF: **Sales order number**
Internal data type: CHAR
Internal length: 000010
Position in structure: Offset: 0119. External length: 000010

14. KDPOS: **Item number in sales order**
Internal data type: CHAR
Internal length: 000006
Position in structure: Offset: 0129. External length: 000006

15. KDEIN: **Delivery schedule (sales order)**
Internal data type: CHAR
Internal length: 000004
Position in structure: Offset: 0135. External length: 000004

16. SHKZG: **Debit/credit indicator**
Internal data type: CHAR
Internal length: 000001
Position in structure: Offset: 0139. External length: 000001

17. WAERS: **Currency key**
Internal data type: CHAR
Internal length: 000005
Position in structure: Offset: 0140. External length: 000005

18. DMBTR: **Amount in local currency in CHAR format**
Internal data type: CHAR
Internal length: 000015
Position in structure: Offset: 0145. External length: 000015

19. BWTAR: **Variation type**
Internal data type: CHAR
Internal length: 000010
Position in structure: Offset: 0160. External length: 000010

20. ERFMG: **Quantity in unit of entry**
Internal data type: CHAR
Internal length: 000015
Position in structure: Offset: 0170. External length: 000015

21. ERFME: **Unit of entry**
Internal data type: UNIT
Internal length: 000003
Position in structure: Offset: 0185. External length: 000003

22. BPMNG: **Quantity in order price quantity unit**
Internal data type: CHAR

Internal length: 000015
Position in structure: Offset: 0188. External length: 000015

23. BPRME: **Order price unit (purchasing)**
Internal data type: UNIT
Internal length: 000003
Position in structure: Offset: 0203. External length: 000003

24. EBELN: **Purchasing document number**
Internal data type: CHAR
Internal length: 000010
Position in structure: Offset: 0206. External length: 000010

25. EBELP: **Item number of purchasing document**
Internal data type: NUMC
Internal length: 000005
Position in structure: Offset: 0216. External length: 000005

26. ELIKZ: **"Deliver completed" indicator**
Internal data type: CHAR
Internal length: 000001
Position in structure: Offset: 0221. External length: 000001

27. SGTXT: **Line item text**
Internal data type: CHAR
Internal length: 000050
Position in structure: Offset: 0222. External length: 000050

28. WEMPF: **Goods recipient**
Internal data type: CHAR
Internal length: 000012
Position in structure: Offset: 0272. External length: 000012

29. ABLAD: **Unloading point**
Internal data type: CHAR
Internal length: 000025
Position in structure: Offset: 0284. External length: 000025

30. KOSTL: **Cost Center**
Internal data type: CHAR
Internal length: 000010
Position in structure: Offset: 0309. External length: 000010

31. AUFNR: **Order Number**
Internal data type: CHAR
Internal length: 000012
Position in structure: Offset: 0319. External length: 000012

32. ANLNI: **Main asset number**
    Internal data type: CHAR
    Internal length: 000012
    Position in structure: Offset: 0331. External length: 000012

33. ANLN2: **Asset subnumber**
    Internal data type: CHAR
    Internal length: 000004
    Position in structure: Offset: 0343. External length: 000004

34. RSNUM: **Number of reservation/dependent requirement**
    Internal data type: NUMC
    Internal length: 000010
    Position in structure: Offset: 0347. External length: 000010

35. RSPOS: **Items number of reservation/dependent require-ment**
    Internal data type: NUMC
    Internal length: 000004
    Position in structure: Offset: 0357. External length: 000004

36. KZEAR: **Indicator: final issue for this reservation**
    Internal data type: CHAR
    Internal length: 000001
    Position in structure: Offset: 0361. External length: 000001

37. UMMAT: **Receiving/issuing material**
    Internal data type: CHAR
    Internal length: 000018
    Position in structure: Offset: 0362. External length: 000018

38. UMWRK: **Receiving plant/issuing plant**
    Internal data type: CHAR
    Internal length: 000004
    Position in structure: Offset: 0380. External length: 000004

39. UMLGO: **Receiving/issuing storage location**
    Internal data type: CHAR
    Internal length: 000004
    Position in structure: Offset: 0384. External length: 000004

40. UMCHA: **Receiving/issuing batch**
    Internal data type: CHAR
    Internal length: 000010
    Position in structure: Offset: 0388. External length: 000010

41. KZBEW: **Movement indicator**
Internal data type: CHAR
Internal length: 000001
Position in structure: Offset: 0398. External length: 000001

42. WEUNB: **Indicator: goods receipt nonvaluated**
Internal data type: CHAR
Internal length: 000001
Position in structure: Offset: 0399. External length: 000001

43. LGNUM: **Warehouse number/complex**
Internal data type: CHAR
Internal length: 000003
Position in structure: Offset: 0400. External length: 000003

44. LGTYP: **Storage type**
Internal data type: CHAR
Internal length: 000003
Position in structure: Offset: 0403. External length: 000003

45. LGPLA: **Storage bin**
Internal data type: CHAR
Internal length: 000010
Position in structure: Offset: 0406. External length: 000010

46. GRUND: **Reason for manual valuation of net assets**
Internal data type: CHAR
Internal length: 000003
Position in structure: Offset: 0416. External length: 000004

47. EVERS: **shipping instructions**
Internal data type: CHAR
Internal length: 000002
Position in structure: Offset: 0420. External length: 000002

48. EVERE: **Compliance with shipping instructions**
Internal data type: CHAR
Internal length: 000002
Position in structure: Offset: 0422. External length: 000002

49. IMKEY: **Internal key for real estate object**
Internal data type: CHAR
Internal length: 000008
Position in structure: Offset: 0424. External length: 000008

50. KSTRG: **Cost object**
Internal data type: CHAR

Internal length: 000012
Position in structure: Offset: 0432. External length: 000012

51. PAOBJNR: **Number for business segment (CO-PA) in CHAR format**
Internal data type: CHAR
Internal length: 000010
Position in structure: Offset: 0444. External length: 000010

52. PRCTR: **Profit center**
Internal data type: CHAR
Internal length: 000010
Position in structure: Offset: 0454. External length: 000010

53. PS_PSP_PNR: **Work breakdown structure element (WBS element)**
Internal data type: NUMC
Internal length: 000008
Position in structure: Offset: 0464. External length: 000008

54. NPLNR: **Network number for account assignment**
Internal data type: CHAR
Internal length: 000012
Position in structure: Offset: 0472. External length: 000012

55. AUFPL: **Planning number for transactions in the order in CHAR format**
Internal data type: CHAR
Internal length: 000010
Position in structure: Offset: 0484. External length: 000010

56. APLZL: **Counter for distinguishing DB entries**
Internal data type: CHAR
Internal length: 000008
Position in structure: Offset: 0494. External length: 000008

57. AUFPS: **Number of order item in CHAR format**
Internal data type: CHAR
Internal length: 000004
Position in structure: Offset: 0502. External length: 000004

58. VPTNR: **Partner account number**
Internal data type: CHAR
Internal length: 000010
Position in structure: Offset: 0506. External length: 000010

59. FIPOS: **Commitment item**
Internal data type: CHAR
Internal length: 000014
Position in structure: Offset: 0516. External length: 000014

60. GSBER: **Business area**
Internal data type: CHAR
Internal length: 000004
Position in structure: Offset: 0530. External length: 000004

61. BSTMG: **Good receipt quantity in order unit in CHAR format**
Internal data type: CHAR
Internal length: 000015
Position in structure: Offset: 0534. External length: 000015

62. BSTME: **Order unit (purchasing)**
Internal data type: UNIT
Internal length: 000003
Position in structure: Offset: 0549. External length: 000003

63. EXBWR: **Posting amount in local currency entered externally**
Internal data type: CHAR
Internal length: 000015
Position in structure: Offset: 0552. External length: 000015

64. KONTO: **G/L account number**
Internal data type: CHAR
Internal length: 000010
Position in structure: Offset: 0567. External length: 000010

65. RSHKZ: **Debit/credit indicator**
Internal data type: CHAR
Internal length: 000001
Position in structure: Offset: 0577. External length: 000001

66. BDMNG: **Requirement quantity in CHAR format**
Internal data type: CHAR
Internal length: 000015
Position in structure: Offset: 0578. External length: 000015

67. ENMNG: **Issued quantity in CHAR format**
Internal data type: CHAR
Internal length: 000015
Position in structure: Offset: 0593. External length: 000015

68. QPLOS: **Inspection lot number**
Internal data type: NUMB
Internal length: 000012
Position in structure: Offset: 0608. External length: 000012

69. UMZST: **Status of receiving batch**
Internal data type: CHAR
Internal length: 000001
Position in structure: Offset: 0620. External length: 000001

70. UMZUS: **Status of receiving batch**
Internal data type: CHAR
Internal length: 000001
Position in structure: Offset: 0621. External length: 000001

71. UMBAR: **Valuation type of transfer batch**
Internal data type: CHAR
Internal length: 000010
Position in structure: Offset: 0622. External length: 000010

72. UMSOK: **Special stock indicator for physical stock transfer**
Internal data type: CHAR
Internal length: 000001
Position in structure: Offset: 0632. External length: 000001

73. LFBJA: **Fiscal year of a reference document**
Internal data type: NUMC
Internal length: 000004
Position in structure: Offset: 0633. External length: 000004

74. LFBNR: **Document number of a reference document**
Internal data type: CHAR
Internal length: 000010
Position in structure: Offset: 0637. External length: 000010

75. LFPOS: **Item of a reference document**
Internal data type: NUMC
Internal length: 000004
Position in structure: Offset: 0647. External length: 000004

76. SJAHR: **Calendar year for monthly WS generation**
Internal data type: NUMC
Internal length: 000004
Position in structure: Offset: 0651. External length: 000004

77. SMBLN: **Number of a material document**
Internal data type: CHAR

Internal length: 000010
Position in structure: Offset: 0655. External length: 000010

78. SMBLP: **Item in material document**
Internal data type: NUMC
Internal length: 000004
Position in structure: Offset: 0665. External length: 000004

79. EXVKW: **Sales value specified externally in loc.currency (CHAR-FORM)**
Internal data type: CHAR
Internal length: 000015
Position in structure: Offset: 0669. External length: 000015

80. QM_ZUSTD: **Batch status with status changed in QM (internal)**
Internal data type: CHAR
Internal length: 000001
Position in structure: Offset: 0684. External length: 000001

81. POSNR: **Delivery item**
Internal data type: NUMC
Internal length: 000006
Position in structure: Offset: 0685. External length: 000006

82. VBELN: **Delivery**
Internal data type: CHAR
Internal length: 000010
Position in structure: Offset: 0691. External length: 000010

83. QM_UMZST: **Status of receiv.batch when status changed in QM (intern.)**
Internal data type: CHAR
Internal length: 000001
Position in structure: Offset: 0701. External length: 000001

84. BWLVS: **Movement type for Warehouse Management**
Internal data type: NUMC
Internal length: 000003
Position in structure: Offset: 0702. External length: 000003

85. UMREZ: **Numerator for converting to base unit of measure**
Internal data type: DEC
Internal length: 000003
Position in structure: Offset: 0705. External length: 000005

86. UMREN: **Denominator for conversion to base units of measure**
Internal data type: DEC
Internal length: 000005
Position in structure: Offset: 0710. External length: 000008

87. VFDAT: **Shelf life expiration date**
Internal data type: DATS
Internal length: 000008
Position in structure: Offset: 0715. External length: 000008

88. DABRZ: **Reference date for account settlement**
Internal data type: DATS
Internal length: 000008
Position in structure: Offset: 0723. External length: 000008

List of Segment Documentation

E1MBXYH: Goods Movements for Mobile Data Entry (Header Data)

1. BLDAT: **Date of the document**
Definition: The document date is defined in order to include the issue date of the original document.

2. BUDAT: **Posting date in the document**
Definition: Date used when entering the document in Financial Accounting or Controlling. Use: The fiscal year and the period for which an update of the account specified in the document or cost elements is made; derived from the posting date. When entering documents, the system checks whether the posting date entered is allowed by means of the posting period permitted. Note: The posting date can differ from both the entry date (day of entry into the system) and the document date (day of creation of the original document). Dependencies.

3. XBLRN: **Reference document number**
Definition: The reference document number contains the document number of the customer/vendor. Use: The reference document number is used as a search criterion for displaying or changing documents. In correspondence, the reference document number is sometimes printed in place of the document number.

4. BKTXT: **Document header text**
   Definition: The document header text contains explanations or notes that apply to the document as a whole that is, not only for certain line items.

5. FRBNR: **Number of bill of lading at time of goods receipt**
   Definition: Number identifying the bill of lading of the goods that have been received. The bill of lading is the document issued by the sender that accompanies the goods.

6. XABLN: **Goods receipt/issue slip number**
   Definition: Number that—in addition to the material document number—uniquely identifies a goods receipt/issue slip. This number can be assigned both internally and externally. Use: This GR/GI slip number only has been designed for use in those countries (e.g., Italy) whose legislation requires specification of this number for goods that leave the plant and are transported on public roads. In other countries, the material document number printed on the GR/GI slip (in the standard system) is usually sufficient. To enter external documents, you can use the field Material slip or Delivery note. What to do: If the number assignment for GR/GI slips is active for the plant, you can proceed as follows: Enter a number manually; enter no number; in this case, the system assigns a number automatically.

7. TCODE: **Session: Current transaction code**

   Definition: The name of the currently active SAP™ transaction.

E1MBXYI: Goods Movements for Mobile Data Entry (Items)

1. BEAKZ: **Indicator: line already edited**

   Values
   "X" Yes
   "   No

2. XSTOB: **Flag: Reverse posting**

   Values
   "X" Yes
   "   No

3. MATNR: **Material**
   Definition: alphanumeric key uniquely identifying the material.

4. WERKS: **Plant**
   Definition: Number uniquely identifying a plant.

5. LGORT: **Storage location**
   Definition: Number of the storage location where the material is stored. A plant may contain one or more storage locations.

6. CHARG: **Batch number**
   Definition: Number that uniquely assigns a material manufactured in batches or production lots to a specific batch.

7. BWART: **Movement type (inventory management)**
   Definition: Key for the type of goods movement. Each goods movement (e.g., "purchase order to warehouse") is allocated to a movement type in the system.

8. INSMK: **Stock type**
   Definition: Indicator specifying to which stock the given quantity is posted. Possible stocks are: unrestricted-use stock, stock in quality inspection, blocked stock.

   Values
   "X" Quality inspection
   "S" Blocked
   "2" Quality inspection
   "3" Blocked
   "   Unrestricted-use
   "F" Unrestricted-use

9. SOBKZ: **Special stock indicator**
   Definition: Indicator specifying the special stock type. Use: If certain stock (e.g., consignment stock) of a material needs to be managed separately, the stock type in question is identified with this indicator).

10. KZVBR: **Indicator: consumption posting**
    Definition: Indicator specifying that the consumption is to be posted to a consumption account (V) or an asset account (A). Dependencies: The indicator is used in the case of goods receipts for purchase orders and is derived from the account assignment category of the purchase order.

    Values
    "   No consumption
    "V" Consumption
    "A" Asset
    "E" Sales order
    "P" Project

11. LIFNR: **Vendor (creditor) account number**
Definition: Alphanumeric key that uniquely identifies "the.

12. KUNNR: **Customer number**
Definition: Key with which the customer can be identified within the SAP™ system.

13. KDAUF: **Sales order number**
Definition: Key that uniquely identifies a sales order.

14. KDPOS: **Item number in sales order**
Definition: Number that uniquely identifies an item within a sales order.

15. LDEIN: **Delivery schedule (sales order)**
Definition: Number that uniquely identifies an item within the delivery schedule for a sales order.

16. SHKZG: **Debit/credit indicator**
Definition: Shows on which side of the account (S = debit, H = credit) the update of the transaction figures is carried out.

Values
"H" Credit
"S" Debit

17. WAERS: **Currency key**
Definition: Currency key for amounts in the system.

18. DMBTR: **Amount in local currency in CHAR format**

19. BWTAR: **Valuation type**
Definition: Key uniquely identifying stocks of a material subject to split valuation. Dependencies: The valuation category determines which valuation types are permissible for a material. Example: If a material is valuated according to its origin (valuation category H), you can define the possible countries of origin as valuation types).

20. ERFMG: **Quantity in unit of entry**

21. ERFME: **Unit of entry**
Definition: Unit of measure in which the goods movement or inventory count is entered. What to do: Enter a unit of measure here only if it is different from the default unit of measure. There are the following default units of measure: the order unit for goods receipts with reference to purchase orders; the production unit for goods receipt with reference to production orders; the

unit of issue for other goods movements. If the default unit of measure has not been defined in the material master record, the system will suggest the stockkeeping units.

22. BPMNG: **Quantity in order price quantity unit**

23. BPRME: **Order price unit (purchasing)**
Definition: Unit of measure to which the order price relates. Example: 100 pcs are ordered at a price of 10 $/kg. The order unit is "piece." The order price unit is "kilogram."

24. EBELN: **Purchasing document number**
Definition: Alphanumeric key that uniquely identifies a purchasing document.

25. EBELP: **Item number of purchasing document**
Definition: Number that uniquely identifies an item within a purchasing document.

26. ELIKZ: **"Delivery completed" indicator**
Definition: Indicator showing that the purchase order item is to be regarded as closed. Use: If the "delivery completed" indicator is set at the time of goods receipt or in the purchase order, no further goods receipts are expected in respect of this order item. What to do: The "delivery completed" indicator can be set either at the time of goods receipt or in the purchase order or outline agreement item. Dependencies: If a delivery is received that is within the under/overdelivery tolerates, the "delivery completed" indicator is set automatically.

Values
"X" Yes

" No

27. SGTXT: **Line item text**
Definition: In this field you can store an explanatory text for the line item. Line item texts can be used internally and externally. To be able to distinguish between these, you must begin texts for external use with "*." These can then be printed on all correspondences, dunning notices, payment advice notes, and so forth. The asterisk is removed when the test is printed.

28. WEMPF: **Goods recipient**
Definition: Recipient for whom the material or the service is destined.

29. ABLAD: **Unloading point**
Definition: Point at which the material is to be unloaded (e.g., dock 1).

30. KOSTL: **Cost Center**
Definition: Key uniquely identifying a cost center.

31. AUFNR: **Order Number**
Definition: Number that identifies an order within a client.

32. ANLNI: **Main asset number**
Definition: The number that, together with the asset subnumber, identifies a fixed asset in Asset Accounting.

33. ANLN2: **Asset subnumber**
Definition: The number that, together with the asset main number, uniquely identifies a fixed asset in Asset Accounting. Using the asset subnumber, you can: provide for separate management of later acquisitions to assets; represent complex fixed assets with their component parts.

34. RSNUM: **Number of reservation/dependent requirement**
Definition: Alphanumeric key that uniquely identifies a reservation or a dependent requirement.

35. RSPOS: **Item number of reservation/dependent requirement**
Definition: Number that uniquely identifies an item within a reservation or a dependent requirement.

36. KZEAR: **Indicator: final issue for this reservation**
Definition: Indicator serving to identify a reservation item as "completed." Further goods movements in respect of this reservation item are not anticipated (although they are still possible). Use: It is set automatically for a goods movement when the total reserved quantity has been withdrawn or delivered. In the case of a partial delivery, the indicator can be set manually if no further goods movements are expected in respect of the relevant items.

Values
"X" Yes
" No

37. UMMAT: **Receiving/issuing material**
Definition: The receiving material is the material number under which the quantity to be transferred is to be managed. The issuing material (in the case of a reversal) is the material whose stock

is reduced by a given quantity. Note: The material entered here does not determine the value of the transfer posting, but the material specified in the Material field. Dependencies: For the receiving/issuing material, the following should be considered: the material must exist; the material must be managed in the same stockkeeping unit as the issuing material.

38. UMWRK: **Receiving plant/issuing plant**
Definition: The receiving plant is the plant or internal department/section that is to receive the goods. The issuing plant (in the case of a reversal) is the plant whose stock is reduced by a given quantity. Note: The plant entered here does not determine the value of the transfer posting, but rather the plant entered in the Plant field.

39. UMLGO: **Receiving/issuing storage location**
Definition: The receiving storage location is the storage location that is to receive the goods. The issuing storage location is the storage location whose stock is to be reduced by a given quantity.

40. UMCHA: **Receiving/issuing batch**

41. KZBEW: **Movement indicator**
Definition: Indicator specifying the type of document (e.g., purchase order, delivery note) that constitutes the basis for the movement. Use: This indicator is necessary, for example, to enable a distinction to be made between a goods receipt for a purchase order and a goods receipt for a production order. These two movements result in different data and account updates in the system. Dependencies: The movement indicator is derived from the SAP™ transaction.

Values
" Goods movement w/o reference
"B" Goods movement for purchase order
"F" Goods movement for production order
"L" Goods movement for delivery note
"K" Goods movement for kanban requirement (WM—internal only)
"O" Subs. adjm. of "mat.-provided" consumption

42. WEUNB: **Indicator: goods receipt nonvaluated**
Definition: Indicator specifying that the goods receipt for this item is not to be valuated. Use: Set the indicator if goods receipts involving this material are not to be valuated. The valuation of the purchase order item will then take place at the time of invoice

verification. This indicator must be set in the case of multiple account assignment for example. Note: If the indicator has been set for a material item with the material type "nonvaluated," the quantity recorded in Inventory Management is liable to differ from the value in Financial Accounting during the period between goods receipt and invoice receipt, since the value is not updated in the Accounting system until the time the incoming invoice is posted.

Values
"X" Yes
"   No

43. LGNUM: **Warehouse number/complex**
Definition: Number that identifies a complex, physical warehouse structure within the Warehouse Management system. Use: All activities within a warehouse, for example, goods movements and physical inventory, are assigned to a specific warehouse number. The physical warehouse, where these activities take place, is identified by the warehouse number.

44. LGTYP: **Storage type**
Definition: The storage type is a subdivision of a complex, physical warehouse. Different storage types are identified by the warehousing technique, form of organization, or their function. A typical warehouse could have the following storage types: goods receipt area; picking area; high-rack storage area.

45. LGPLA: **Storage bin**
Definition: The storage bin (sometimes referred to as a "slot") is the smallest addressable unit in a warehouse. It identifies the exact location in the warehouse where goods are stored or can be stored. A storage bin can be further subdivided into bin sections. Several different materials (quants) can be stored in one bin at the same time.

46. GRUND: **Reason for manual valuation of net assets**
Definition: Using this key, you can define the reason for manual valuation of net assets in the asset master record.

47. EVERS: **Shipping instructions**
Definition: Key denoting the packaging and shipping instructions issued to the vendor. What to do: Enter the key for the relevant shipping instructions.

48. EVERE: **Compliance with shipping instructions**
Definition: Key indicating to what extent the vendor has complied
with shipping instructions. Example: Key 1 means that the vendor has supplied the material in the stipulated packaging. Key 3
means that the vendor did use the stipulated type of packaging,
but the packaging was damaged on arrival of the goods. Key 10
means that the vendor used a different type of packaging than
the stipulated or that the packaging was so damaged as to render
the shipment unacceptable.

49. IMKEY: **Internal key for real estate object**

50. KSTRG: **Cost object**
Definition: Term that identifies the cost object ID. Use: Cost
objects are the activity units of the company. Costs are allocated
to them in accordance with their cause. The R/3™ System distin-
guishes between: Cost objects represented by a cost object ID;
Cost objects represented by objects of other applications, such as
production orders, sales orders, or projects. Cost objects are represented by cost object IDs in the following area: Activity-Based
Costing, for which the overhead costs are first posted to cost cen-
ters and then allocated to the processes; from there they are allocated to the cost objects as process costs. Cost Object Controlling
with Intangible Goods: When intangible goods are produced,
direct costs are allocated directly to the cost objects. Overhead
can be allocated to the cost objects either by means of overhead
surcharges or through Activity-Based Costing. Cost Object Controlling with Repetitive Mfg/Process Mfg: In repetitive manufacturing and process manufacturing, you can create a cost object
hierarchy to collect actual costs that cannot be collected at the
material or order level. The nodes of the hierarchy can represent
such things as production lines at which material components are
staged without reference to an order. These costs can either be
distributed to the assigned orders or settled to stock as price differences. Information System: In order-related production, you
can represent product groups with cost object IDs. You create a
cost object ID for each product group and assign materials to the
cost object ID. The costs for the materials are summarized in the
information system and reported for each product group. What to
do-Examples-Dependencies: The cost object category determines
what functions can be performed on this cost object. Functions

can be performed on cost object hierarchies only when the cost object entered represents the top of the hierarchy.

51. PAOBJNR: **Number for business segment (CO-PA) in CHAR format**

52. PRCTR: **Profit center**
    Definition: Key that uniquely identifies the profit center in the current controlling area.

53. PS_PSP_PNR: **Work breakdown structure element (WBS element)**
    Definition: Key identifying a WBS element.

54. NPLNR: **Network number for account assignment**
    Definition: Key identifying the network used for account assignment

55. AUFPL: **Planning number for transactions in the order in CHAR format**

56. APLZL: **Counter for distinguishing DB entries**

57. AUFPS: **Number of order item in CHAR format**

58. VPTNR: **Partner account number**

59. FIPOS: **Commitment item**
    Definition: Alphanumeric code of the commitment item that you are creating, changing, and displaying, or to which you are assigning budget.

60. GSBER: **Business area**
    Definition: The business area is an organizational entity for which balance sheets as well as profit and loss statements can be created for internal reporting. Unlike the company code, the business area is not a legally independent entity and is therefore not subject to the legal requirements for external reporting.

61. BSTMG: **Goods receipt quantity in order unit in CHAR format**

62. BSTME: **Order unit (purchasing)**
    Definition: Unit of measure in which the material is ordered.

63. EXBWR: **Posting amount in local currency entered externally**

64. KONTO: **G/L account number**
    Definition: The G/L account number identifies the G/L account in a chart of accounts.

65. RSHKZ: **Debit/credit indicator**

    Definition: Shows on which side of the account (S = debit, H = credit) the update of the transaction figures is carried out.

    Values
    "H" Credit
    "S" Debit

66. BDMNG: **Requirement quantity in CHAR format**

67. ENMNG: **Issued quantity in char.format**

68. QPLOS: **Inspection lot number**

    Definition: Number that uniquely identifies an inspection lot. What to do: The inspection lot number is assigned by the system.

69. UMZST: **Status of receiving batch**

    Definition: Indicator describing the status of the transfer batch.

70. UMZUS: **Status key of transfer batch**

    Definition: Key specifying the status of a transfer batch (e.g., unrestricted-use, restricted-use, etc.).

71. UMBAR: **Valuation type of transfer batch**

    Definition: Key used in the "split valuation" of materials (i.e., the separate valuation of different stocks of the same material) to permit stocks of a transfer batch to be differentiated according to various criteria.

72. UMSOK: **Special stock indicator for physical stock transfer**

    Definition: Special stock indicator of the second posting line of a document item posted with this movement type. Use: This indicator is used, for example, in the case of the physical transfer of a consignment material and when consignment material is transferred from the vendor's stock to the company's own stock.

73. LFBJA: **Fiscal year of a reference document**

74. LFBNR: **Document number of a reference document**

    Definition: Number that uniquely identifies a reference document. The document number is unique per company code and fiscal year. When you enter an accounting document, the number can be assigned by the user or by the system (from a predefined number range). The permitted document number ranges are specified via tables for various document types.

75. LFPOS: **Item of a reference document**

    Definition: All items in an accounting document are assigned a number that allows them to be uniquely identified. The numbers are assigned consecutively when the document is created.

76. SJAHR: **Calendar year for monthly WS generation**
Definition: Calendar year (YYYY)

77. SMBLN: **Number of a material document**
Definition: Alphanumeric key that uniquely identifies a material document. Number of the material document with which a goods movement was posted. Together with the material document, year, the document number constitutes the key which a material document is accessed.

78. SMBLP: **Item in material document**
Definition: Number that uniquely identifies an item within a material document.

79. EXVKW: **Sales value specified externally in loc.currency (CHAR-FORM)**

80. QM_ZUSTD: **Batch status with status changed in QM (internal)**

81. POSNR: **Delivery item**
Definition: The number that uniquely identifies the item in a delivery.

82. VBELN: **Delivery**
Definition: The number that uniquely identifies the delivery.

83. QM_UMZST: **Status of receiv.batch when status changed in QM (intern.)**

84. BWLVS: **Movement type for Warehouse Management**
Definition: Key for the type of warehouse movement. Each warehouse movement (e.g., goods receipt, goods issue, stock transfer) is processed in the system by means of a movement type. Use: The movement type influences the creation of the transfer order in many ways (e.g., printing, defining the interim storage area confirmation, and so on).

85. UMREZ: **Numerator for converting to base unit of measure**
Definition: Numerator of the quotient that specifies that ratio of the alternative unit of measure to the base unit of measure. Use: To convert a quantity, whose unit of measure is not the same as the base unit of measure, into the base unit of measure, the system requires a quotient: Quantity (in alternative unit of

measure) = quotient*quantity (in base unit of measure). What do you do: Enter the number of units of the alternative unit of measure (denominator) that corresponds to the number of units of the base unit of measure (numerator). Example: The alternative unit of measure is kilogram (kg). The base unit of measure is piece (PC). 5 kg correspond to 3 pieces. 5 kg-3 PC→1 kg = 3/5 PC. In this case, the quotient is therefore 3/5 (the numerator being 3 and the denominator 5). Note: You may enter only whole numbers in the numerator and denominator fields; that is, if 3.14 m^2 correspond to one piece, you must enter integer multiples (314 m^2 = 100 PC). In this case, the quotient is therefore 100/314 (the numerator being 100 and the denominator 314).

86. UMREN: **Denominator for conversion to base unit of measure**
Definition: Denominator of the quotient that specifies the ratio of the alternative unit of measure to the base unit of measure. Use: To covert a quantity, whose unit of measure is not the same as the base unit of measure, into the base unit of measure, the system requires a quotient: Quantity (in alternative unit of measure) = quotient*quantity (in base unit of measure). What to do: Enter the nubmer of units of the alternative unit of measure (denominator) that corresponds to the number of units of the base unit of measure (numerator). Example: The alternative unit of measure is kilogram (kg). The base unit of measure is piece (PC). 5 kg correspond to 3 pieces. 5 kg = 3 PC → 1 kg = 3/5 PC. In this case, the quotient is therefore 3/5 (the numerator being 3 and the denominator 5). Note: You may enter only whole numbers in the numerator and dominator fields; that is, if 3.14 m^2 correspond to one piece, you must enter integer multiples (314 m^2 = 100 PC). In this case, the quotient is therefore 100/314 (the numerator being 100 and the denominator 314).

87. VFDAT: **Shelf life expiration date**
Definition: This is the shelf life expiration date. Use: What to do: Examples Dependencies: The date is set by the system upon receipt of the goods—either you enter it direct upon receipt of the goods or you can enter a data of production upon receipt of the goods and the system then calculates the shelf life expiration date from the date of production plus shelf life in days (from the material master record).

88. DABRZ: **Reference date for account settlement**
Definition: The reference date is used to identify the accounting
period for an invoice accounting assignment.

IDoc Type Structure of ZKNVHM01

Customer Hierarchy Basic IDOC for ALE Distribution

- **Z1KNVHM: Customer Hierarchy Base Segment**
  Status: Mandatory
  Min. number: 1, max. number: 999999

List of Segment Structures

Z1KNVHM: Customer Hierarchy Base Segment
Segment Release 31H

1. MSGFN: **Function**
   Internal data type: CHAR
   Internal length: 000003
   Position in structure: Offset: 0055. External length: 000003

2. HITYP: **Customer hierarchy type**
   Internal data type: CHAR
   Internal length: 000001
   Position in structure: Offset: 0058. External length: 000001

3. KUNNR: **Customer number of the customer hierarchy node**
   Internal data type: CHAR
   Internal length: 000010
   Position in structure: Offset: 0059. External length: 000010

4. VKORG: **Sales organization**
   Internal data type: CHAR
   Internal length: 000004
   Position in structure: Offset: 0069. External length: 000004

5. VTWEG: **Distribution channel**
   Internal data type: CHAR

Internal length: 000002
Position in structure: Offset: 0073. External length: 000002

6. SPART: **Division**
Internal data type: CHAR
Internal length: 000002
Position in structure: Offset: 0075. External length: 000002

7. DATAB: **Start of validity period for assignment**
Internal data type: DATS
Internal length: 000008
Position in structure: Offset: 0077. External length: 000008

8. DATB1: **End of validity period for the assignment**
Internal data type: DATS
Internal length: 000008
Position in structure: Offset: 0085. External length: 000008

9. HKUNNR: **Customer number of the higher-level customer hierarchy**
Internal data type: CHAR
Internal length: 000010
Position in structure: Offset: 0093. External length: 000010

10. HVKORG: **Higher-level sales organization (customer hierarchy)**
Internal data type: CHAR
Internal length: 000004
Position in structure: Offset: 0103. External length: 000004

11. HVTWEG: **Higher-level distribution channel (customer hierarchy)**
Internal data type: CHAR
Internal length: 000002
Position in structure: Offset: 0107. External length: 000002

12. HSPART: **Higher-level division (customer hierarchy)**
Internal data type: CHAR
Internal length: 000002
Position in structure: Offset: 0109. External length: 000002

13. GRPNO: **Number of the routine used for copying**
Internal data type: NUMC
Internal length: 000003
Position in structure: Offset: 0111. External length: 000003

14. BOKRE: **ID: Customer is to receive rebates**
    Internal data type: CHAR
    Internal length: 000001
    Position in structure: Offset: 0114. External length: 000001

15. PRFRE: **Relevant for pricing ID**
    Internal data type: CHAR
    Internal length: 000001
    Position in structure: Offset: 0115. External length: 000001

16. HZUOR: **Assignment to hierarchy**
    Internal data type: NUMC
    Internal length: 000002
    Position in structure: Offset: 0116. External length: 000002

List of Segment Documentation

Z1KNVHM: Customer Hierarchy Base Segment

1. MSGFN: **Function**

   Values
   "003" Delete: Message contains objects to be deleted
   "004" Change: Message contains changes
   "005" Replace: This message replaces previous messages
   "009" Original: First message for process
   "023" Wait/Adjust: Data should not be imported
   "018" Resend

2. HITYP: **Customer hierarchy type**
   Definition: Specifies the type of customer hierarchy (e.g., pricing, statistics). Use: The customer hierarchy type is used for the following purposes: To identify the purpose of a particular hierarchy; to determine which account groups are allowed in a hierarchy; to determine which organizational data is allowed in a hierarchy. What to do: If you are maintaining a hierarchy, enter the relevant hierarchy type. In the standard system, customer hierarchy type A (standard hierarchy)has been defined. However, you can define your own hierarchy types in Customizing in the chapter "Define Hierarchy Types."

3. KUNNR: **Customer number of the customer hierarchy node**
   Definition: Number that uniquely identifies the node in a customer hierarchy. A node can be defined for an existing customer

master record an organizational unit in the customer's structure. In this case, you need to create a master record for the organizational unit. Note: When you create a master record for a node in a customer hierarchy, you are creating a kind of scaled down customer master record. If a node represents a particular organizational unit in the customer's own structure (e.g. a regional sales office), you can specify basic information, such as address and contact person data as well as indicators to say whether the node is relevant for pricing and rebate processing.

4. VKORG: **Sales organization**
   Definition: An organizational unit responsible for the sale of certain products or services. The responsibility of a sales organization may include legal liability for products and customer claims. Use: You can assign any number of distribution channels and divisions to a sales organization. A particular combination of sales organization, distribution channel, and division is known as a sales area.

5. VTWEG: **Distribution channel**
   Definition: The way in which products or services reach the customer. Typical examples of distribution channels are wholesale, retail, or direct sales. Use: You can maintain information about customers and materials by sales organization and distribution channel. Within a sales organization you can deliver goods to a given customer through more than one distribution channel. You can assign a distribution channel to one or more sales organizations. If, for example, you have numerous sales organizations, each sales organization may use the "Wholesale" distribution channel. Note: For each combination of sales organization and distribution channel, you can further assign one or more of the divisions that are defined for the sales organization. You can, for example, assign "Food" and "Nonfood" divisions to the "Wholesale" distribution channel. A particular combination of sales organization, distribution channel, and division is known as a sales area.

6. SPART: **Division**
   Definition: A way of grouping materials, products, or services. The system uses divisions to determine the sales areas and the business areas for a material, product, or service. Use: A product or service is always assigned to just one division. From the point of view of sales and distribution, the use of divisions lets you organize your sales structure around groups of similar products

or product lines. This allows the people in a division who process orders and service customers to specialize within a manageable area of expertise. Example: If a sales organization sells food and nonfood products through both retail and wholesale distribution channels, each distribution channel could then be further split into food and nonfood divisions.

7. DATAB: **Start of validity period for assignment**
Definition: Specifies the starting date from which the assignment of this node or customer is valid in the customer hierarchy. Use: If you wish, you can create customer hierarchy assignments in advance. For example, if the structure of your customer is changing at a specified date in the future, you can create new assignments to be effective from that date.

8. DATBI: **End of validity period for the assignment**

9. HKUNNR: **Customer number of the higher-level customer hierarchy**
Definition: Number that uniquely identifies the higher-level node to which this node is assigned.

10. HVKORG: **Higher-level sales organization (customer hierarchy)**
Definition: Identifies the sales organization of the sales area in which the higher-level node is maintained. Note: If you allow nodes within a customer hierarchy to be maintained in different sales areas, the valid combinations of sales area can be defined in Customizing for Sales.

11. HVTWEG: **Higher-level distribution channel (customer hierarchy)**
Definition: Identifies the distribution channel of the sales area in which the higher-level node is maintained. Note: If you allow nodes within a customer hierarchy to be maintained in different sales areas, the valid combinations of sales area can be defined in Customizing for Sales.

12. HSPART: **Higher-level division (customer hierarchy)**
Definition: Identifies the division of the sales area in which the higher-level node is maintained. Note: If you allow nodes within a customer hierarchy to be maintained in different sales areas, the valid combinations of sales area can be defined in Customizing for Sales.

13. GRPNO: **Number of the routine used for copying**
Definition: Number of a subroutine (= form routine) that checks
a requirement at a specific time. Use: The standard system contains some standard routines for checking requirements when
copying. You can also define your own routines according the
needs of your company. Example: If you copy a quotation to a
sales order, the system can check every quotation item to ensure
that the customer had not rejected them for any reason. What to
do: The system proposes a routine for checking copying requirements according to the type of document to be copied. If you do
not want to use the proposed routine you can do one of the following: Enter the number of another routine; change the routine
yourself and define specific requirements that should be checked.
(Before you change a routine, you should check if it is used some-
where else, in order to avoid unwanted changes at another point.)
You can find the available routines in Customizing for copy controls for each document (e.g., maintain copy control for sales documents).

14. BOKRE: **ID: Customer is to receive rebates**
Definition: Indicates whether a customer may be granted a
rebate. What to do: If you want a customer to be able to receive
rebates, mark the field.

Values
"X" Yes
"   No

15. PRFRE: **Relevant for pricing ID**
Definition: If the master record represents a node in a customer
hierarchy, the pricing indicator determines whether the node is
relevant for pricing. Use: You can indicate that a node is pricing-
relevant and create condition records for it. If the node is part of
the hierarchy path that the system determines for a sales order,
the system takes the corresponding condition records into account
during pricing. What to do: If you are maintaining the master
record for a customer hierarchy node and you want to create pricing condition records for the node, set the indicator.

Values
"X" yes
"   No

16. HZUOR: **Assignment to hierarchy**

    Definition: Using this field, you can assign a fixed hierarchy level
    to a customer so that this customer master record always has the
    same (fixed) hierarchy level assignment for all hierarchy types
    when it is used as a hierarchy node. Only levels 01 to 10 can be
    assigned. This field is used only in the transfer structures for con-
    trolling and the sales information system, that is, this fixed level
    assignment need not correspond to the actual hierarchy level as
    not every node is relevant for CO/PA or SIS. Sample hierarchy
    with level assignments: Customer A | Customer B / Level 01 |
    Customer C | Customer D / Level 02. Only nodes B and C are rel-
    evant for CO/PA or SIS. They are copied into the corresponding
    structures with the fixed levels 01 or 02.

INDEX

ABOUT THE AUTHOR

Rajeev Kasturi (Basking Ridge, NJ) is a leading SAP™ consultant who implements and teaches ALE/EDI/IDOC technologies at client sites. A professional in information technology for more than eight years, he has a background in mechanical engineering, nuclear engineering, dataprocessing systems analysis and design, and database administration. Rajeev has successfully spearheaded multiple ALE/EDI implementations at Fortune 500 companies, and he runs a consulting practice, Rajcast Inc., that focuses on ALE, EDI, and Workflow technologies for SAP R/3™.

Rajeev welcomes comments, feedback, and suggestions on this book, and he can be contacted at aleedi99@hotmail.com.